LEFT OF CENTRE

LEFT
OF
CENTRE

Kamal Morarka in Parliament

Edited by
Lina Mathias

Foreword by
Pritish Nandy

RUPA

Published by
Rupa Publications India Pvt. Ltd 2013
7/16, Ansari Road, Daryaganj
New Delhi 110002

Sales centres:
Allahabad Bengaluru Chennai
Hyderabad Jaipur Kathmandu
Kolkata Mumbai

Copyright © Kamal Morarka 2013
Foreword copyright © Pritish Nandy 2013

ISBN: 978-81-291-2976-5

10 9 8 7 6 5 4 3 2 1

The moral right of the author has been asserted.

Samajwadi Janata Party (Rashtriya) president and
hailing from a well-known industrialist family of
Mumbai, **KAMAL MORARKA**
was a union minister in the Chandra Shekhar
government and a Rajya Sabha member during
the tumultuous 1990s. As a parliamentarian
(1988–94) and minister, Morarka's speeches
and replies reflected his vast reading, knowledge
of the economy and, more importantly,
his concern that the ordinary citizen should
not get short shrift from the lawmakers
and bureaucrats. As an industrialist, newspaper
proprietor (*Afternoon Despatch & Courier*
and *Chauthi Duniya*), politician and part
of the think tank Centre for Policy Analysis,
he continues to read voraciously, intervene
effectively in issues of concern and follow the
ideas of Dr Ram Manohar Lohia, Jayaprakash
Narayan and Acharya Narendra Dev. He has
also served on several government committees.
He was president of All India Manufacturers'
Organisation, president of Indian Council
of Foreign Trade, vice president of
All India Association of Industries and president
of National Alliance of Young Entrepreneurs.

Morarka chairs a number of non-governmental
organizations that work for water conservation
and harvesting in Rajasthan, wildlife research
(he is an avid photographer), arts and crafts,
and organic farming and research. He blogs
on www.kamalmorarka.com.

BY THE TIME THEIR TERM IS OVER [THIS GOVERNMENT] WOULD HAVE SOLD THE PUBLIC SECTOR OFF AND USED ALL THAT MONEY FOR REVENUE EXPENDITURE AND NOTHING WOULD BE LEFT FOR THE LEGACY.

Former parliamentarian and minister Kamal Morarka has always been someone who speaks his mind. *Left of Centre*, a collection of his speeches in Parliament, reflects his extensive knowledge on a variety of subjects, his clarity of thought, his oratorical excellence and, most importantly, his concern for the ordinary citizen. Although economic and financial matters were his forte, as the speeches in this book will reveal, he was extremely well-versed on all the hot topics of his time.

With witty observations and practical suggestions, this thought-provoking collection showcases Morarka's views on tumultuous and significant events of the 1990s, including the Bofors scam, the liberalization of the economy, the Babri Masjid demolition, the Harshad Mehta scam and more.

Parliament is not a *congress* of ambassadors from different and hostile interests; which interests each must maintain, as an agent and advocate, against other agents and advocates; but Parliament is a *deliberative* assembly of *one* nation, with *one* interest, that of the whole; where, not local purposes, not local prejudices, ought to guide, but the general good, resulting from the general reason of the whole.

—Edmund Burke, Speech to the Electors of Bristol,
3 November 1774

CONTENTS

FOREWORD

I entered Parliament four years after Kamal Morarka left it, but his reputation had survived the intervening years.

I knew Kamal, of course, from his days with Chandra Shekhar. I was then barely into my thirties and editor of *The Illustrated Weekly of India*, apart from heading *The Times of India* as publishing director. He was on the other side of the fence: an ardent socialist who had stepped away from his successful family business to argue that India's future lay in exploring the romance of a more just and egalitarian society, not in chasing the dream of laissez-faire that most businessmen of that era thought (and many still do) would instantly fix all of India's economic problems. So, instead of lobbying for causes that could have enhanced his many businesses, Kamal threw in his lot with Chandra Shekhar, the saturnine Young Turk of the Congress who had quit the ruling party during the Emergency, when he was imprisoned by Indira Gandhi, to carve out his own niche in Indian politics, following the ideology of Acharya Narendra Dev.

Unlike others who floundered after quitting the Congress, Chandra Shekhar grew in stature, becoming one of India's most respected Opposition leaders. Even I, a hard-nosed journalist who rarely had a good word to say for most politicians, found myself admiring him for his plain-speak and no-nonsense attitude. Chandra Shekhar also had a cutting-edge integrity which I found quite charming in a political environment ruled by what looked like only boring, double-faced Geminis.

When, through a series of apparently impossible political events, Chandra Shekhar became India's eighth prime minister with barely sixty-four MPs in his fold, to lead a government that was possibly the shortest in independent India's history, he chose Kamal to be his minister of state in the Prime Minister's Office. It was a job Kamal did with amazing sangfroid and yes, incredible as it may sound today, without the slightest hint of scandal. He was obviously inspired by the fact that his mentor had finally proved himself to be the man of destiny we all hoped he would be. So he did his best during those few months to restore the sanctity of the Prime Minister's Office. You must realize how difficult that was in the immediate aftermath of the Bofors years when anything, from rice sales to Russia and over-priced howitzers, was reportedly being transacted in the PMO, and not exactly transparently.

The way Kamal ran the office, as anyone will tell you, was worth applauding, especially in the context of today's times, when corruption has become as commonplace as outrage and out-priced onions. His speeches in the Rajya Sabha won him much applause as well. Whatever he spoke about—and he spoke on many subjects, but largely on matters of finance and economics—won him plaudits even from those who chose to disagree with him. For he spoke with conviction and rare insight into the subjects he chose. Even today, if you read his speeches, some of which have been compiled here by Lina Mathias of the *Economic & Political Weekly*, you will discover how perceptive they were, how prescient. Some of the ideas he articulated and the points he raised, for example on Kashmir, are still pertinent. Proving the axiom that the more things change, the more they remain the same. At least, India's problems do.

That is exactly why this book deserves to be read.

There is no rocket science here. In fact, India's problems do not need rocket science to resolve. They need only an empathic understanding of what makes this nation tick. And, perhaps more important, what the 1.2 billion people of India *actually* want. As distinct from what our politicians, safely ensconced in their Lutyens bungalows, *think* they want. Kamal attempts to bridge the hiatus. He offers simple, easy insights, untainted by doublespeak. In fact, they are often so simple that we miss out on their importance. He reiterates the basic compulsions that drive the way we think, behave, act and retain faith in the great institutions Nehru had the foresight to build in the early years of this nation's history, which his successors have often tried to dismantle, luckily not always with great success.

It is this Nehruvian spirit of liberalism, this faith in democratic institutions, this commitment to the greater good, which Kamal describes as the Left of Centre position, a position from which Indian politics appears to be veering away in this century. That is what this book is about. The dream that inspired Indian politics for half a century after Independence, a dream that faded away when Narasimha Rao (and his Sancho Panza, Manmohan Singh) began their half-hearted reforms twenty-two years ago. Governments have come and gone since then. But the issues that Kamal raised in Parliament remain to remind us that no government that does not consider the greater good as its ideal can ever hope to find long-lasting, durable solutions, least of all economic ones. India has clearly abandoned the path of Gandhi and, now, moved even further away from what Nehru had dreamt of.

Curiously, this shift has been most pronounced under the rule of the very party Nehru had once led and which his family continues to lead. Not under those who are seen to be his detractors.

This begs the questions: Has the Congress failed India? Or did Nehru fail India by taking a path today's reformists believe was a road to sure disaster? Can India ever swing back from its current sojourn in la-la land to a position Left of Centre? Or will socialism forever remain a dirty word, discarded by history? Read these speeches. Maybe you will find answers here.

Pritish Nandy

INTRODUCTION

Kamal Morarka's spacious book-lined office in Mumbai holds a world of erudition, witty observations on the country's current situation and anecdotes about his experiences in the course of his political career—as Rajya Sabha MP and union minister of state in the Prime Minister's Office (PMO) in the Chandra Shekhar government. His conversation has an unhurried grace to it, but is never pointless or meandering. As president of the Samajwadi Janata Party (Rashtriya); chairman of the Gannon Dunkerley Group engaged in civil engineering, mechanical and general engineering; chairman of the board of directors of Mumbai's evening daily, the *Afternoon & Courier*; and owner of the Hindi and Urdu *Chauthi Duniya*, he straddles many worlds. And his uncanny ability to get to the nub of any issue, state it with an almost forgotten elegance coated with dry wit, is a sheer delight to behold.

During his term in the Rajya Sabha (3 April 1988–2 April 1994) and as union minister in 1990–91, he has spoken on issues that range from the Rent Control Bill to Kashmir to Delhi University, tax reforms and the public sector. He was also a member of various parliamentary committees like those on public undertakings, direct taxes, newsprint, public accounts, etc.

To go through these speeches now is to get a perspective that is backed by painstaking study, an eye for detail and a lucid presentation of complex issues that plague Indian polity and society. But most importantly, one thread runs through them all consistently:

concern for the ordinary citizen's problems when he or she deals with the state, whatever be the level of the bureaucracy or politicians. His is not a dry analysis crammed only with facts and figures, but one that considers its application to the average Indian's daily life.

To read them now is to understand a slice of Indian history when the nation's economy was undergoing a huge change and other tumultuous events were buffeting its society and polity. Morarka has sat and spoken in the august House from both sides, the Opposition and the Treasury benches. His speeches and statements on issues like the Bofors investigation, the stock market scam of ₹600 crore, the 6 December 1992 Babri Masjid demolition and the mayhem that followed are filled with deep anguish and a call to reason and humanity. His participation in the debates on income tax, appropriation bills and the public sector show his practical knowledge of the world of Indian business and no-nonsense, down-to-earth suggestions to deal with bottlenecks and leakages.

It is no secret that public disenchantment with the falling levels of debates and discussions in the Indian Parliament began some time ago and has intensified greatly of late. The events of the past few years have shown that the Indian society and its expectations from those at the helm of the state have changed dramatically. Parliament's relationship, whether with the public at large, the judiciary, the media or the executive, too, is undergoing changes.

As Morarka observes, 'The hallmark of a good Parliament is that the Opposition must be responsible and the government should be responsive. Unfortunately, this government is not responsive and therefore the Opposition has to use other tactics. The problem is with the treasury benches who try to avoid the main issues and then derail the debates. Opposition members are not alert enough to bring back the debate to the main track.'

Morarka considers Jawaharlal Nehru to be India's best prime minister to date and he was influenced greatly by India's eighth prime minister, Chandra Shekhar, whom he met when he was twenty-one years old. Writing of Chandra Shekhar after he passed away, veteran journalist Vir Sanghvi said, 'I miss his sincerity, his warmth and his view that there was a space between the Congress and the BJP. Now, that space has vanished.' On 4 May 2010, Vice President Mohammad Hamid Ansari unveiled a lifelike portrait of Chandra Shekhar in the Central Hall of Parliament House, donated by Morarka. The same portrait, painted by R.D. Pareek, adorns his Mumbai office.

Morarka grew up (he was born on 18 June 1946 in Bombay) in a home with a background of entrepreneurs and interest in active politics. The participants in the shaping of the India that was emerging post-Independence were familiar visitors. Apart from this vibrant influence, he studied the works of Acharya Narendra Dev, Dr Ram Manohar Lohia and Shri Jayaprakash Narayan, which left him deeply impressed with socialism and its principles. More importantly, it made him that rare creature—a successful industrialist and a committed politician who swears by socialism.

His parents, Mahavirprasad R. Morarka and Belabai M. Morarka, brought him up to value simplicity of lifestyle and high thinking. He recalls an incident when he was nine years old that left a permanent impression. Every student of the Cathedral School in Mumbai (he did his primary schooling there and later at the John Cannon School) was supposed to be taken to the church on the Founder's Day. Any student not interested in doing so had to get his parent's signature. His father asked him to go to church. He was told that temple, church and mosque were all the same. After doing his Inter Science from St Xavier's College, Mumbai, in 1966, he married Bharati at the age of twenty. They have two daughters.

However, politics and business do not overshadow everything else for Morarka. He is a wildlife photography enthusiast, a voracious reader and chairs non-governmental organizations (NGOs) that work in the fields of wildlife research and conservation, rural development, health, and arts and crafts. Water conservation (in the Shekawati region of Rajasthan), horticulture, organic farming, popularizing India's traditional arts and crafts and growing orchids are particular passions. He is also a member of the think tank Centre for Policy Analysis.

AS A PARLIAMENTARIAN

Kamal Morarka's journey in active politics and as an effective and responsive parliamentarian began with his getting elected to the Rajya Sabha from the Janata Dal (Secular) on 3 April 1988. He remained a member of the Rajya Sabha for six years, up to 2 April 1994.

He has about 1,094 questions to his credit in his six-year span. Starting from agriculture, commerce, finance, railways, power and energy, industry and mines, his questions in Parliament stretch to matters such as planning, rural and urban development, labour, education and external affairs, to mention a few.

Subject-wise break-up of questions:

Subject	No. of Questions	Per Cent (%)
Finance	154	(14.07%)
Industry and Mines	87	(7.95%)
Commerce	70	(6.39%)
Agriculture	50	(4.57%)
Railways	49	(4.47%)
Petroleum and Natural Gas	48	(4.38%)
Textiles	46	(4.20%)
Power and Energy	45	(4.11%)
Planning	43	(3.93%)
Environment and Forests	40	(3.65%)
Civil Aviation	39	(3.56%)
Communication	37	(3.38%)
Home	37	(3.38%)

Surface Transport	33	(3.01%)
Defence	31	(2.83%)
Food	27	(2.46%)
Urban Development	26	(2.37%)
External Affairs	22	(2.01%)
Science and Technology	20	(1.82%)
Health and Family Welfare	19	(1.75%)
Information and Technology	19	(1.75%)
Steel	19	(1.75%)
Rural Development	1	(1.46%)
Labour	16	(1.46%)
Chemical and Fertilizers	15	(1.37%)
Water Resources	15	(1.37%)
Personnel	12	(1.09%)
Education	11	(1.0%)
Civil Supplies	10	(0.91%)
Law, Justice and Company Affairs	10	(0.91%)
Human Resource Development	9	(0.82%)
Tourism	6	(0.54%)
Welfare	5	(0.45%)
Electronics	4	(0.36%)
Culture	3	(0.27%)
Youth Affairs and Sports	1	(0.09%)
Total	**1,094**	

AS A MINISTER

When Shri Chandra Shekhar was the prime minister of India, from 10 November 1990 to 21 June 1991, he inducted Kamal Morarka into the council of ministers as a minister of state in the PMO. Morarka held this office from 21 November 1990 to 21 June 1991. He remained devoted to the jobs and responsibilities he was delegated by the prime minister and replied to the questions related to the PMO under his direct responsibility. He ensured that the PMO worked efficiently, without unnecessary interference and intervention of different ministries, to get optimal results. He also replied to the debates in both Houses of Parliament as and when the need to that regard arose, or otherwise when asked to do so on behalf of other ministries. As a minister, subject-wise classification of questions as replied to by Morarka with number and percentage is as follows:

Subject	No. of Questions	Per Cent (%)
Industry	111	(46.05%)
External Affairs	48	(19.91%)
Personnel	39	(16.18%)
Planning	15	(6.22%)
Atomic Energy	13	(5.39%)
Science and Technology	13	(5.39%)
Ocean Development	1	(0.41%)
Power	1	(0,41%)
Total	241	

TAKING THE 'SOFT' OPTION

What did the government do in 1991 to deal with the fiscal imbalance? It took the soft option, says Morarka, in this debate on the Finance Bill No. 2 on 18 September 1991. In statements that echo the public sentiment in the country today, he points out to the then finance minister (Dr Manmohan Singh) that there seems to be no attempt to curtail wasteful government expenditure. This is true of the security for VIPs or obsolete projects, for instance. The only emphasis is on selling public-sector shares and corporate taxation, he says, as he points out that there should be no sacred cows, not even defence expenditure under the guise of security.

I am glad that the finance minister[1] is here today when I am making my submission on the Finance Bill. At the outset, I must say that the biggest problem facing the country is the balance of payments (BoP) problem. And most of the policies that this government has announced are purportedly to help solve that problem.

I feel that the balance of payments in the long term can be solved only by a favourable balance of trade. Over the last ten years, we have had an increasing deficit in the balance of trade and that is why the balance of payments position is bad. Sir, we have the figures given by the Reserve Bank of India. And now we have the figures given by an international body, the Organisation for Economic Co-operation and Development (OECD), which carried

---

[1]Dr Manmohan Singh

out a study on the debt of various countries. On an objective analysis, it is very clear that 1987 was the watershed year for the Indian debt to go out of control. The figures are very clear.

In 1986, the total short-term debt of the Government of India was 2.9 billion dollars. In 1987, it went up to 4.9 billion dollars. We increased our short-term debt by 2 billion dollars in one year. We must understand that we have to reverse what happened between 1985 and 1989. Two things that have happened between 1985 and 1989 definitely need to be reversed. One is, we have obviously taken loans, short-term loans, for long-term purposes. It is no use blaming/asking who did it or why he did it. It is the country's debt.

> The finance minister [...] must shed excess baggage instead of privatizing ONGC or the Steel Authority or Indian Oil, which is very easy to privatize because they are making money and anybody can get up and say he will run it.

What is the best way to organize this debt into long-term? It is short-term again. Taking an International Monetary Fund (IMF) loan will be a long-term one but the debt will have to be repaid by generating your own surplus. Talking about the import-export surpluses, Eximscrip is a welcome move. It could have been done five years ago. If five years ago we had a link between import and export, we would not have come to this situation today. I would request the honourable finance minister to use his clout to see that non-oil export-import balance should generate a minimum surplus as fixed by him. And that can be easily done by monitoring the Eximscrip ratio.

OIL OF OUR OWN

On the question of oil imports, the most unfortunate aspect is that over the last four or five years the indigenous oil output is not going up. Instead of giving in to the IMF or the World Bank, let us have the US oil companies coming and exploring oil and at least, let us guarantee that in the next five or six years we will have another 10 million tonnes of oil of our own.

The second point is about the fiscal imbalance. Though the finance minister is trying to stick to 6.5 per cent of the gross domestic product (GDP), as Shri Yashwant Sinha had announced in February, and if he finds it difficult because of his fertilizers' subsidy—all my sympathies are with him for this—but unfortunately, again we are taking the soft option. There is absolutely no effort to cut down government expenditure. We are only talking of retaining the fiscal deficit to 6.9 per cent by other methods, by selling public-sector shares, by corporate taxation, which is welcome, but not by cutting government expenditure. Government expenditure, even to the layman, is absolutely wasteful and has gone out of all proportion.

CURB WASTEFUL DEFENCE AND GOVERNMENT EXPENDITURE

Take the police, for instance—security to VIPs. There are so many obsolete projects being run by various ministries, which serve no useful purpose. But I understand that the finance minister would find it very difficult, because every ministry will say: 'We cannot cut it because this is essential'; and they will give reasons for everything. This is where the surgeon's knife should be converted into the butcher's knife. We are a poor country. We must learn to live within our means.

I come now to the defence expenditure. Defence is the holy cow. At one time when the Congress party was in the Opposition, they started saying that if you cut defence expenditure, you are against the security of India. It is not so. Within the defence ministry there is a lot of wasteful expenditure. Again I come to a very sensitive subject. In buying armaments there should be no politics. There was a committee under Shri Arun Singh set up by Prime Minister V.P. Singh. I don't know what has happened to the report. But I am sure Shri Arun Singh must have made some useful suggestions.

If defence expenditure can be curbed, all efforts should be made to do that.

HOW TO MANAGE THE PUBLIC SECTOR WELL

The third thing is for augmenting income and correcting fiscal balance. Everybody agrees that the public sector is not doing well. The oil sector, petrochemical sector, electronics sector are doing well selectively. Indian Drugs and Pharmaceuticals Limited (IDPL) is doing equally well compared to the private-sector companies. The public textile sector is sick; in fact it has grown out of the private sick sector. So, the ownership by itself cannot guarantee or cannot affect the functioning of the unit. It is the market condition and management of the unit.

In the 1970s when Smt. Indira Gandhi came to power with the 'Garibi Hatao' programme, there were two shifts in thinking. One was that the public sector should enter the consumer industry. So, the government entered that area. The India Tourism Development Corporation (ITDC) hotels were expanded. Modern bakeries making bread and soft drinks were promoted. Then the government went to trade, State Trading Corporations (STC), Minerals and Metals Trading Corporation (MMTC), etc. Then whichever units in the private sector were sick, the government began taking them over. In the textile sector, you have taken over 120 sick units; many engineering units in Calcutta.

Now, if we have come to the conclusion that it is not possible to run such an unwieldy public sector, my first submission to the finance minister is that he must shed excess baggage instead of privatizing Oil and National Gas Corporation (ONGC) or the Steel Authority or the Indian Oil, which is very easy to privatize because they are making money and anybody can get up and say he will run it. Please auction out the unviable textile mills. But from the next day, it is the liability of the private entrepreneur to run it. India is a country well-placed in entrepreneurship. That is one thing in this country. Take a cobbler on the street—you will find he has made some gadgets to make his job easier. Technology development is very natural in this country; may not be hi-tech, but people develop their own. So, if these mills are handed over, somebody will run them and run them reasonably profitably. Perhaps he may not be able to employ all the labour. That brings me to the next point.

WHAT DOES THIS EXIT POLICY MEAN?

With the industrial policy that you have announced, the private sector is talking about the exit policy. What does this exit policy mean? If we are going to put 500,000 workers out of employment, it will create a socio-economic unrest which this government will not be able to tolerate. Please don't do it; please don't start any socio-economic unrest among the organized labour, as you will not be able to withstand it. There is the Board of Industrial and Financial Reconstruction (BIFR), which itself is a good exit mechanism. They examine a project and whenever they find that labour has to be reduced, they call the labour union, and my knowledge is, most of the labour unions are cooperating in the rationalization programme. So, the exit policy exists already.

What the industrialists probably want is a blanket exit policy so that they can just close down the unit and put workers out of employment. In a welfare state like India, it is totally out of the question. We should not think of allowing the so-called exit policy; it should be banned. The government should not even use such words. You cannot think of putting lakhs of people out of employment. But if the excess baggage of the public sector is unloaded and selectively you get out of the consumer industry, I am sure the core sector can be well run by the public sector. We have good sets of managers in the public sector. Given proper authority and autonomy, where the government should be like the owner, like in the private sector, they should show better results.

After all, the big private houses also employ managers to run their companies; it is not the family members who run them. They appoint managers, give them proper authority and responsibility and proper remuneration, and they get results. The government should do the same. I see no reason why government companies cannot be run well, provided proper work culture is developed.

Dr Vikram Sarabhai—I pay my tribute to him; he is no more, he died twenty years ago—made a study of control and management of public sector undertakings (PSU). He enunciated how public-sector management can be made autonomous while control can be retained by the government. Control and management are two different things. Unfortunately, in our system, the government itself starts managing, or interfering in day-to-day activities, and it becomes an alibi for the manager. Business is business. It has to be run like business. Profit will go to the owners i.e. the government, as happens in the private sector.

GO FOR PRESUMPTIVE TAXATION

My final point is on taxation and banking. I have nothing much to say on the tax proposals which the finance minister has brought. In fact, I feel that this must be only an ad hoc taxation. He has set up a committee, the composition of which gives me great confidence because that committee is supposed to propose taxation reforms. I do not know what the committee will do. I will just give a few suggestions. For instance, if you take the expenditure tax, which Shri Jagesh Desai criticized, apart from the logic whether air-conditioned restaurants should be taxed or not, I feel that with the present tax system, it is not possible for you to administer the collection of taxes at so many points.

The entire system has become corrupt. I may be pardoned for saying this. I am not passing judgment against anybody. But the fact is that you will find it difficult in the system as it exists today, unless the points of collection are reduced. At the same time, you will have to widen your tax base. The correct method is to go in for presumptive taxation.

Even small restaurants, laundries, eating houses, even paanwallas, all of them have incomes beyond the exemption limit. My friends keep on asking for an increase in the exemption limit, which you are not increasing. Who is paying this tax on income beyond ₹18,000? Except [for] the salaried class—pardon me for saying this—no self-employed man is honestly paying his tax. So ultimately, the crushing burden falls on the salaried man. Inflation affects only the salaried man. The person who is self-employed manages his affairs in a manner that he does not need to pay tax.

So, the correct answer is, you must put presumptive taxation on self-employed people. Every person who is self-employed must pay tax. It may be ₹500 every year. It may be a flat rate. The previous finance ministers have done it in some cases, like timber, liquor, etc. All the small business people must pay a fixed tax irrespective of their income, because you will never be able to monitor their income.

APPOINT COMPETENT PEOPLE IN BANKS

On the banking side, I must congratulate the finance minister. Some of the actions he has taken really create confidence in the honest man. If a bank chairman's performance has been bad, he should be sacked; he should certainly not be given an extension and should certainly not be put in a bigger bank. In our system, lots of pressures are there. We are all familiar with those kinds of pressures. I think the finance minister should be firm. Please clean the banking system.

The State Bank of India is a premier banking institution of this country. It is surprising that the last two or three governments thought it fit to appoint as chairman of the State Bank a person from outside the State Bank. At the same time, State Bank officers are appointed as chairmen of other banks. It is an irony. It happens due to various pressures, which I need not explain here.

The finance minister has himself been a bureaucrat for more years than I can remember. He can choose a competent person. It is not possible to eliminate corruption. The committee that has been set up under Shri Narasimham, what is it for? I do know what kind of instructions he has given. Restructuring in India is not easy. Even in regard to the seven subsidiaries of the State Bank of India, how many times have I asked for their merger into one bank or two banks? But it is not possible to do it. I do not know whether all the nationalized banks will merge into three or four banks. And I don't know what the committee will suggest in the first place. But please make an effort to see that competent people are put in the correct place, and that can be easily done. You do not need any committee or anybody for advice. The finance minister himself can do this.

I am finishing with just two suggestions. One is on the wealth tax. There is a lot of discussion [on it]. Prof. Nicholas Kaldor came to India and he had given a report on which the whole taxation structure is working today. Wealth tax was not meant as a tax for revenue. It was meant to cross-check if a man has evaded tax over the years. His idea was, if you have to show the assets and liabilities year after year for wealth tax, the income tax officers can see whether that person is not adding too much wealth on which he has not paid tax.

TAX WEALTH THAT IS NOT GENERATING INCOME

Over the years, as it usually happens in a deficit economy, it has become a source of revenue. When it becomes a source of revenue, it becomes a source of tax evasion. Now there is some reduction in the wealth tax. I think, in a progressive taxation, a signal should be sent. There should be a differential wealth tax. Wealth which generates income should be exempted from tax. Wealth which does not generate income should be subjected to wealth tax. Those who hold jewellery, hold gold, hold cash, should be taxed, because they are just keeping it and it has no relation with the economic activity of the country. But those who are investing money in business, in shares, depositing it in banks, etc., are getting income from this and it is taxed. Therefore, you should not tax them again. You should exempt them from wealth tax.

But wealth tax on all income-bearing investments should be totally abolished. This will be a proper signal, this will be a correct signal, to the taxpayers, and the money will be channelized into investment and production, which is the aim of this whole exercise. There is a big shift in the GDP to the services sector without any corresponding increase in employment. This kind of GDP growth is a phoney growth and we should not be misled by it.

THROW OUT THIS UNEQUAL TAX SYSTEM

'Who is paying tax?' asks Morarka, whilst speaking on the Finance Bill, 1992, on 11 May 1992, pointing out that 'we started out to tax the rich but we are taxing an entirely different entity.' Only that section ends up paying tax which cannot escape doing so—the salaried class. The class that spends heavily seems to be outside the tax system. Also, income is taxed on the amount, regardless of how it is earned. So, throw out the taxation system as it is and ensure that taxing is done according to the type of income rather than just having slabs, he suggests.

We may or may not agree with the type of liberalization or the features of the various policies that he (Dr Manmohan Singh, the finance minister) has undertaken. At this point of time, I feel, it would be appropriate if we judge what has happened after the presentation of the budget in the last two and a half months. I first want to quote the deputy chairman of the Planning Commission. Only yesterday he has said that the fiscal adjustment programme is not going as expected. He feels that it is a disquieting feature of the economy.

THE FINANCE MINISTER CAN REST ON HIS LAURELS

He has further said, and very rightly so, that the entire Eighth Plan depends on the following things: a reasonable degree of price stability, exports to grow at 13.6 per cent, imports to be limited to 8.4 per cent, savings to be achieved at 21.6 per cent and the dissavings to be limited to 1.1 per cent. He has said that these are the figures that we should be able to achieve, without which, to quote Shri Pranab Mukherjee, 'The plan will be in serious trouble.'

From what I can understand, some of these figures are very ambitious, especially the export figures. The finance minister will bear me out. In spite of devaluation, in spite of better exchange rate because of the 60:40 ratio, in spite of other measures that the government has taken, the export growth has still not reached what the finance minister would like it to be. Ultimately, the BoP is a reflection of the balance of trade. Today, if the balance of payments is good, barring 800 million dollars, the rest of it is all debt. Eight hundred million dollars, as far as I know, is non-repatriable; the rest of it in one form or other is only added to our debt. I had said then that a time had come when having improved the BoP position and having some breathing time, the government can rethink whether we should go in for another tranche of the IMF loan, because the other conditionalities may be more difficult to implement.

If I have ₹10 lakh or ₹5 lakh and am getting bank interest of ₹50,000 per year sitting at home while the worker who sweats for ten hours earns ₹50,000 a year—why should our tax be the same?

I think a time has come when the finance minister can rest on his laurels. Having brought the country out of a difficult situation of BoP, he can now think of what is the best strategy, what is the optimum strategy to be followed in the months and years to come. That is my first request to him.

The other feature, apart from BoP, is the money supply. Money supply is 19.5 per cent, as I understand. I do not know whether these figures are correct, but apparently, liquidity in the economy is still more than desirable. One of the reasons that we can trace is that the monetized deficit is still running high, much more than what the finance minister had anticipated. This means [that], again we go back to square one, and that the revenue expenditure has to be controlled. I am surprised that the non-interest revenue deficit is also ₹400 crore. I can understand, interest is a legacy inherited by the finance minister. It is not easy to reduce interest overnight, but you have to keep other expenditure controlled and controlling expenditure is an unpleasant thing to do. The finance minister has to become unpopular with his other colleagues, but there is no shortcut.

BE STRICT WITH OTHER MINISTRIES

This year he has to maintain the revenue expenditure at a level which has been projected in the budget. So, he has to be very strict. Secondly, in spite of the best efforts to achieve 6.5 per cent fiscal deficit, we have seen, he had to resort to a cut in capital expenditure. Revenue expenditure has still gone up, much more than what he would like the figures to be. So, my request to him is that right from now—we are in the month of May—he has to show a very high degree of strictness with the other ministries and be ruthless in cutting expenditure and augmenting revenue.

The other ambitious figure is, this dissavings has to be limited to 1.1 per cent, which means, translated into simple language, the public-sector losses have to be cut down. Now, this subject has been discussed again and again. I don't think it is practical in the present policy to make workers from fifty-eight undertakings jobless. The Krishnamurty Committee[1] is looking into it but a method should be found as to how we can reduce the losses of the public sector, how the dissaving can be limited to this figure without any mass socio-economic dislocation, because I fear that

---

[1] V. Krishnamurthy Committee on Disinvestment of Public Sector

we have a lot of problems on hand. We should not have employed workers becoming unemployed and going to the streets because that will be a problem which is more than the finance minister will be able to handle.

I wish to draw the attention of the finance minister to the taxation aspect. Income tax, when it was introduced in the 1930s in this country, was a tax on the rich. The rich used to have income and naturally the state would like to have a part of that income. What happened in the last forty to fifty years is an eye-opener. Income tax is no more a tax on the rich. The income tax has gone down because indexation has not taken place. Even this year there is a hue and cry on the exemption limit. The finance minister has his own problems, which I understand.

But let us see what happened in the past fifty years. If you take the value of the rupee in 1938–39, and the value of the rupee in 1992, the cost of living index has gone up from 100 to 5,263—fifty-two times. If indexation of taxation was done without any increase or decrease in taxation, without any change in the slabs—today, even the 20 per cent slab would apply to people earning ₹10 to ₹12 lakh. So, whatever rates of income tax the finance minister has been able to rationalize, they continue to be far higher than what they used to be fifty years ago.

ONLY THE SALARIED PAY INCOME TAX

What has happened meanwhile? The government has not indexed the slabs and the exemption limits. But the taxpayers have done it themselves. The richer sections of the assessees have indexed the taxes: they have decided how much they will pay and how much they will not pay. So they don't show the income in their returns. What is the result? The result is that the real revenue is coming, not from the top bracket, but it has started moving downwards and an ironic stage has come when it is the trade unions which are asking for an increase in exemption limits. Twenty years ago it was the Federation of Indian Chambers of Commerce and Industry (FICCI) or other associations which used to ask for increase in exemption limits. Today, that section is not concerned with the exemption limit.

Unfortunately, and I say this with anguish, people who are spending heavily in this country do not pay tax. They are outside the tax system.

Who is paying the tax? Income tax today is a tax on the middle class, specially the salaried class. Only that section of the population is paying tax which cannot escape tax because you are deducting their tax at source and paying to the government. I think it is a very unfair thing to do. I understand the dilemma of the government that today the main chunk of the revenue comes from the salaried class.

What I am going to suggest may sound revolutionary. I feel that when you have taken such big steps, things which we could not think of one year ago—I think, in the field of taxation, when your Direct Tax Code comes, it would be worth trying to abolish taxation on certain sections of the people. For instance, the worker who is doing manual labour should be exempted from income tax. Instead of only having a slab, the type of income is important. If I have ₹10 lakh or ₹5 lakh and am getting bank interest of ₹50,000 per year sitting at home while the worker who sweats for ten hours earns ₹50,000 a year—why should our tax be the same?

> I think, what is required to be done is to have a hard look and remove certain sections of the people from the tax net. You still have an army of revenue collectors. Let us give them the task of chasing those who are spending money.

Whatever slab you put to me is fine, but I suggest that at the lower end of the slab, the manual worker should be exempted from income tax, whatever his income may be, because that is really hard-earned income—he has earned every rupee of it in the hardest possible way. It may be a complicated tax system, but it will be definitely more equitable because today equity has gone. Today, I am surprised that in the pre-budget memorandum it is the trade unions which are asking for an increase in the exemption limit, a subject which, according to me, should not have concerned them.

Twenty years ago, my driver was not in the tax bracket. The labourer in a factory was not in the tax bracket. Today, they are in the tax bracket. But those who are seen to spend money don't appear to be paying tax. So, I feel that the income tax, as it is today, is highly unequal and it needs a total revolutionary change.

THROW OUT THE PRESENT TAX SYSTEM

I have seen the interim report of the Chelliah Committee. Some of the recommendations are very good. They seek to rationalize, simplify, even make the tax equitable. But it suffers from one major constraint and that is, it is trying to correct the imbalances in the existing system. In my opinion, this system should be thrown out, this whole tax system which is existing today. We had started out to tax the rich, but we are taxing an entirely different entity. It was probably beyond the terms of reference of Raja Chelliah. I think, what is required to be done is to have a hard look and remove certain sections of the people from the tax net. You still have an army of revenue collectors. Let us give them the task of chasing those who are spending money.

There are two suggestions in the Chelliah Committee report. One is on presumptive tax, which the finance minister has introduced in a moderate way this year for shopkeepers and others. The second is on an Estimated Income Scheme (EIS), which the Chelliah Committee has given but the finance minister has not introduced. I suggest that this EIS should be introduced for the upper income people in this country, who are seen to spend money but not pay tax. The revenue officials should put them under an estimated income. If you are spending so much money, we estimate that this must be your income and if you don't think it is so, please explain.

Unless you do this, I am afraid, in this system every year we [will] have a debate on 28,000, 30,000, 22,000, 80L, 80CCA. I feel that this entire debate is totally misdirected. Having said that, on the provisions that you have already introduced, 80L—the finance minister has kindly restored a part of it—but one of the good points of the Indian economy, in spite of all its trouble, has been the savings rate. The household savings rate in India, among the developing countries, is still quite high, and this is because of our Indian ethos. The Indian ethos is to save. So, no saving instrument should be taken away. I know, even a saving instrument can be misused. That is always there. But whatever provision you have for encouraging savings should not be taken away.

> Taxation should be only in the case of the partners and as per their shares in the firm. That way, most of the spurious concerns will go. You will have more honest or more reasonable tax returns.

Whether it is 80L [or] 80CCA, merge them into 88. But the basic fact is that by giving a flat reduction out of the total income, what the Raja Chelliah Committee has suggested and the finance minister has done is not very prudent because you are telling the assessee, 'You pay us less and less, and we don't mind what you do with the money that you save.' Instead of that, it is better that you say, 'If you are going to put it into a savings instrument, less tax is chargeable to you; otherwise, you pay more.' I think the saving habit should be encouraged. Expenditure can be frowned upon that way. Over the years we have seen that saving instruments have done well. Finance ministers, one after another, make some change in it. I feel that the Direct Taxes Board can simplify it in a way that every year we do not change these sections, because it only adds to the confusion.

ABOLISH TAX ON ALL FIRMS

The other provision they have made is a tax on firms. I think the step is in the right direction. In 1989 there was a bill in this House, which was a good bill. But there was such a hue and cry among the business community that you threw the baby out with the bath water. Instead of amending the provisions, you repealed that bill. I was present in the House when you repealed that entire bill, which was totally uncalled for. But in a way, Raja Chelliah has done a lot of work on firms, partners and how evasion of income can be arrested. A part of it has been implemented. I am sure in respect of firms the basis should be clear. No individual should be allowed to evade tax by having multiplicity of firms or multiplicity of assessments or entities. So, if you make the individual as the basis…in fact, what you should do is that you should go a step further and say that taxation should be only at the level of the individual. This business of registered firms should be abolished, which Chelliah has recommended. Please abolish tax on all firms. Taxation should be only in the case of the partners and as per their shares in the firm. That way, most of the spurious concerns will go. You will have more honest or more reasonable tax returns. I think this is one of the recommendations of the Chelliah Committee which should be accepted in full.

PRODUCTIVE AND NON-PRODUCTIVE TAX

Regarding presumptive taxation, you have made a good beginning. I think it should be extended to the truck operators, laundries and small bakeries, where lakhs of people are involved and whose income is definitely above ₹28,000, but they are not in the tax bracket. They will not come in the tax bracket because they are not maintaining accounts in the manner that the income tax people want them to do. You will never be able to collect tax from them. The best way is presumptive taxation, according to the type of investment, according to the size of the unit and the location.

It is not difficult for the assessing officer to know that a person having a shop in Chandni Chowk or Connaught Place will be earning some minimum amount. You can still get a lot of revenue from those who are today escaping from taxation. The other type is wealth tax, which is very progressive. You have differentiated between productive and non-productive [tax]. It is very good. Please take it further. This is the suggestion which I have been giving for the last two or three years, that wealth which generates income should be treated differently and wealth that does not generate income should be treated separately. Somebody wants to keep his money in the form of gold or ornaments or cash. He should pay a part of it to the exchequer. If that money had been in the economy, he would have got some money out of it. So the rationale is very good. It should be carried to its logical conclusion. Care should be taken in the drafting so that we don't add to the litigation because that will not help us.

Coming to the other two forms of tax, I want to say something about the gift tax and the estate duty, which has been abolished. I feel the Gift Tax Act can go. You must have a simple provision in the Income Tax Act. Apart from income of various types, any accretion to wealth—a part of it should go to the exchequer. If a father is leaving a legacy to his son, the son has got some money without doing anything—a part of it he must pay to the exchequer. If somebody has received some money in the form of a gift from his relatives—everybody has got an uncle or cousin in America—abroad, from whatever source, he is richer to that extent. So, he must pay a part of it to the exchequer. That part of it may be 20 per cent or 25 per cent. That is up to the finance minister to decide. But please make it simple.

The then finance minister, Shri Madhu Dandavate, had introduced a bill for gift tax on donees. But that bill lapsed because of a change in the government. That was also a complicated bill. I say, in the Income Tax Act, please add one more section that apart from the other income, any accretion to a person's wealth, he must pay so much to the exchequer. Make that 20 per cent, I don't mind. But see to it that anybody who is becoming rich shares it with the exchequer.

IS IT THE WORLD BANK AND IMF IDEOLOGY?

On excise and customs duties, I differ with this government. I do not understand the rationale of increasing the excise duty and reducing the customs duty. Is it the World Bank and IMF ideology? Do they feel if customs duty is reduced, your competitiveness will go up and industry will be able to compete? I think all that is far-fetched. In India iron ore, tea, cotton and jute are the only things that we can export. In spite of the best attempts of the government they have not kept pace. People are producing TV sets or other so-called hi-tech products for export. But they become obsolete before they can export them.

The issue is very simple—your traditional exports are the only items, ultimately, on which you have to depend. You have reduced customs duty. Give it a try and see. As far as we are concerned, we are very clear that compression of import is the answer to your problems. On allowing imports there was a debate. The then finance minister, Shri Yashwant Sinha, had compressed imports. The commerce minister, Shri Chidambaram, says to the press that last year our balance of trade has been the least in deficit. It is because Shri Sinha had compressed the imports.

The other debate is [that] industrial production has fallen because of import compression. There is no empirical data. Either the government should give us the data or they should not tell us that because imports were restricted, the industry did not run. I have tried to figure out from industrialist friends and others who know. Nobody has been able to give me a concrete instance of the import restriction affecting production. They wanted to give me some macro-economic figures. It did not help me. I said, 'Has your industry suffered because of import restrictions?' The answer was 'no'. Basically, I have not found a single person coming forward and telling me that because he could not import components or because he had difficulties as the LC (Letter of Credit) margin was 200 per cent, he had suffered. His import might have become costlier. But I do not think that basically industrial production or even export production has been affected. Well, after all, import for export is still allowed. That has taken care of you by a 60:40 ratio by REP (Replenishment licences) or Eximscrips. Import for export was always allowed.

KEEP A FINGER ON THE THIRTIETH OF EACH MONTH

But should we have import for the running of your industry? I am not sure. I feel that you should have a second look at import compression. All this liberalized trade policy is good. But the finance minister should keep a finger on the thirtieth of every month to put, if necessary, import curbs. In a country like India, import should be restricted. You should not have free imports because people are importing all sorts of fancy gadgets. It is a drain on the foreign exchange.

On customs and excise, there was a sub-committee of the finance consultation committee when Shri Rajiv Gandhi was himself holding the finance portfolio. That sub-committee had come to the conclusion that the ad valorem rates should not be reverted to because there was a lot of evasion, there was a lot of corruption and there was a lot of litigation. The sub-committee came to the conclusion that after all, the ad valorem rates helped the revenue because when the prices went up, the government got more money. The committee gave a report—which Shri Rajiv Gandhi had accepted—that we should have specific rates and the tariff value could be revised periodically.

In the case of cigarettes, one of your ex-chairmen of the CBEC has written an article that the tariff value should be revised every six months or every three months, so that there would be no loss of revenue. But in this budget, you have made a major change, not in cigarettes thankfully, but in other items, from specific to ad valorem. I think theoretically it may be a progressive measure, but in Indian conditions, it is a regressive measure. We, again, will have people who will not pay tax; we will have litigations; we, again, will have a heap of problems which can be avoided. On excise and customs, these are my views.

To conclude, I have seen the figures on income tax. Twenty years ago, 25 per cent of the non-agricultural net domestic product (NDP) was reflected in the person's income tax returns. Later on, it became 15 per cent. Today, only 7 to 8 per cent of the non-agricultural NDP is being returned by personal assessees. This shows how much we are adding to the pool of black money every year. In 1988–89, out of thirty lakh assessees—personal assessees, not corporate—only one lakh assessees were showing an income above ₹1 lakh. It is not possible that in this country, there are only one lakh of people with an income of more than ₹1 lakh.

With the consumer boom, with Maruti cars selling like hot cakes, with all the new gadgets selling like hot cakes, there are only one lakh of people whose annual income is more than ₹1 lakh? This is absolutely transparent tax evasion and the entire system should be changed.

Even as a percentage of the NDP, 2.7 per cent used to constitute personal tax. It is now only 1.7 per cent. All these figures are well known to the finance minister. I would only request him, if the Direct Taxes Code is coming—Shri Rameshwar Thakur used to mention it in every form, but recently, I have seen him silent on it; I do not know whether it has been postponed—please bring it in such a manner that we do not have this rampant evasion and have more revenue with least pain. Certainly, we should not cause pain to the people who are working with their hands.

THE CONSTITUTION IS MEANT TO PROTECT THE MINORITY

Morarka makes a lucid and passionate plea to realize—post 6 December 1992—the true spirit of Hinduism, which has flourished for more than 4,000 years and does not require the hatred of other religions to continue to do so. The Bharatiya Janata Party's (BJP) quest for power, he says, is understandable; what is not is the manner in which they are attempting to get it. He says 'The issue today is not of secularism or communalism, the issue is of the rule of law or vandalism. A civilized India or a barbaric India—that is the central issue facing us today.' And then he asks, 'Because 85 per cent of the Indian population is Hindu and because Hindu tradition talks of religious tolerance, you are able to have this polity. So, what is wrong with it? Why are we developing an inferiority complex today? Why do we want to change it?' He was speaking on 11 March 1993 in the Mention of Thanks on the President's Address. Twenty years later, his questions continue to demand answers.

The central point which is engaging the attention of the country, consciously or subconsciously, is of the polity that is being developed in the country with the events of 6 December. It has been discussed before in this House, but I say with a lot of anguish that after the event, in the last three months the kind of tone and tenor that is being adopted has a very, very serious foreboding for the future of this country. I say that with all seriousness.

I stay in Bombay (Mumbai). What has happened in Bombay

in January, if I recount it in this House, I am sure people will be shocked beyond belief. A lot has been printed in newspapers. I do not want to go into the details of these incidents. But suffice it to say, for a person like me who was born at the dawn of Independence, I feel we have taken a lot of things for granted. We have grown up in free India. Democracy is a way of life, which we have accepted from birth. For a person like me, the issue today is not of secularism or communalism, the issue is of the rule of law or vandalism. A civilized India or a barbaric India—that is the central issue facing us today.

> The issue today is not of communalism. The BJP is not just a communal party in my opinion. It is anti-Constitution. What the BJP is trying to do today is to demolish the entire structure that has been built ever since the dawn of Independence.

ENLIGHTENMENT IS DIFFICULT, IGNORANCE IS EASY

In a political process, different parties have different views. The BJP is accusing the Congress of being communal, has accused the Janata Dal and us of being pro-minorities. We have been accusing them of a particular line of thinking. But after 6 December all that has changed. The issue today is not of communalism. The BJP is not just a communal party, in my opinion. It is anti-Constitution. What the BJP is trying to do today is to demolish the entire structure that has been built ever since the dawn of Independence. I think the Parliament, both Houses of Parliament, and the people in general must start debating this point.

I do not support the steps taken by the government immediately after 6 December. We have held the government guilty of inaction before 6 December and of over-action and wrong type of action after 6 December. For instance, dismissal of the three governments, other than Uttar Pradesh—we see no logic in doing it. Banning of organizations—when democracy is in full play, unless there is an emergency, banning of organizations is impracticable—all that we have opposed. But that is not the issue. We know that the leader of Opposition in the Lok Sabha enjoys a cabinet minister's status. There were a lot of objections when he was arrested. We ourselves thought that, probably, when Parliament is in session, he should have been allowed to attend it. But what happens in the meantime?

On 7 December, people who are defensive about what has happened...when these leaders are released from jail, the entire atmosphere is changed; they adopt a militant tone. Enlightenment is difficult. To go into darkness is very easy; ignorance is very easy. I am one of those who believe that our freedom struggle threw up the greatest of leaders that any part of the world could be proud of. I believe that our Constitution, as adopted in 1950, is one of the most enlightened and incontrovertible documents that could be produced in any part of the world.

THE MOST FANTASTIC ADVENTURE

Over the last forty-five years, we have had a lot of difficulties. We have amended the Constitution. We are trying to make it work. But I would plead that India is engaged in one of the most fantastic adventures in world history: we are trying a peaceful socio-economic transformation of one-sixth of the world's population by the democratic process. Nowhere else in the world can anybody claim to be doing even a part of this experiment. The only other country is China, and they do not have a democratic process.

> I have no objection if the BJP, as a political party, wants to try to come to power. But what they are doing now is to take the country backwards—into darkness. What they are today trying to tell us is that a part of us are lesser Indians than the rest of us.

In all the developing countries, from Iran to South Asia, democracy has been extinguished. India is a country where democracy has been in full play.

Every five years and recently, unfortunately, every two or three years, there have been Lok Sabha elections—free and fair elections. I have no objection if the BJP, as a political party, wants to try to come to power. After all, they are in the political process: one day they want to come to power. I have no grievance about that. But what they are doing now is to take the country backwards—into darkness. What they are today trying to tell us is that a part of us are lesser Indians than the rest of us.

THE MYTH OF APPEASEMENT

I am a Hindu; I am proud to be a Hindu. But after 6 December—mark my words—when I meet people from another community, especially a Muslim friend of mine, I have to hang my head down. I have to admit before him that some of my brethren have done him wrong. What are the issues that are being raised every day by them? They are petty issues—which they call appeasement of minorities. Their entire tone is that the minorities have had it too good in this country; the Constitution is for the majority. They have got it all wrong. The Constitution, as a document, is only meant to protect the minority. The majority elects Parliament. Why do we need a Constitution? We don't need a Constitution: normal rules are enough. But the Constitution is meant precisely for this purpose: it is to protect those who are not in a majority.

> If we go by their thesis that the majority must have its own way then why talk only of a religious majority, why not an economic majority?

Parliament, even by unanimity, can pass a law. An aggrieved citizen can go to the Supreme Court, and the Supreme Court can strike it down. The majority will and can, unanimously, pass a law and still it can be struck down. That is enlightenment. The Constitution-makers have kept a provision that when a minority is sought to be trampled upon by the majority, the court will protect them. If their thesis is correct—that this structure was a disputed structure, the courts took too much time and so we went and took control of it—by this doctrine, in the case of a disputed property, 200 people can enter a house and say, 'The court is taking too much time and we are taking possession.' And then if somebody tries to intervene, their logic is, 'No, no, if we are doing something wrong, let's take a vote.'

> After 6 December 1992 the issue is whether we are going to run this socio-economic process, which we have adopted in 1947, by this system or we are to bring about some basic changes in which the democratic process itself is extinguished.

You cannot decide disputes properly by a vote. The voting process is meant to elect a government. Having put a government into place, the voting process comes again when its term ends or when the government loses majority in Parliament. Every issue cannot be put to the people. This is a very dangerous doctrine. If we go by their thesis that the majority must have its own way then why talk only of a religious majority, why not an economic majority? Why should not the slum dwellers of Delhi be allowed to enter others' houses and say that the houses belong to them? Why should not all the jhuggi/jhonpari wallahs say, 'Let's take a vote whether all these housing colonies should belong to us or not?'

AN ARTIFICIAL FRENZY AND MUSCLE POWER

Are we living in a civilized society? That is the issue today. The issue is not of communalism, the issue is not of fundamentalism. Those issues are behind us, those issues are prior to 6 December.

After 6 December 1992 the issue is whether we are going to run this socio-economic process, which we have adopted in 1947, by this system or we are to bring about some basic changes in which the democratic process itself is extinguished.

They are very senior leaders. I have great personal respect, not only for their competence but for their integrity. I may not agree with them, but I have great respect for them. But something has gone wrong. And what has gone wrong? A very simple thing is that they see power coming. There is religious frenzy. It is like holding a plebiscite in Kashmir. I put it to them: are they prepared to agree that there should be a plebiscite in Kashmir? Why not? If people's will is going to determine everything, why do we not allow a plebiscite in Kashmir? Why not? No, because they know that a plebiscite in Kashmir cannot be free and fair. The entire atmosphere is charged with religion. So, the issue will be obfuscated.

> Because 85 per cent of the Indian population is Hindu and because Hindu tradition talks of religious tolerance, you are able to have this polity. So, what is wrong with it? Why are we developing an inferiority complex today? Why do we want to change it?

They have created an artificial frenzy and showed the muscle of the majority to trample upon the minority, and they want a vote to be taken. I belong to a party which has opposed this government on its economic policies. It is they who supported this government. When we said that our ethos of forty-five years should not be extinguished by notifications, and if Jawaharlal Nehru and Indira Gandhi had taken so much time to build an economic structure, not to demolish it by notifications, they did not listen to us. Why? Because the party of the leader of the Opposition and the Congress together have about 400 MPs in the Lok Sabha. Shri Advani said, 'This is the best prime minister the country has ever had.' They supported the economic policies. When they were supporting them, they were basking in the glory of the support of the Opposition party.

CONVERTING INDIAN CULTURE INTO A STRAITJACKET

Four thousand years of philosophy and culture cannot be wiped out by all of us who are pygmies in this process. What we are seeking to do is to convert Indian culture and history into a straitjacket which is envisaged by a few of us. It is not possible. There is substance in some of the things they say. Only their inferences are wrong. For instance, they say that India is secular because it is predominantly Hindu. They are correct.

Because 85 per cent of the Indian population is Hindu and because Hindu tradition talks of religious tolerance, you are able to have this polity. So, what is wrong with it? Why are we developing an inferiority complex today? Why do we want to change it? I am proud of it. Eighty-five per cent of our population—largely illiterate, in poverty, suffering privations, wants to live in dignity and allow others to live in dignity. I think this is a proud thing.

But they say today that 85 per cent of us are allowing the rest of the 15 per cent to live here. That is not true. India was never a Hindu country. India was India. If at all they want to use a word, they must use 'Sanatan Dharm'. The very meaning of 'Sanatan Dharm' is what is perpetual, what is true for all times to come. The Hindu philosophy is one philosophy where there is not one book, not one guru, not one final authority. I am a Hindu, I can never be expelled from Hinduism. The Shankaracharya cannot expel me. Nobody can expel me. Ashok Singhal certainly cannot.

I do not understand this. We have the Vedas, the Upanishads, the Bhagwad Gita, the Ramayana, the Mahabharata. We have got a treasure house of wisdom in the Hindu pantheon. Today I find that somebody has got an organization, got it registered under the Societies Act, and wants us to believe that he has the last word on the interpretation of Hinduism. This is not acceptable. They may not agree with me today.

If their only aim is to win elections, they already had governments in four states. In the electoral process, somebody wins and somebody else loses, but they will never be able to change the ethos of the Hindu mind. Aurangzeb ruled here. It is history. Aurangzeb did not tolerate the way of worship by the Hindus and their religion. In spite of that, he could not convert the Hindus to become anti-Muslim. What Aurangzeb could not do, I am sure the Rashtriya Swayamsevak Sangh (RSS) and the Vishwa Hindu Parishad (VHP) cannot do. They are trying to convert the Hindu mind and to make India a Hindu version of Pakistan. It is not possible. They are barking up the wrong tree.

WHAT IS THE FIGHT ABOUT?

The very things they want to do, they keep on denying. Shri Advani will say in a press conference that India can never become a Hindu country. They are trying to say this was always a Hindu Rashtra. Then they say the Indian Muslims should call themselves Muhammadi Hindus. I don't understand this. If they have got such a large heart that they are prepared to agree that Muslims here are also part of the same ethos, then what is the fight about? The RSS says it wants to unify the Hindus. If they can really unite the 85 per cent, then all the 100 per cent will get unified. I don't understand against whom they want to unify the Hindus. If you want to unify all the countrymen against a foreign aggressor, I can understand that, but the moment you say you want to unify the Hindus, it means against those who are not Hindus. They may go on saying they are not anti-Muslim but every step of theirs leads you only to that.

> Aurangzeb [...] could not convert the Hindus to become anti-Muslim. What Aurangzeb could not do, I am sure the RSS and the VHP cannot do. They are trying to convert the Hindu mind and to make India a Hindu version of Pakistan.

I am sorry Sushma Swarajji is not here today. Day before yesterday she spoke very well. But see how the mental attitude comes out. She said: 'We are proud of our heritage; we are proud of our culture where a king imprisons his father. We do not have a culture where the king kills his brother to get to the throne.' There she was referring to Aurangzeb. But Ashoka was not on her consciousness. He killed a hundred of his brothers to get to the throne. Was he part of the culture or not?

We are not educating our masses today. We are de-educating them. For 4,000 years they themselves have got a natural feel. Those who do not speak in Parliament and those who are not articulate—even they understand that the ethos of Hinduism is to live and let live. That cannot change. I do not understand what is the big change after 6 December. Till 6 December, Shri Narasimha Rao was the best prime minister the country ever had. And after 7 December, they say, his government must go and elections must be held. I do not understand this transformation. They have grounds to feel that suddenly the Hindu inferiority complex has been awakened successfully by them and they will be able to garner the Hindu votes.

OPEN A DIALOGUE WITH THE MUSLIMS

This is not correct. We are doing a lasting damage to this country. Posterity will never forgive us. I do not grudge their coming to power. Many of them are very competent people. Let them rule in the states and let them rule at the Centre if the people elect them, but let them not destroy the heritage of this country, for which the people suffered imprisonment and shed their blood. It is my earnest request to them that the BJP as a political party must revise its stand and try to undo the damage that had been done on 6 December. If they are serious about solving the problem, the ball is in their court. They must open a dialogue with the Muslim community and heal their wounds. If they want to show patriotism, it is their patriotism which is on test.

They cannot say that a Muslim in India has to prove his patriotism. I mention this with anguish. Shri Satish Pradhan is not here. In Bombay, the statements made by the Shiv Sena chief[1] were uncivilized. He told the *Time* magazine that the Muslims have to be kicked out of this country. The next day he clarified by saying that he did not say that. What he meant was that Pakistanis and Bangladeshis and also those who help them must go. So his clarification is not much of a clarification. He feels Muslims have no place in this country. Then he adds that those who are patriotic can stay. Now, who is going to give a certificate of patriotism?

We are living in a civilized country. If anybody does anything anti-national, there are enough laws. Please book him, lodge an FIR, try him in the courts, whether he is a Muslim or a Hindu. You cannot decide suddenly about patriotism, saying because somebody was seen clapping at a cricket match for a Pakistani player, his patriotism is in doubt, if he is a Muslim. If I say Imran Khan is a good bowler, my patriotism is not in doubt, since I am [a] Hindu. But if a Muslim claps for Imran Khan, immediately eyebrows are raised, why was he clapping for a Pakistani bowler? Can there be anything more petty? This is not childish, this is churlish.

THIS IS BLASPHEMY

Then they say namaz was being held on the streets and on loudspeakers and they occupied the roads. As a counter, in Bombay, maha aarti was started. In Islam, there is a concept of collective prayer on Friday; in Christianity, there is a concept of collective prayer on Sunday. In Hinduism, there is no such concept. They gather as a crowd in a front of a small Ganesh mandir. And just to carry on the aarti for three hours, they sing aarti of all the gods. This is blasphemy. What are they trying to tell us about religion? They want to create a law and order situation. They want to make

---

[1]Shri Balasaheb Thackeray

a normal Hindu feel, 'Look here, the Muslims have had it too good. You better come with us.' There is an air of terror in them.

If I say Imran Khan is a good bowler, my patriotism is not in doubt, since I am [a] Hindu. But if a Muslim claps for Imran Khan, immediately eyebrows are raised, why was he clapping for a Pakistani bowler? Can there be anything pettier?

After 6 December, I see a normal Hindu is not able to speak up; he is not able to say that what they are saying is wrong. My concept is, Hindu religion, Hindu philosophy is tolerant. I will end by saying what their concept is. Their concept is, 'We believe in Hinduism. The Hindu religion is very Catholic in its spirit. We are very tolerant. If you don't agree with us, we will beat you up.'

KASHMIR MUST BE TREATED DIFFERENTLY

'No political solution is possible unless you talk. Talking is elementary to any political solution,' Morarka declares in the discussion on a statutory resolution, Seeking Approval of President's Rule in Jammu & Kashmir, on 27 August 1991. He points out that if the people there face callous treatment from the government, find no jobs and take up guns, the retaliation cannot be to take away their right to change the government. 'There cannot be a bigger travesty of truth than this,' he says of the statement that the problem is that Kashmir has been treated differently and it should be treated like any other state.

The issue of Kashmir has come up for discussion in this House again and again and, unfortunately, for the last two or three years, wherever we have discussed Kashmir, we have been discussing the extension of President's Rule. Before that, there was the Governor's Rule. Across party lines, it will be said by everybody that a political solution to the Kashmir problem should be found, that Pakistan is playing mischief in Kashmir and that the political process should again begin in Kashmir.

But some basic and fundamental facts are always overlooked and unless we solve that basic problem, I am afraid we will not make any headway in Kashmir. We will have to again extend the President's Rule which, I am sure everybody agrees, is not a democratic solution or a desirable thing in our present scheme of the Constitution. Kashmir has a long history. Unfortunately, my BJP friends are not here. Yesterday, Shri Krishan Lal Sharma said that according to him, the problem is that Kashmir has been treated differently; it should be treated like any other state in India. There cannot be a bigger travesty of truth than this.

KASHMIR IS HISTORICALLY DIFFERENT

Kashmir, historically, is different and it has to be treated differently. The integration of Kashmir into India is legally and constitutionally complete, but if we have problems with the population there and if that problem has to have a solution, it can be had only if we, on our part, respect whatever promises and pledges we have given to the Kashmir people at the time of accession of Kashmir to India.

> **It may surprise the people to know that Kashmir is the only place where there were no communal riots, not even at the time of Partition.**

The question of Article 370 crops up again and again. It is very clear that the accession of Kashmir to India is on the basis of certain conditions which have been incorporated under Article 370. I do not understand how abrogation of Article 370 can ever achieve integration of Kashmir into India.

If the psychology of the Kashmiri has to be changed, or if we have to motivate them into remaining integrated, emotionally integrated, with the rest of India, it is incumbent on our part not only to fulfil whatever has been promised to them but also in our conduct to prove that India is a secular state.

Kashmir was the only Muslim majority state in the whole of India which decided to accede to India and not to Pakistan. Because we rejected the two-nation theory, because we said, 'India is going to have a secular Constitution. Every Indian is going to live here with dignity.' After forty years if we turn around and say,

'No, all that is wrong, and we will have dominance of one religion over another, we are going to have disputes like we have in other parts of the country'—what is the message that you are sending to the people of Kashmir by this? It is that the ethos of India, the ethos of the Government of India which was there at the time of Independence, has undergone a change.

By this, you cannot have the willing cooperation of the Kashmiri people. These are fundamental facts. When there is an all-party meeting, I think we should talk to our friends. We should bring them round. If we have made the pledge to a whole population in one part of the country, on the basis of which you promised them and they agreed to accede to us, we should do nothing to create the remotest doubt that we are trying to negotiate our pledge.

EMPLOYMENT AND PROSPERITY

Kashmir has become a complex problem today. If we want a peaceful and orderly socio-economic transformation, there are certain basic conditions. The first condition is: are you able to give employment and prosperity to the people? In a country like India it is difficult to make changes which are visible. The population is large. We have limitation of resources.

> **As is likely to be, if an army stays in a place for a long time, there are going to be complaints.**

When the people feel that the rulers have become insensitive, that there is rampant corruption, that the limited resources are being frittered away, when they see every day that their due right is being denied to them, then there is the third thing, and they feel, 'We must have the right to change the government. If the government is not behaving properly, if it becomes insensitive, we have the right to change the government.'

The real problem now in Punjab and Kashmir is that even

the third thing has been taken away. Even their right to change the government has been taken away from them. When you take that away, when the people's lot cannot be changed, when the government is seen to behave in a callous manner and the people do not have a right to change their government, then they take up guns and arms. This is the fundamental truth in any part of the world. Now what is the argument? We say, 'Because you have taken to guns, we will not give you the right to vote. Because you have taken to guns and terrorism, conditions are not normal. So, we will not allow you to vote.' That means you are going to perpetuate the state of affairs.

Unless you allow them to have a government of their own choice, passions are not going to cool down, whether it is in Punjab or in Kashmir or in Assam or anywhere. The Constitution-makers themselves thought that a situation may arise that for a short time the central rule may have to be directly applied to a state.

SUBSIDIES ARE NOT REACHING THE PEOPLE

The Constitution-makers never envisaged that by the amending power of the Constitution you will make central rule a perpetual state of affairs, to the extent that people in Punjab or in Kashmir will start thinking that they are a colony of Delhi. You have an army there. As is likely to be, if an army stays in a place for a long time, there are going to be complaints. One small incident is going to be blown out of proportion. There will be a general atmosphere of this kind because you have censorship. Journalists cannot go there and there is no political activity. There is a general air of suspicion.

If our own population in Kashmir is disenchanted with the central government, that is our fault. Surely Pakistan must be doing something nefarious, but unless the central government is able to create confidence in the Kashmiri people that we are going to abide by whatever promises we have given to them, we won't make headway.

Another argument that is given here is that Kashmir is already pampered. So many subsidies are going to Kashmir. Already Kashmir is getting aid disproportionate to its population, compared to other states. But the lot of the people has not improved in spite of your aid. You are subsidizing all right. But successive administrations in Kashmir have been run in such an inefficient manner, to use a mild word, that the people feel that they have got a raw deal.

Unemployment and poverty is more rampant in Kashmir than in any part of the country. The argument given by our friends is that since Kashmir is being treated in a special way, it is high time that special arrangement is terminated. That Kashmir's integration will be complete the moment you remove Article 370. That argument falls flat on its face.

COMMUNAL POLITICS INTRODUCED FOR THE FIRST TIME

I do not want to go into the history of Kashmir. From 1947 to 1987, there has been a series of mistakes we have made. But the present situation can be directly traced to certain mistakes we made in 1984. A popular government was dismissed. There were defections and a new chief minister was appointed there[1]. He has the dubious credit of introducing communal politics in Kashmir for the first time. It may surprise the people to know that Kashmir is the only place where there were no communal riots, not even at the time of Partition.

Communalism was introduced in the state of Jammu and Kashmir. This poison was introduced courtesy the puppet chief minister whose government was installed in 1984. There was an election in 1987. There was a Muslim United Front which got 35 per cent of the popular vote. They got around five seats in the Assembly. I do not know—I have not been to Kashmir—how the

---

[1] In 1984, the Farooq Abdullah government was dismissed by the governor, and Ghulam Mohammad Shah, who was pro-Congress, took his place.

elections were conducted. But there is a widespread belief that those elections were rigged. If elections are rigged, the discontentment will surface immediately. We have seen it happening in Pakistan. We have seen it happening in our own Assam. In Kashmir the November 1989 Lok Sabha elections in the entire Valley witnessed a 2 per cent voting. This means the boycott of the elections is complete.

> The argument given by our friends is that since Kashmir is being treated in a special way, it is high time that special arrangement is terminated. That Kashmir's integration will be complete the moment you remove Article 370. That argument falls flat on its face.

I do not even know the members of the Muslim United Front, but the fact remains that if they have a following of 35 per cent in the Valley, they are a relevant force to speak on behalf of the citizens of the Valley. Then what happened? Because of the persistent attitude of the local government, all those forces have gone underground. Now we are trying to search with whom to talk. We heard Shri Kapil Verma of the Congress (I) just now telling us, 'If you talk to one group, the other group will eliminate you.' All these problems happen whenever democracy is subjugated, whenever you are going to do artificial things.

COMMITTING A CARDINAL SIN

Now your problem is bigger. If you had allowed elections to be conducted properly, probably we would have had a legitimate government, which would have solved the problems there locally. Even now the Kashmir imbroglio can be solved only by returning the power to the people. Without that nothing is possible. My last point is: what is this government doing? One can say there is a long history. So many governments have changed.

Now look at the cardinal sin that the government has committed—it invites a British Labour Party leader, Mr Gerald Kauffman. He comes to India. He is the shadow foreign secretary. As usual, our mental slavery of forty years persists. The white-skinned man is very important to us. He was welcomed and allowed to go to the Valley. First of all, that should be banned because Indian leaders are unable to go there. Why did you arrange a visit of the shadow foreign secretary of the UK? What was the statement that he gave? He said, 'Plebiscite is the only solution for Jammu and Kashmir.' On the one side we have our friends who are saying, 'Abolish Article 370 and forget about Kashmir as a problem.' On the other side, the government wants to invite a foreigner who comes and tells us that the issue of accession is still open. I don't understand this. I do not know whether the prime minister knew about this. I do not know whether the foreign minister knew about it. Of course, from the statement the government has given recently over the Russian developments, I feel no government is functioning.

I come to the final point. When we were in power for a very short time, we initiated a dialogue with the extremists or the militants in Punjab. In Kashmir, we tried to make contacts, but it was not so easy. No political solution is possible unless you talk. Talking is elementary to any political solution.

GIVE A DOG A BAD NAME AND HANG IT

The public sector is everyone's favourite whipping boy. Speaking on Disinvestment in the Public Sector on 5 May 1992, Morarka makes a dispassionate assessment of the government's treatment of this sector, pointing out the lopsided policies, the unrealistic expectations and what could be done to remedy the situation. As he had said then, 'Fifteen years ago, nationalization was the panacea... Today, the pendulum has swung the other way. Privatization is the panacea.' Neither, he observed, is the solution. Questioning the selling of public-sector equity at premium rates and using it for revenue expenditure, he likens it to selling the family silver to pay grocery bills.

Ever since the government[1] has come to power, they are systematically adopting a policy where a large part of this ministry has already become redundant. Obviously, with 80 per cent of the work going away, they do not have any work. We have said enough on the economic policy. We do not agree with the main postulates of their policy. I want to test them on the touchstone of their own policy.

THIS IS OUR BENT OF MIND

For the Khadi and Village Industries Commission (KVIC), a new department was created, called the Department for Small-scale, Agro

---

[1] The P.V. Narasimha Rao government that came to power in 1991.

and Rural Industries. This was created when the National Front government was in power and when Ajit Singh was the industry minister. Today, what do we find? It is a part of the Department of Industrial Development. It is not even a separate department recognized enough to have a separate report of its own.

> Tell them that employment generation is their main business. And if they cannot do that, they must become unemployed first. There is no use having an army of officers sitting in Udyog Bhavan who have no work to do. Please send them to the rural areas.

This is not a small lapse [that] I am pointing out. This is our bent of mind. The small-scale, rural and agro industries take a back seat. They are nowhere in our priority of things. It is clear from all the records that the best ratio (investment employment) of the maximum employment generation with the minimum investment is in the small industry, in the khadi and village sector. Anybody who wants to restructure the industry—even by their policy—should have thought and acted in a way where the KVIC would be used as the nodal point for creation of employment. You are going to dislocate industrial employment. Avowedly, the policies are anti-employment.

Please do not do it. Please have an alternative employment strategy. What is being done (within your department)? Please tell them to go to the villages. Tell them that employment generation is their main business. And if they cannot do that, they must become unemployed first. There is no use having an army of officers sitting in Udyog Bhavan who have no work to do. Please send them to the rural areas. This should be the first reorientation [and] restructuring of this department.

THE FASHION OF THE DAY IS TO DISOWN NEHRU

The public sector consists of hundreds of industries in different sectors of the economy, with different units and different locations. Bunching them together and discussing their performance is very foolish. Then it should be the same for the private sector also. I am sorry to say that today we are talking about the public sector in such a way as to give the dog a bad name and then hang it. First, we invented the public sector as being special to India. It was done by Jawaharlal Nehru who called them 'Temples of Modern India'. Today, there is the fashion of Nehru-baiting. The last Congress speaker has criticized Nehru more eloquently than anybody else can. The order of the day is to disown Nehru. People like Mahatma Gandhi, Jawaharlal Nehru and Sardar Patel have passed into history. They are beyond criticism by the pygmies of today.

Let us come to the basics. We have a public sector. We have made this large investment. It is the ground reality. What do we propose to do?

Yes, we have a lot of problems. First, the public sector as a whole is not generating money. The finance minister is rightly concerned that apart from the taxes from the private sector, he should get some money from the public sector. The public sector is not all under the ministry of industries. It is distributed in the petroleum sector, the fertilizer sector, coal sector and energy sector, in a wide spectrum of ministries.

Which are the public-sector units that are not doing well? Why are they not doing well? Can they be improved? Fifteen years ago, nationalization was the panacea. Today the pendulum has swung the other way. Privatization is the panacea. Let us understand that neither nationalization nor privatization can be the panacea. Every unit has a problem of its own that must be solved on its own merits.

MANAGEMENT, TECHNOLOGY, PRODUCTIVITY, MARKETING

What is relevant is management; what is relevant is technology; what is relevant is productivity and what is relevant is marketing.

These are relevant aspects, and not who owns the shares, because the shareholders get only the dividends. As one speaker pointed out, in the private sector also, the person who controls the company owns 4 per cent or 5 per cent or 7 per cent of the share of the company.

In the public sector also, there are good managers and bad managers. The unfortunate thing about the public sector is that we try to governmentalize it, which we should not have done. Most complaints that we make in Parliament are not of a criminal nature. They are of impropriety. The managing director (MD) either misuses his power or favours somebody or has done some unethical practice. Your joint director sits on the board of the public sector undertaking. He knows what has happened. If the MD has done something wrong, sack that MD and appoint a new one. The country is full of MDs who want to serve the public sector.

PARLIAMENT IS THE OWNER

But in the government we have a system. First, we won't appoint a person, we will go on processing files. Having appointed a person, we will not remove that person. I am not talking of the IAS and the cadre posts. But in a business enterprise, accountability is the crux of the matter. A CMD (chairman and managing director) who cannot give you the results must go. He must make way for somebody else. That is the only criterion.

You are the owner. Parliament is the owner. The unit has to be accountable to Parliament through the government. The government must appoint the managers. Of course, a manager has to function within his constraints. These constraints are also in the private sector. After all, Tata Iron and Steel Company Limited (TISCO) is a Tata concern only in name. It is managed by [the] people who get a salary. The board of directors lays down the policy. If you can't do the job, they will sack you and put somebody else.

The government is the owner. The president of India, in fact, is the owner. I do not understand what is the dichotomy and why we get confused. We get confused because we are afraid of taking the right decision at the right time.

YOU START BLAMING THE WORKERS

We have been procrastinating things for too long. A stage has come today when the country's finances are in trouble. So we are trying to find scapegoats. If a public sector undertaking is not doing well, you start blaming the workers. Are there different set of workers in the country for the public sector and the private sector? Are there different trade union leaders? The private sector is also dealing with their trade unions. They are doing it successfully. They are having collective bargaining.

Again, the crux of the matter is that the private-sector managers are afraid to face the trade unions because the managers themselves are indulging in unethical practices.

I am happy that all Central Daily Allowance (CDA) has been effective from 1 January 1987. It is very good for workers. But whose money are you giving? And why should the same wage apply across the board? Workers of a good unit are definitely entitled to ask for higher wages. They must share the prosperity of their unit. What will happen in an inefficient unit? The workers will gherao the manager. Today, none of your managers' lives are made miserable. The man who is making losses is also sitting pretty. He immediately concedes to the labour union's demand. But who is paying?

PRODUCTIVITY WILL IMPROVE BY TALKING TO THE WORKMAN

The day your managing directors in the state unit come to terms with the fact that you will not be able to run an industrial unit without the cooperation of the workers, that day you will see prosperity; otherwise not. Unfortunately, during the last forty years, what has been happening is that your MD is sitting in his own ivory tower and you cannot get productivity by attending seminars. Productivity will improve only by sitting with the worker and talking to him.

> You cannot do an inefficient thing and cover it under some social clause. They have sold ₹2,500 crore of equity at whatever price and used that money for revenue expenditure. That is like selling your family silver to pay your grocery bills!

Unfortunately, the trend now is that after Nehru-baiting and public-sector-baiting, we have now taken to worker-baiting. This will not work. We are just running away from the problem. The workers are not to be blamed at all. There has to be an 'exit policy' for the management and not for the workers. Workers do not make an exit because they did not come there voluntarily, but were employed. If you over-employ and the technology has changed, the workers have to be rationalized and the trade unions fully understand this.

The BIFR is sitting down with the MDs and workers and I can assure the minister that the BIFR has not found the trade unions uncooperative. They have found the financial institutions uncooperative, they have found the state governments uncooperative and sometimes, they have found the promoters not willing to put more money. But they have not found a single cause where the workers of the trade unions have not cooperated to resurrect the industry.

BELLIES TOO BIG TO TIGHTEN BELT

You cannot have corrupt managements who are openly taking bribes or doing wrong things or indulging in wrong practices and then you want the workers to tackle them. The workers will not listen. This is not only with the public sector; in the private sector, too, the case is the same. If the company is doing well, everybody must share its prosperity. If the company is not doing well, everybody must tighten his belt. But people who say that you should tighten your belt are those having bellies so big that they cannot tighten the belt at all!

In the case of the public-sector disinvestment, what has been done? Last year, ₹2,500 crore worth equity was sold. If the public sector was not doing well, how was the equity sold at a premium? We have sold all our profit-making companies whose equity the mutual funds or the banks were prepared to buy. Who has fixed the price? Why have the mutual funds determined the price? If you believe in market economy they must first get the shares quoted by the stock exchange.

LIKE SELLING THE FAMILY SILVER TO PAY GROCERY BILLS

You cannot do an inefficient thing and cover it under some social clause. They have sold ₹2,500 crore of equity at whatever price and used that money for revenue expenditure. That is like selling your family silver to pay your grocery bills! By the time their term is over [this government] would have sold the public sector off and used all that money for revenue expenditure and nothing would be left for the legacy. I am for a healthy public sector. I am not against disinvesting a part of the public sector. But do it at the best price and use that money for getting assets and put them back in the economy or [for] extinguishment of the foreign debt.

The World Bank or IMF have said that the second tranche would not be coming if forty-eight PSUs are not closed down. But let it be very clear. Dis-employment of that kind of number is not possible in this country. We will not allow it to happen.

BOLDNESS, BRAZENNESS AND BRAVADO

Let me put this government on warning. If, to please their World Bank and IMF bosses, they think they can play havoc with this country's socio-economic structure, we will not allow this. Everybody will be on the streets. It will be the duty of all major political parties to stop this mismanagement of economy and complete sell-out of all that the freedom struggle stood for.

Whatever you want to do, please take the trade unions into confidence and do it slowly. Boldness is one thing, brazenness is another and bravado is a third thing. They should not indulge in brazenness and bravado.

AGAINST ALL CANONS OF FINANCIAL LAWS

Last year (April 2012) the media reported that twenty years of disinvestment has together yielded ₹113,031 crore. The government's arbitrary and unplanned strategy of disinvestment in the backdrop of a volatile stock market was seen as disastrous for state revenue collection. On 16 March 1992, during a **Special** *Mentions speech, Morarka said, 'My request to the government is [that] they should come out with a clear-cut procedure where the government realizes the best price for the shares.'*
Participating in the Short Division Discussion on 28 July 1992 and again on 30 November 1992, he says that the selling of public-sector shares should be under the scrutiny of Parliament.

Last year in the budget, there was a provision to disinvest shares of selected public sector undertakings to the extent of 20 per cent and the government had calculated that it would receive ₹2,500 crore by way of revenue. What has actually happened is that the realization from the shares, which were decided to be sold, has been much more. The government has got ₹3,000-odd crore. The companies which are selected are companies which are doing well, whether they are Indian Oil Corporation (IOC) or Steel Authority of India Ltd (SAIL) or ONGC or Mahanagar Telephone Nigam Ltd (MTNL).

These are the companies which the government has earmarked,

where part of the equity will be sold just now, to begin with, to the mutual funds and later on to the public. There are a few points to which I want to draw the attention of the government. While there may be nothing objectionable in disinvesting part of the government equity, now there is talk that in view of the experience the disinvestment may go up to 49 per cent.

Since the government is considering disinvestment to such a large extent, a few points should be borne in mind. When you sell your own shares to the public, it is one-time revenue that you get because once you sell the shares, they are gone forever. It is, therefore, necessary on the part of the government to ensure that you get the best price. I don't know why they have not come forward to tell us about the method of calculation of the price at which they are selling the shares. Okay, let us consider that the shares are being sold to the mutual funds. But tomorrow they will also go to the public.

WHY THE SECRECY?

Even a private-sector company, when it goes public, fixes a premium which is vetted by the Controller of Capital Issues (CCI) or the ministry of finance. In PSUs there should be a method by which the Parliament must know the price the government has fixed for the shares of those PSUs. In fact, it would be much more advantageous and it would be the correct procedure to follow if there is some sort of a tender or public issue of these shares so that the government could realize the best price. Why should there be secrecy?

There should be total transparency in the transaction. The government should come out with a position paper giving details such as what are the names of the undertakings; whether they have already sold the shares which they proposed to sell; what are the number of shares they sold; what is the price fixed; who were the buyers and what was the method followed in selling those shares? I understand from the speech of the finance minister in the budget that for the next year they are going to evolve some guidelines and procedures.

> It is very well known that when any private entrepreneur sells capital assets, the procedures used are either to buy another capital asset or to repay debts. Unfortunately, because of the difficult financial situation of the government, the money collected last year has been spent on expenditure. It is a very dangerous thing.

HAVE A CLEAR-CUT PROCEDURE

My request to the government is, they should come out with a clear-cut procedure where the government realizes the best price for the shares and the shares are widely distributed to the public, in case they are going to make it a public issue. My other point, apart from the high realization, is about the use of money so collected. It is very well known that when any private entrepreneur sells capital assets, the procedures used are either to buy another capital asset or to repay debts. Unfortunately, because of the difficult financial situation of the government, the money collected last year has been spent on expenditure. It is a very dangerous thing.

It may be a very extreme view to take but the fact remains that if you sell all your premium shares of PSUs and use that money for your current year expenditure, then it is very bad financial management. I request the finance minister that this year, whatever the realization out of the proceeds of PSUs the shares should be strictly used either to acquire another asset or to repay debt so that liabilities of the government come down to that extent. It is prudent financial management to use the accretion on capital account for either another asset on the capital account or a debt repayment on the capital account. This is my request to the finance minister. I hope he will consider it.

◆

PUBLIC SECTOR UNDERTAKINGS *(Participating in the Short Division discussion in the Rajya Sabha on 28 July 1992)*

It is sad for the country that the public sector is being discussed ever since this government came to power. First, let me, for the sake of record, say that we seem to be confused. The general trend and the tone in the last one year is that for the last forty years we have been pursuing wrong policies, which need to be corrected. There is a hint that socialism is out of date.

> This public sector was due to the far-sightedness of Jawaharlal Nehru. When the steel plants were set up, when these modern complexes were set up, apart from any other economic activity, the biggest resource that was created in India was managerial talent—middle-level managerial talent.

The confused thinking, which obfuscates the facts, holds that this public sector, this whole welfare model, everything that was introduced by Jawaharlal Nehru, is out of date. The world has marched forward [and] we must integrate into the market economy, global economy, integrate with the West, etc. Let us forget these forty years and instead of talk of the ten years since 1980. For the information of the House, the total investment in the public sector stands at ₹113,000 crore today. In 1980 when Smt. Gandhi came back to power, it was only ₹18,000 crore. It increased from ₹18,000 crore to ₹42,000 crore in the Sixth Plan period (1980–85) and when Shri Rajiv Gandhi came to power, with his modern outlook and in his wisdom he increased the investment in the public sector from ₹42,000 crore to ₹99,000 crore. After Rajiv Gandhi, the National Front government[1] came to power.

Just to remind the House, when the public sector started in 1955, what was the scenario in India? The total industrial sector

---

[1]Led by Shri V.P. Singh

consisted of a few families who used to run enterprises. There was nothing like professional management. This public sector was due to the far-sightedness of Jawaharlal Nehru. When the steel plants were set up, when these modern complexes were set up, apart from any other economic activity, the biggest resource that was created in India was managerial talent—middle-level managerial talent. Thousands of young men—technocrats, managers, accountants, cost people—got trained in running, organizing and putting up industries and large complexes.

> **Today, we are talking of over-staffing. In fact, if the public sector is guilty, it is guilty of not creating employment opportunities.**

Take the Food Corporation of India (FCI). I have got a lot of complaints about how it is being run today—that is a different matter—but tell me of one company in India, one private enterprise in India, that can organize food procurement and distribution on that scale throughout the country. It is the public sector which has done it. Take the IPCL.[1] It is a petrochemical complex anybody would be proud of. The private sector in India is copying it. Large houses, who are today getting into petrochemicals, are vying with each other to copy the IPCL.

What is the anatomy of the public sector? At the time when ₹18,000 crore was the total investment in the public sector, the total employment was 19.39 lakh. When investment has gone up from ₹18,000 crore to ₹113,000 crore, employment has gone up from 19.30 lakh to 22 lakh. What is the ratio? Today we are talking of over-staffing. In fact, if the public sector is guilty, it is guilty of not creating employment opportunities.

There are only twenty-five enterprises which account for 86 per cent of the total profits. So, it is these twenty-five enterprises which you must concentrate on; run them more profitably. Now,

---

[1]Indian Petrochemicals Corporation Ltd

to run twenty-five companies is not a gigantic task. Similarly, there are twenty loss-making companies, which account for 80 per cent of the losses. What we have to do is to have a Parliamentary Committee—either the Committee on Public Undertakings or a special committee for this purpose—which should go, unit by unit, into these loss-making companies and decide what to do with them. The other aspect, which is being much talked about these days, is about closure, on which this whole debate has started. My friend, Shri Narayanasamy, said that 3.5 lakh people would be affected by the closure of fifty-eight units listed by the Department of Public Enterprises (DPE).

> On the one side, the government says it is short of money and there is a resource crunch. On the other side, we are in a hurry to sell our assets at a highly undervalued price. This is absolutely untenable by any canons of financial law.

There is a situation, and the solution is very simple. If they have identified, unit-wise, the people who are surplus, all that they have to do is, for the next two or three years, not to fill up the vacancies. They will get adjusted. There is no need to make people jobless and create panic. It is an inhuman thing to do, and in a welfare state, an unacceptable thing to do. It [the government] must come out with a White Paper on what exactly it wants to do and give Parliament a chance. About disinvestment—it has nothing to do with privatization. Even if old furniture, broken furniture in a government office is to be sold, tenders are invited. If tenders are not invited, the comptroller and auditor general (CAG) will pass strictures. It is no surprise that today in the bank scam we find that public-sector shares have also been involved. This is bound to be, because people know that government shares can be obtained without giving the highest offer. If you offer them for a song, there are enough people with money who will come and buy them.

If they sell out 20 per cent of the equity of the twenty-five top profit-making companies at the normal price earnings ratio of equity which is applied to private companies, on 20 per cent disinvestment the government will realize ₹18,000 crore. I will end by telling the minister, please take it into your own hands and see that the workers who are employed in a unit are paid their wages in time. Your government is running in a deficit. You are not going to save much by saving a few crores of rupees from the salaries of the workers. Please see that justice is done to the workers and the public sector is handled in a proper way and not in this crude and arbitrary manner.

◆

(*Rajya Sabha Debate, 30 November 1992,* 154)

In last year's budget, the government had decided to disinvest public sector unit shares to the extent of ₹3,500 crore. That was the revenue expected during this year. They have already sold two or three lots this year and recovered ₹600 crore. In December they are going to sell shares worth another ₹3,000 crore. Why I am bringing this to the attention of the government is that the first three lots have been undersold to a large extent. I will just give two or three examples so that it is very clear. In the first round the average price of shares of the Steel Authority of India Limited was ₹13.24. In the third round it was increased to ₹40.40, a three-fold increase by their own methods. But the price quoted in the stock exchange is ₹200.

There is no reason why the government should sell its own assets at less than the market value. On the one side, the government says it is short of money and there is a resource crunch. On the other side, we are in a hurry to sell our assets at a highly undervalued price. This is absolutely untenable by any canons of financial law. If government furniture, second-hand furniture, is sold without calling for tenders, the official is hauled up and punitive action is taken. Here, shares worth thousands of crores of rupees are being sold by a so-called committee whose chairman is Shri V. Krishnamurthy. Now a second committee has been constituted. The government officials are going to determine the price and sell shares, worth thousands of crores of rupees and there is nobody to question.

I demand that any further sale of public-sector shares should be under the scrutiny of Parliament, either by a specially constituted parliamentary committee or the Joint Parliamentary Committee (JPC) can look into it. I have no objection. But the government must realize the full value for whatever assets it wants to sell.

SCANDAL BIGGER THAN SCAM

The Institute of Public Enterprises made a study about last year's public-sector disinvestment and came to the conclusion that money realized was ₹3,000 and some odd crore. The value realized should have been ₹6,536 crore and the government realized less than half the value available in the market. People are ready to pay. I suggest the government issue shares in the market. Let 10,000 to 20,000 investors take advantage of it. The government will get more money and it will not be accused of allowing three or four or ten people to take advantage of it.

The finance minister has reportedly told the press that public issue takes a long time. I can understand why last year they were in a hurry. But they had this whole year on hand. Even between now and March, a public issue can be easily organized.

The private entrepreneurs do it in three months. There is no reason why you cannot do it. Why should mutual funds make money at the expense of the government? Shri V.P. Singh has asked for an inquiry and has said that a JPC should inquire into it. I am not going to that extent. But I do feel [that] if the public sector disinvestment method, especially the December package, is not stopped and if the government does not follow a proper procedure, it will become a scandal bigger than the scam. We are selling shares and there is a difference between the market price and the price you have realized.

PROTECT THE SMALL SHAREHOLDERS AND DEPOSITORS

'A typically bureaucratic bill which only encourages more paperwork,' says Morarka in this debate on sending the Companies (Amendment) Bill, 1987, to a Select or Joint Committee, on 27 April 1988. In its wholesome form, this legislation should stop the harassment of the small investor, encourage the medium entrepreneur and discipline the big companies. However this bill is 'one of the most poorly drafted pieces of legislation that I have come across,' he says as he points to its many shortcomings.

This amendment bill is a very half-hearted one. In fact, it has got certain features which confuse the investors. The purpose of the act is to protect the creditors, depositors and shareholders in a much wider sense than those who have a bigger stake in the company. We find that in this particular amendment bill, certain provisions have been made to protect the depositors by way of giving powers to the new Company Law Board in respect of fixed deposits. At the same time, a very important right of the investors has been taken away and that is, to get an annual report on the functioning of the companies. A new feature is being introduced in the Companies Act which was never there in the Companies Act 1956, or in the various amendments that have been made since 1956. Only an abridged form of the profit and loss account and the annual report will be sent to the shareholders and on payment of a fee, he will be entitled to get the full report, as he is getting now.

If the Honourable Minister looks into the representations from various shareholders' associations over the years, he will find that even the existing requirement of information to be provided to the shareholders is not enough. In fact, shareholders' associations have already represented that the information given to them should be much more specific.

> The small depositors and the shareholders will always be left at the mercy of a certain government bureaucrat or a certain department.

We find a bill that has been ostensibly brought to protect these very small shareholders and depositors, which takes away even the existing rights being given to them. It is a very, very serious matter. This particular act, which is the main one governing the administration of the companies in the corporate sector, cannot be effective, in spite of over 600 sections and a vast army of company law administration officials all over the country. The small depositors and the shareholders will always be left at the mercy of a certain government bureaucrat or a certain department.

HOW HAVE WE GOT MASSIVE CASES OF DUPING?

For instance, in spite of all these powers which the Company Law Board enjoys, this particular amendment bill says that certain powers will be shifted from the High Court to the Company Law Board. It makes no difference. The ultimate executing authority is the government. The Company Law Board will be executing its decisions through the government. If the Company Law is effective, then how have we got massive cases of duping? The investors are totally taken for a ride. M/s Sanchayita[1] and M/s Peerless[2] are cases

---

[1] In 1980, around one lakh depositors lost over ₹120 crore in the Sanchayita Investments. Only a few have got their money back.
[2] The Kolkata-based Peerless General Finance and Investment Co. Ltd was India's oldest residuary non-banking company (RNBC).

which come to my mind. These are cases where the number of people affected are in thousands and in lakhs. I do not think that this particular bill in its present form will take into account the real problems of the investors. Therefore, my amendment is that we should refer it to the Select Committee.

I can only recall to memory that in the time of Jawaharlal Nehru, all acts which were complicated were invariably referred to the Select Committee by a motion brought forward by the government itself.

I want to go specifically into a few clauses apart from this abridgement of the annual report which is a very serious matter affecting the common man. There are certain things which are quite contradictory. For instance, on small- and medium-sized companies, the policy of the government is that even in the corporate sector, we will give encouragement to small-scale industries, small entrepreneurs, new entrepreneurs.

Unless the law is made effective, the administration will remain loose. Now the law, as it is today, applies to over one lakh companies. It is not possible to administer small companies which have a share capital of ₹1 lakh, ₹5 lakh or ₹10 lakh effectively. What the nation is concerned with is where public money is involved in a big way, in companies having a large share capital, capital over ₹10 crore or ₹5 crore, which today get the same treatment as small simpliciter companies.

SMALL COMPANIES SHOULD HAVE MINIMAL FORMALITIES

The law should be amended in a manner that the small companies should have very minimal formalities, whereby the company law administration does not have to waste time on them. Only then the law will become effective in the case of large companies where we will be able to protect the shareholders, creditors and depositors.

They have said [in the amending bill], companies having a share capital of more than ₹25 lakh will have to have a managing director or a full-time director. This is wholly uncalled for. This should be for the companies which have a share capital of over ₹5 crore where we can think of these positions, the perks and the salaries the company can afford. Small- and medium-sized companies, if they are closely held companies—we should not burden them with more and more formalities which do not help us in any way to achieve the objective of this bill.

> **Penalty should act as a deterrent. How far are we able to deter the large companies from violating the law?**

It has been provided in this bill that private limited companies, who accept fixed deposits, will be deemed to be public companies. Now, I see, an amendment has come that this will not apply to companies getting deposits from relatives. But I venture to say that there are small family companies which can raise deposits from their own friends and associates. Why should they become public companies? They are not getting money from the public in the wider sense. If they are getting loans, they are small loans from commercial banks against securities. By bringing or by roping in all these companies, really, what we are doing is that we are not applying the law to these companies but allowing law to become ineffective in the case of big companies, and this is precisely what is happening. For instance, in Bombay or Calcutta (Kolkata), there are big corporations, big companies, which deserve to be closely monitored [to see] whether they are following the Companies Act or not.

This cannot be done every year, howsoever great our desire may be, with a limited number of staff. We probably can go on increasing the personnel in the company law department. But the administration or the act cannot be effective unless we do an ABC analysis and see that only those companies where public money is really involved are closely monitored and therefore I say, I am totally against this whole concept where we go on providing penalties for infringement. Penalty should act as a deterrent. How far are we able to deter the large companies from violating the law?

Here I see a very strange amendment, that in case the government has not approved the managing director's appointment, the managing director will be fined ₹500 per day for the number of days that he refuses to vacate the office. I do not understand this logic. The law should be that government has not approved the managing director's appointment and the managing director should therefore have vacated the office from the moment the government has disapproved of it. But to provide a penalty of a few hundred rupees in the event of his continuing in office for the period when the government has disapproved the appointment is very strange.

DEPOSITS ARE NOT LOANS

After the present government came to power, it announced policies which were very liberal to the corporate sector. Liberal does not mean that they can break the laws. Liberal means that the government lays down the framework of the industrial policy and within the framework of that policy the government wants to give the corporate sector a little leeway to operate. But here I find under Section 370 or Section 372 a whole new definition is given to inter-corporate deposits.

Deposits within the meaning of 'loan' create trouble for the corporate sector. Under no stretch of imagination can a deposit be termed as loan. We are making deposits in banks. They cannot be called loans. We are not giving loans under inter-corporate deposit. To include it under the term 'loan' is an atrocity and it will only affect the small and medium entrepreneurs. The bigger companies can get enough loans from companies, from government institutions.

In spite of our talk of socialism and decentralization, it is always the bigger companies which get the larger cake out of the government resources, and it is the small and medium people who are hard hit by this provision. While ostensibly it is meant to protect the small man, the people who are really hit by the tenor of this bill are the small and medium entrepreneurs. The Monopolies and Restrictive Trade Practices Act (MRTP) and Foreign Exchange Regulation Act (FERA) companies are not affected by this bill at all. I do not suggest that there should be any restrictions put on MRTP and FERA companies which are not realistic.

The Industrial Policy Resolution [exists] from the time of Jawaharlal Nehru which the government still professes is a relevant document. I feel in terms of fulfilling those objectives there should be restrictions only on MRTP and FERA companies. Small- and medium-sized companies should be outside the orbit of most of these restrictions. Only then will the company law administration be effective; otherwise, this series of amendments only adds to the plethora of amendments that we have been adding from year to year. We have two sets of companies; those who want to violate the law with impunity and those who want to follow the law, in letter and spirit. It is to the latter category, that is, those who follow the law of the land, that you should give them leeway.

> Today, the law should be amended to the effect that if the director's relatives or those connected with the company are employed by the company, details should be given.

OUTDATED PROVISIONS

I come to another provision. In the Statement of Objects and Reasons, one of the objects mentioned is 'reducing unnecessary cost or burden by requiring companies to attach only an abridged form of prospectus to the application form...' I would like to know specifically from the Honourable Minister which section of companies has represented that the cost of printing the balance sheet is prohibitive and they want to reduce it. In the annual report as presented today there is a whole section dealing with listing of employees getting salaries of over ₹3,000 and I find that over the years this figure of 3,000 has not increased. In this amending bill there is some provision resulting in large companies having thousands of such employees and they are listing those employees, which itself takes up thirty or forty pages of the balance sheet.

Merely deleting that provision can bring down the cost of printing and that will not affect the small investors in any way. Instead of doing that, they have taken powers [which] now suggest that it should be deleted altogether. A small shareholder is not interested in who is employed and what salary he is getting. He is only interested in knowing whether a director's relative has been employed or not. This was inserted in the 1960s when it was found that the wives or relatives of the managing directors of companies were appointed on high salaries. So, a provision was inserted. At that time, ₹3,000 was a very high salary. It was said that with regard to people drawing above ₹3,000 details should be given.

DETAILS OF DIRECTOR'S RELATIVES

Today, the law should be amended to the effect that if the director's relatives or those connected with the company are employed by the company, details should be given. Probably, after this provision, nobody's relative will be employed because it will come to the adverse notice of the government. But abridging the whole balance sheet to reduce costs is not good. We are seeing larger corporations, instead of just giving information as required by the Companies Act, printing fancy balance sheets, [with] colour photographs, offset printing, printing on paper, etc. Certainly, they are not worried about the cost.

It is a strange thing that the government is worried about reducing the cost, unless we are talking about the balance sheets of the public-sector companies, which is a different matter. But in the private sector, the companies which are doing so take pride in printing coloured balance sheets and in the name of reducing costs you cannot bar vital information from us. So, he cannot say—it is a very vague submission of the Honourable Minister—that the government felt it necessary to do so as a result of the representation. We want to know, as a result of representation from whom?

KEEP SMALL PRIVATE COMPANIES OUT OF PURVIEW

In spite of the Companies Act, our experience has been that most of the violations which are technical in nature are taking a lot of time of the Company Law Board, and we find notices being sent to the private limited companies, we find late presentations of returns, late holding of annual meetings, etc. And even about the simpliciter companies in which the husband and wife are the directors—why the hell should the government be worried about whether they hold a meeting at all?

The partnership firms, proprietary firms, private limited companies are nothing but glorified partnerships and the act should be amended in such a manner that the small private companies are kept outside the purview of this department. Only then the government department can concentrate on the really larger violations where companies have started doing badly, but the balance sheet does not reflect that, with the result that more people start putting deposits and face difficulties later.

There are investment companies about which the people do not know, and they do not know whether they have the approval of the Reserve Bank of India or not, and by the time the government machinery acts, a large number of people find themselves duped by these companies and these companies cannot be stopped unless the company law department is vigilant. But the company law department cannot be vigilant in the present system because the present system is conducive to the harassment of the small man and I find nothing in this amending bill, which either disciplines these companies or stops the harassment of the small men or encourages the medium entrepreneur. Look at the provision regarding abridging the balance sheet, giving less information to the shareholders on the accounts. Why should the annual report contain, according to this bill, information 'on conservation of energy, technology absorption'? Now, are these subjects in which a small investor is interested? Will he even understand it? It is highly technical.

With this kind of contradiction, I think this bill is a typically bureaucratic bill which only encourages more paperwork. It is good for the bureaucracy. But the small man will have to go again and again to the government, which is probably good in the scheme of things, but which is contrary to the avowed objects and reasons of the bill. It is totally contradictory to the spirit of the Sachar Committee, which had a very socialist approach. It is contrary, I may submit with your permission, to the thinking of their own prime minister. I do not understand who the author of this bill is. I do not understand how this kind of omnibus bill without direction has been brought. This is one of the most poorly drafted pieces of legislation that I have come across.

NOBODY IS LISTENING TO THE SMALL DEPOSITORS

I have seen in the administration of companies [that] for smaller things they are very punctilious. If a company is not filing some paper on time, promptly they will send a notice. But there are some other companies which I know of, which are not repaying their depositors. Depositors are knocking at their doors. And nobody is listening to them. This kind of anomaly must be corrected, since this is a very important act, in the sense that the entire corporate sector is administered by this act. If the government has any powers to discipline companies, it is through this act. And if this act is treated in such a callous manner, I am at my wit's end to understand how larger companies will ever come within the framework of any discipline at all.

Whenever any controversy starts, we start the controversy of the public sector and the private sector. This is a needless controversy. In this country, we need the private sector and we need the public sector. In this country we need large companies and we need small companies. Everybody must play his role as per the scheme of the Constitution, as per the scheme of various resolutions. We in the Opposition may or may not agree with the government's policies. But the government policies must adhere at least to what their own avowed objectives are. This bill does not even conform to their own pattern.

I do not understand how these provisions have found their way into this bill, especially in relation to the entire corporate deposits and loans, just because a few High Court judgements have clearly stated that a loan is different from a deposit. The reason you are giving is that this bill also includes the provision to plug loopholes and remove some lacunae. This is not a loophole or a lacuna. Loans and deposits are two different things. But by an act of Parliament, we are trying to change the context and the meaning of the entire corporate operations.

Recently we have seen companies whose turnover was, let us say, ₹10 crore, and let us say they had to pay excise of 20 per cent, which is ₹2 crore. We could see that some companies paid 10 per cent less excise or 10 per cent more. Now, we find that there are corporate bodies which, the excise department says, owe excise which they will not be able to pay even if they sell their whole company. Now, either the companies are indulging in a massive fraud, in which case the company law department is not functioning, or if these are not real dues, the excise department is not functioning properly.

PEOPLE WILL LOSE FAITH IN THE SYSTEM

For the common man today it is not a healthy practice in democracy. People will lose faith in this entire system. If there are companies which owe excise duties of ₹500 crore or ₹10,000 crore, well, I do not think it is a healthy practice in democracy or for corporate functioning.

I request the minister that the government of its own motion should bring a Joint Select Committee of both Houses of Parliament, which can give a thought to this over the next few months and come out with a concrete bill which will be less cumbersome, less complex but more effective.

WE ARE PROMOTING A CULTURE OF CORRUPTION

Speaking in the debate on the Prevention of Corruption Bill, 1987, on 10 August 1988, Morarka begins with a statement that is witty but disquietingly insightful. He goes on to point out that decentralization and taking away the disproportionate discretionary powers of petty officials is the key to reducing corruption. Besides, if we ridicule the honest and promote the corrupt, what message are we sending out? 'We are building a society in which the small thief is hanged by the neck, and we are taking our hats off to [the] bigger ones.'

The speaker just before me has very graphically illustrated how corruption is prevalent in all walks of life, including the lower courts. Incidentally, the raison d'etre of this bill almost disappears because if this is how the courts are going to function then the purpose of this bill—of setting up special courts—is totally defeated.

I will begin by quoting Gunnar Myrdal in the *Asian Drama* where he mentions that in developing countries, the incentive in economic affairs is reduced because of controls on profits, unlike the Western countries where there is great incentive in economic activity, where if a man works more, he earns more and taxation is less. On the other hand, he has noted that in the developing countries there is much greater incentive in administrative activity, which is almost missing in the Western countries. Of course, he has gone on to illustrate how right from getting an industrial licence to opening the gates of railway track, money has to change hands, with specific reference to India.

DEARTH, DELAY AND DISCRETION

I feel that if we analyse the present social structure and the points at which corruption takes place, there are three main reasons, the three Ds—dearth, delay and discretion. At the level of the common man, it is the shortage of commodities—whether it is rations, edible oil, getting a ration card, a railway ticket—this corruption is the direct result of dearth. The total supply is less than demand. Unless shortage disappears, corruption will remain.

Only you can change the point at which you want corruption to take place. If you have open trade in foodgrains, the local bania will be corrupt; he will be charging black-market rates and probably the administrative machinery can act on him. But in the public distribution system, if the shortage persists, it is the government's own people who are corrupt and action becomes even more difficult. So, unless shortage disappears, the corruption which affects the common man cannot go away. No amount of courts, no amount of administrative machinery, no amount of special judges or courts will be able to bring relief to the common man as far as his daily necessities go.

> In today's India, I do not find any justification for having so many levels through which a file should go. The point is, because there are small government officials who can delay our work and there is a regular army of self-employed people who will take money and can get your file moving fast, corruption takes place.

The second level at which corruption takes place is due to delay. In government offices, right from the undersecretary to the minister, the file goes to seven levels. I do not know; it must be a legacy of the British rule; they may be having a seven-tier system of management. In today's India, I do not find any justification for having so many levels through which a file should go. The point is, because there are small government officials who can delay our work and there is a regular army of self-employed people who will take money and can get your file moving fast, corruption takes place. So, unless you eliminate the delay you cannot eliminate corruption, and this delay takes place because of the inherent structure of our tax system. If we can straighten the system, I am sure, a lot of corruption, at various levels, can be reduced.

REDUCE DISCRETIONARY POWERS

The third level of corruption is discretion—and that is where high-level corruption comes. Say, there is a particular licence or a particular permit or a particular import technology which the government has to give and there are five applicants. All the applicants being business houses, all applicants are influential, all of them are rich and the government has to select one or two. Here is a discretionary power. Whether the discretionary power is wielded by the minister or the secretary or by any other high official, that is where corruption in high places takes place.

In a democratic system like India, unless discretionary power is reduced, corruption will remain. You take the revenue officials. The amount of discretionary power under the Direct Taxes Bill, under the Income Tax Act and even under the new act which we passed last year and which is due for amendment again, incidentally; the amount of discretionary power wielded by an income tax commissioner, by an income tax officer or by a sales tax officer is immense. It is totally disproportionate to his own status in life.

> Whether the discretionary power is wielded by the minister or the secretary or by any other high official, that is where corruption in high places takes place.

I agree with the previous speaker, that hardly 1 per cent of people can resist succumbing to a situation. Here, there is an excise inspector in a factory, and your law gives him power, which can make a difference of crores of rupees. His own judgment, his own discretion, can make a difference of crores of rupees to the owner of a factory, and his own salary is only ₹1,000 or ₹2,000. It is not hard to see that corruption will take place.

DECENTRALIZATION IS THE KEY

Unless there is a basic restructuring where discretionary power has to have direct proportion or direct relevance to the status of the person who is wielding that power, I am afraid corruption cannot go.

Now, society being what it is and these reasons being what they are, one may well ask, what is the solution? The first solution is that the common man's daily necessities must be available in good quantity. Number two: we should try to decentralize. The common man should not be made to travel and meet one particular person. The goods should be taken to the common man. The common man must not go and stand in the queue, because it is where corruption starts.

Decentralization is the key—I do not know if it is a key to removal of corruption—but definitely to reduction of the corruption. More centralization means more corruption. Even the Soviet Union has opted for 'perestroika'. If you read the proceedings of the Communist Party of Soviet Union (CPSU), Mikhail Gorbachev has himself come up against long queues, for restructuring of the party system. Of course, they have a one-party system. We have an open democratic system. But he has also felt that if the system is too much closed, malpractices set in and the common man stands to lose.

In a system like India, in a society based on the dreams of Mahatma Gandhi, we have no business to go on centralizing the system, introducing controls, making petty officials in charge of things by which, willy-nilly, they will succumb to the temptation to make money. The other thing is the value system that we are trying to institutionalize. Today, I am sorry to say, the honest man is looked down upon while another, no matter how he has earned the money, gets respectability.

THE CORRUPT GET PROMOTED

Smt. Indira Gandhi, after becoming prime minister, called for social boycott of black marketeers, and social boycott of corrupt people. That was twenty years ago. Today, forget about boycott, a corrupt government official is getting promoted.

> We have controls. So, we have corrupt officials. Then, to catch the corrupt officials we have the Vigilance Squad. To see that the Vigilance Squad does not become corrupt, we have the Anti-Corruption Bureau. To see that the Anti-Corruption Bureau does not become corrupt, we have the state CID. If that does not help, the CBI is there.

To know that a government official is corrupt, no inquiry is required, no judge is required. Everybody in the mohalla knows it. Everybody in the Udyog Bhavan knows it. I don't want you to take action. But certainly, in the matter of promotion, merit must be recognized, honesty must be recognized. A person is living in a style which is disproportionate to his income. Maybe, the Central Bureau of Investigation (CBI) has not raided him. You don't need to raid a person to know that he is living beyond his means.

We are promoting a culture of corruption. We have promoted a value system where dishonesty pays over honesty. Unless this system is changed, unless this environment is changed, no amount of these laws will help.

What is happening today? We have controls. So, we have

corrupt officials. Then, to catch the corrupt officials we have the Vigilance Squad. To see that the Vigilance Squad does not become corrupt, we have the Anti-Corruption Bureau. To see that the Anti-Corruption Bureau does not become corrupt, we have the state Central Investigation Department CID. If that does not help, the CBI is there. The number of cases recorded by the CBI in 1975 was 1,078; in 1980 it recorded 1,073 cases. Even in 1985, after eleven years, the cases were 1,082. Are we to believe that with the increasing population, increasing economic activity, the corruption percentage has gone down?

It is difficult for the common man to swallow. There are cases of some sub-judge taking ₹2,000 or some sub-inspector taking ₹5,000. In today's society this is petty change. This is not corruption which the CBI should be after. I will be happy if the CBI, instead of a thousand, catches only a hundred cases. But let them all be of over ₹1 crore each.

But these people are too powerful.

We are building a society in which the small thief is hanged by the neck, and we are taking our hats off to [the] bigger ones. This kind of society is responsible for increasing corruption.

QUALITY OF PEOPLE, NOT THE BILL THAT IS IMPORTANT

Since the bill is there, it is likely to be passed. Its structure is not important. The judges, the special courts, the special judges are not important. It is the quality of the people that is important. At least make sure that the judges whom we select are honest and take people who are of unimpeachable integrity. Shri Chidambaram may not agree with me. Shri Chidambaram himself can select if he sits down with a list of IAS officers. He himself can tick the names of people who are of unimpeachable integrity. They have got sensitive positions. What is that sensitive position? There must be a test for it. For sensitive positions there is a track record and you get a lot of intelligence information.

In my opinion, any position in the bureaucracy, which gives the power to take discretionary decisions, should be taken as a sensitive position and people of unimpeachable integrity should be put there. Then the whole problem will start getting solved in no time. In a small village when a thanedar is posted, no inquiry is required. Within one week the entire village comes to know whether he is an honest man and people flock to him to get their grievances redressed. In the present society where the word of mouth is much more valuable than all this data and objective assessments, my humble submission is, please do something to change the entire environment. If that is done, I am sure, it will go a long way in achieving the objectives with which you brought in this bill.

EDUCATION SYSTEM IS STEEPED IN MEDIOCRITY

Speaking in the debate on The Delhi University (Amendment) Bill, 1988, on 9 August 1988, Morarka eloquently opposes the bill. '[...] because we have a government, which wants to give us Pepsi cola when we do not have drinking water, which wants to give us imported motor cars when we need bicycles and public transport system, which wants to give us computers when there are no blackboards, which wants to give us modern hospitals when people are dying of cholera... So, this entire elitist culture is sought to be introduced in education also,' he says.

I rise to oppose the Delhi University (Amendment) Bill, 1988. The Statement of Objects and Reasons of the Bill says that it is based on the National Policy on Education, 1986. I wish to point out that the concept of autonomous colleges which is being sought to be implemented through this bill is a very modern concept, but it is very premature, inasmuch as the existing education system leaves much to be desired.

NATIONAL POLICY ON EDUCATION IS ELITIST

Before I go into the working of the universities, I would like to point out that the National Education Policy, 1986, as announced by the government, is elitist in nature. The concept of Navodaya Vidyalayas, which has been enunciated with great fanfare, itself provides for selective education up to the district level. In a country where illiteracy is rampant, where what is required is basic education for the masses when the three Rs are required to be taught, I am really sorry that we should try to implement an education policy which seeks to talk in very big terms about modernization of education, of computers and of other modern technology or techniques of education. The prime minister himself has talked of pursuit of excellence. But I am sorry that in the existing system we are steeping into mediocrity and worse.

This bill talks of granting autonomy to colleges and the minister, in his opening remarks, has said that fifty-four colleges would be given autonomy after it is passed. Now I want to bring it to the attention of the House that there are many colleges functioning in an autonomous manner in states other than Delhi. We were told by the minister that this provision is there in all the other places. Delhi [University] is one of the universities where the provision is being put now. Before this autonomy is granted to these colleges, we must examine how the colleges are functioning today.

My friend, Dr Ratnakar Pandey, from the other side, while supporting the bill, has made very good points. He has pointed out the lacunae in the existing system of education. Malpractices are rampant, examination papers are being leaked, the examination system itself is not rational, with the result that we are producing graduates by thousands, who cannot get jobs. When the 10+2 system of education was introduced a few years ago, we were told that the whole idea was that everybody must get education up to the tenth standard. In the two years following, his aptitude could be found out so that only a few people would go for higher education and others would get into various vocations and other streams of work. But nothing of the sort has happened. What has it become? It has become a straight 10+5. Only the name is different.

Now it is junior college and senior college. But the pattern remains the same, with the result that education is not job oriented. For government jobs, also, the minimum qualification is a degree.

And I must say, utterly sorrowfully, that in the case of most of the students who go for arts degrees, what is the content of the programme, what is the content of their studies? Students study either sociology or psychology or philosophy. He may be good for higher research, he may be good for being a lecturer, but unfortunately, he does not get a job in commercial establishments.

WHAT KIND OF AUTONOMY?

The entire education pattern today is unemployment oriented. We are getting more and more degree holders, students or people with big ambitions, who feel frustrated, and I must say that this is a basic cause for most of the frustration and the violence that we see around us today. If the youth today are not channelized in the right direction, I am sorry, we are playing with the future of the country.

Bills like this, I do not understand. What is the conception, what is the idea of the government? I fail even to understand what kind of autonomy they want to give to colleges where basic amenities are still missing. Of course, I must say I am astonished—I am not surprised though—because we have a government which wants to give us Pepsi cola when we do not have drinking water, which wants to give us imported motor cars when we need bicycles and public transport system, which wants to give us computers when there are no blackboards, which wants to give us modern hospitals when people are dying of cholera—which is almost extinct from other parts of the world—which promises to give us satellites, INSAT 1C when ordinary trains and planes do not run on time. So, this entire elitist culture is sought to be introduced in education also.

I am sorry to say, there is absolutely no ground for rushing with this kind of legislation. I would support the move [of] referring it to a Select Committee.

What is required is a comprehensive bill to make education job-oriented. Unless our educational system throws up students or youth who can get settled in society, I am afraid the entire system will collapse. But in the Statement of Objects and Reasons, in a very casual manner we are being told: 'The National Policy on Education, 1986 states that autonomous colleges will be helped to develop in large numbers and that the creation of autonomous departments within universities, on a selective basis, will be encouraged.'

QUALITY OF PROFESSORS AND LECTURERS

I do not understand this. Even universities themselves are hardly autonomous today. There is interference at every stage. Dr Pandey brought out very clearly the effect of trade unionism which he opposed and which, I don't think, is the real reason. But the University Grants Commission (UGC) is there, the ministry of education is there. The present university structure, as it is, needs to work. What we need is efficient working of the present university system rather than superimposing something which is much more modern and which cannot work.

> If the youth today are not channelized in the right direction, I am sorry, we are playing with the future of the country.

Autonomous colleges will be a disaster because what is required is quality of people. If the quality of our professors and lecturers is not good, no amount of restructuring is going to help education. If the basic character of the people involved in the system does not help to motivate the students towards a purposeful life, we are only going to have them running after drugs, drug addiction and then we will get into de-addiction camps and all that sort of thing.

The National Education Policy itself is elitist. What are the bills based on that policy going to create? They are only going to create, as Dr Poddar pointed out very rightly, a caste [hierarchy] of colleges. Some will be very superior colleges. Some will be inferior colleges. Certainly, that is not the aim of the government. Our avowed policy, even the policy of the ruling party, is oriented towards social justice, towards a new socio-economic order. But I am afraid, with bills of this kind, we are trying to accentuate and institutionalize the differences between the elitist people and the ordinary people.

There was a time when we were hearing in the country that public schools would be abolished. But today the time has come when public-school education is looked up to. Those of us who are not from public schools probably have no place in the scheme of things. I do not know in which direction we are going. We talk of one thing, and we try to do exactly the opposite. Of course, a legislation comes and obviously gets passed. But its effects are far-reaching for decades to come.

The quality of education in the present educational system needs to be improved, number one. Number two, we should hold back autonomy till such time when the existing system works efficiently, free from corruption, free from malpractices largely. Thirdly, the entire concept of elitist education, even if there is higher education, even if there is modern education, should be strictly based on merit. Today, that does not happen. Today, all over the country, in every state, we find people who have got less marks are able to muscle through by one means or the other into the engineering colleges and medical colleges.

COMPETENT PEOPLE ARE GETTING FRUSTRATED

About the marks system, when we were students, 60 per cent marks were considered good marks and 70 per cent was distinction but today I am astonished to see that students with 80 per cent marks are not getting admission. What are we trying to do? We are trying to promote a general culture of mediocrity, of corruption. The entire educational system is under strain. Ask any student today.

Good students are having a bad time. The average student or the mediocre student, whose parents are rich, influential, is able to muscle through and get a degree, which in any case he does not need because ultimately he is going to live off [his] father's money.

So, what is exactly happening is, competent people are getting frustrated. If the educational system cannot rectify that, I do not see any reason why they should go on introducing autonomy in colleges.

The last point which I want to make is that the university—I stay in Bombay, so I can talk of Bombay University—standards which were in existence ten or fifteen years ago are not seen these days. Why is it so? The reason is that even at the university management level, politics has crept in even for appointment of registrars, vice-chancellors, etc. It was never so earlier.

With this kind of atmosphere in a country where the guru is supposed to be regarded even higher than God, in a country where tradition has taught us to respect the guru, what is the respect for a school master or a college teacher today? Even the student has no respect for him. It is not because there is something wrong with the teaching staff, but it is the system which is pushing the mediocre into the teaching line. Good people do not want to come into the teaching line, because the entire system is under strain. I am afraid this kind of legislation is not going to take us anywhere.

Therefore, this bill should be referred to a Select Committee not only for the provisions which the government is proposing, but also to have a de novo look at the entire university education system.

THE CASE OF THE MISSING PEPSI COLA AGRO PLANT

To gain licences, big businesses promise the moon and the stars in terms of export performances but fail to deliver once their job is done. During Special Mentions discussing the default in export obligations by corporate-sector companies on 16 December 1991, Morarka warns the government against being taken for a ride and gives the case story of Pepsi cola to prove his point.

I wish to draw the attention of the government, especially the ministry of finance, to the default in the export obligations by the corporate sector. As we know, the balance of payments has been difficult. After this government has come to power, it has taken a series of steps to improve the foreign exchange position. The finance minister, in the House and outside, keeps on saying that difficulties are ahead; we have to see that exports go up and imports are kept under control so that the foreign exchange position is under control.

With respect to this kind of policy statement of the government, it is indeed strange that there are hundreds of companies, which are not keeping their obligations towards export. If I may remind the government, there was a period when a certain industry which was under licencing was not allowed a licence by the government because it contained a lot of import, import of machinery, import of raw material. They got the licence on the express promise that they would match this import expenditure by export. In fact, the government had a ratio. While giving in their licence applications they promised five times, ten times, the foreign exchange earnings by way of export compared to what they were asking the government at the time of putting up of the plant for importing machinery and raw material.

The late Rajiv Gandhi started a special ministry, the food processing industry ministry. His idea was that the farm products should be processed; there should be added value and farmers should get better prices. The intention was very good. How the multinationals defeated the purpose, you see in Pepsi cola.

VERY POOR FOLLOW-UP

The point is that the follow-up is very poor. Units have come up; import of machinery has taken place. Import of raw material will have to take place because industries cannot be closed down. Now, this is a one-way traffic. The Institute of Studies in Industrial Development (ISID)—it has got a link-up with the National Informatics Centre also—has carried out a study and they have made a list of companies in India, which have a net outflow of foreign exchange. This list consists of not only multinationals but also Indian business houses, all the top business houses, and it contains even public-sector companies like Maruti Udyog Ltd.

The total import bill, the total foreign exchange spending of these companies outstrips what they are able to earn. On the one hand, we are having a problem of foreign exchange and we are having all sorts of schemes for foreign exchange to come in; on the other hand, we have large identifiable corporate-sector companies which are not able to meet their obligations. So, the government will have to sit with them and see how they can become foreign exchange-neutral. Maybe, they export at a loss. But these companies must bring in that much foreign exchange which they have promised;

otherwise it will make a mockery of whatever regulations the government makes.

> Stringent steps should be taken to ensure that the corporate sector fulfils the promises that they make because the corporate sector is not a vulnerable section of the society where you can take a compassionate view. If they cannot keep up their promises, they have no business to function.

YE DIL MAANGE AUR ZYADA

The most classic case is the export obligations of Pepsi cola. When this company came up, it told the government that it would put up an agro-research centre. Late Rajiv Gandhi started a special ministry, the food processing industry ministry. His idea was that the farm products should be processed; there should be added value and farmers should get better prices. The intention was very good. How the multinationals defeated the purpose, you see in Pepsi cola. They put up the plant as they promised. The agro-research centre is yet to come. When complaints were made, the government appointed a three-member committee. This committee has given a report to Shri Giridhar Gomang, the food processing minister. The finding of the committee is that no export of products manufactured by Pepsi cola itself has been made.

In the licence, they are supposed to export 40 per cent of their own products. All their export has been what they bought from the market and exported. This is not to the advantage of the country because somebody else would export anything. The second finding is that their soft-drink production is in excess of 25 per cent. There is a ceiling that they can produce soft drink only to the extent of 25 per cent of their total production. They have violated that stipulation. The chief executive of the company has given an interview that the food products—Indian processed foods—have a difficult market because the Indian tomato does not consist of much solids: the potato is very sweet and the citrus is too bitter. That is the end of the matter. He is formally telling you, 'Whatever was the original intention, the fruits or vegetables cannot be exported. They are not what the international community wants.'

CORPORATE SECTOR NOT VULNERABLE SECTION

It is obvious. Just to get the licence and make tall promises [that] you [will] put up an industry and when it comes to fulfilment you do not keep those promises and the government would not take action because you say that employment will be hampered. Then, what will you do with the company? Stringent steps should be taken to ensure that the corporate sector fulfils the promises that they make because the corporate sector is not a vulnerable section of the society where you can take a compassionate view. If they cannot keep their promises, they have no business to function.

I don't know what action the government can take. But in this new era of liberalization a lot of new companies want to come in. If this is the track record, then India is a good green-field area where you can make promises which you never have to keep. I don't think this will give confidence to the honest industrialists in the international community. While it is true that you should not harass the corporate sector, it is equally true that you must be even-handed and if you want the big international companies to come in, you must see that the Indian government is not only liberal but it is also effective in implementing it.

ECONOMY IS FULL OF DISTORTIONS

Speaking from the Treasury Benches on a discussion on the General Budget 1990-91 on 27 March 1991, Morarka makes a minute comparison between the one presented by the then Finance Minister Prof. Madhu Dandavate and the previous Congress-I government's budget. All the issues that we still seem to be grappling with come in here—loan waivers, the right to work, domineering NRIs and the necessity for growth going down directly to the poor instead of the mythical 'trickle-down' effect.

At one point in his speech, Shri S.B. Chavan said that in spite of achievements and growth, etc., this new government is always saying that the economy is in bad shape. Are we really in such a bad shape? I think that is the central question to which we should address ourselves and the part of the Economic Survey 1989–90, which Shri Chavan quoted, is itself an eloquent testimony to the financial and fiscal mismanagement in the five years preceding the last economic survey i.e. the economic survey presented by Shri S.B. Chavan. It gave an account of how the long-term fiscal policy presented in December 1985 had totally failed. I agree with him that the problems that he addressed himself in that economic survey which I had held last year were hardly tackled in the last year's budget. The same problems remain today.

I will have to admit that a drastic financial restructuring that is required has not come about. This government has been in power only for a hundred days. This budget does not financially restructure the economy which is the need of the hour. We must understand that the central question to which we should all address ourselves—it cuts across party lines—is the severe maladies that have crept into the economy in the last eight to ten years, which the Ninth Finance Commission has very rightly pointed out requires 'abolishing the revenue deficit as an absolute fiscal imperative'. Having said that, let us see what the options available to us are. The revenue deficits exist and the need for development too exists. The tax revenues, as the economic survey has shown, have largely kept to the target. There are certain areas like public sector undertakings which have not fulfilled their role as envisaged in the long-term fiscal policy of December 1985. In the Seventh Plan period, which coincided with the period of the previous government, for the first time, we have seen that the entire plan targets have been met either by borrowings or by deficit financing.

> I am saying this because last year this is what I had said when he was the finance minister and in his reply he rebutted everything. And, today, he is repeating everything.

REBUTTAL AND REPETITION

Let us all admit that over the last seven or eight years, severe distortions have crept into the economy. Shri Chavan's own economic survey presented to the Parliament last year, lists the maladies that have entered into the economy. That was presented last year in March and, eight years or ten years prior to that, during that period the same government has been in power. I am sure Shri Chavan, while listing out the maladies, did not ignore these distortions. He read out from the 1985 long-term fiscal policy and mentioned what it projected, and read out from his own economic survey, saying that this has not been fulfilled and there have been severe distortions and now, on that part of the analysis, I totally agree. I really could not understand as to what he was driving at.

I am saying this because last year this is what I had said when he was the finance minister and in his reply he rebutted everything. And, today, he is repeating everything.

Now, the distortions in the economy are known to all concerned. The point that has been made is that there has been growth, that there has been an unprecedented growth during the last few years and yet, the new government is trying to hide that fact. Even when you were sitting here on this side and we were sitting there, you can see the speeches I made at that time. We have not said that there has been no growth. We have got two questions to ask: growth at what cost and growth for whom? These are the basic questions on which we differ. You people now are talking of the growth rate, of the industrial growth rate figure, of 5 per cent or 7 per cent or 10 per cent. Now, you will see from the figures of statistics of industrial growth, that in 1986–87 they had made a major change in the method of calculation of the industrial growth rate figure. The weighted average has been significantly altered and now you cannot compare the growth rates. You are now talking of industrial production in terms of the growth rates, which the statistics show for the 1970s and 1980s. But you cannot compare them.

> In the last five years, is it or is it not a fact that in spite of 40 per cent of the people living below the poverty line, the expenditure on consumer durables, on five-star hotels, on private transport, on various types of luxury gadgets has visibly increased, has significantly increased? How has that happened? It is because of the concessions—tax concessions.

Even leaving aside that, you take the average gross national product GNP—I am glad that Prof. Thakur is here and he is going to speak; I am sure he will deal with this question. You will find this question emerging: is it not a fact that in the total growth figures the proportion of the services sector has significantly changed over the last five years? In the First Plan period, out of the total GNP of the country, 60 per cent was accounted for by the agricultural sector, 24 per cent by the industrial sector and 15 per cent by the services sector.

In the 1985–88 period for which statistics are available, I am sure, the story continues. For the next two years, the agricultural sector contribution came down from 60 per cent to 33 per cent; industrial sector grew from 24 per cent to 27 per cent; and the services sector increased from 15 per cent to 40 per cent. With regard to the growth that we are talking of today, 40 per cent of that consists of the services sector. It consists of defence, communications, transport, banking and insurance, and public administration, and herein lies the clue to the whole mystery. If the growth rate is slow, you step up the government expenditure. If you step up the government expenditure even by deficit financing, even by borrowing, you will achieve the growth rate.

Now, what is it that we have done? We have shown the growth rate to the people and said, 'Look here. Our growth rate is so much. We have achieved it.' But by what methods? By borrowing money, by printing currency notes, thereby fuelling further inflation and reducing the purchasing power of the people. I will come to that later. Now, in this, let us not argue about the facts. We may have disputes on the strategy and we may have differences of opinion. But let us not push the facts under the carpet.

What I am saying is that the growth rate as projected for the last five years is not growth rate which comes as direct addition to the people's income by way of employment generation, productive employment generation or purchasing power in the hands of the people. It is very easy to see and no economist is needed to point it out. In the last five years, is it or is it not a fact that in spite of 40 per cent of the people living below the poverty line, the expenditure on consumer durables, on five-star hotels, on private transport, on various types of luxury gadgets has visibly increased, has significantly increased? How has that happened? It is because of the concessions—tax concessions.

DISTORTED GROWTH

In the last five years' budgets, the tax concessions have gone to a particular section of the population, and that section's purchasing power has definitely increased, and that purchasing power has fuelled the industrial prospects of [a] few limited items. What we are trying to say is that this kind of growth is a distorted growth, merely to show to the people. Whom are we trying to impress? The World Bank? The IMF? Shri Chavan said that we are alarming the international community by saying that the economy is in a bad shape and the coffers are empty. I have great respect for him. But I would like to mention that the international community does not go by our statements. The international community goes by hard facts.

The World Bank, the IMF and the other international institutions know what the exact position of India is, as far as indebtedness is concerned, as far as growth is concerned. By merely changing the figures or the index you cannot impress them. We can only impress ourselves. Yes, that statement has alarmed my friends on the other side. Our creditworthiness in the international market is the same as it was three months ago. It does not change overnight with the change in government. Merely because somebody says the coffers are empty, do you think the international market changes its course? This is a very facile view to take. Shri Chavan talked on two points raised in our manifesto.

> …there was a competition among the Congress-I chief ministers in the last three months to announce bigger bonanzas. Mind you, the central government had some resources, some source of getting money; the state governments have no such recourse. And yet they went on making promises.

LOAN WAIVER SCHEME

One, the loan waiver scheme for farmers and two, the right to work. I shall deal with these two specifically before coming to the general economy. On the loan waiver scheme, he said two things which are contradictory. He said, in the manifesto we had said that we will waive loans of small and marginal farmers. As per the budget speech, the finance minister extended the scope to all farmers except wilful defaulters. On the other hand, he said that they (the current government) are providing only ₹1,000 crore and it appears that it has reduced your scope from the original manifesto promise. Now, both cannot be true.

When the National Front manifesto said that we are going to waive loans of small and marginal farmers—I am glad he has raised the point—there was a competition among the Congress-I chief ministers in the last three months to announce bigger bonanzas. Mind you, the central government had some resources, some source of getting money; the state governments have no such recourse. And yet they went on making promises. Whose calculation is this that to fulfil that promise you require 20,000, 30,000 or 40,000 crore? The fact is that statistics, accurate statistics, are not available instantly on what are the total loans of small and marginal farmers from the various nationalized banks, cooperative banks and regional rural banks. Now, what is the promise?

The promise is to help the small and marginal farmers to get out of the indebtedness. It is not a carte blanche. I can say with all the force at my command that what the finance minister has announced does not mean that rich farmers should go scot-free. I only wish to reiterate that the whole idea is to help the small and marginal farmers within the parameters of the banking system that we have in this country, without the people at large losing confidence in the banking system. After all, it is public money. Let us not have any fear on this account. At the same time, I quite agree that details will have to be worked out in the process.

RIGHT TO WORK

The second question which Shri Chavan raised is: what about the right to work? And he said that the Fundamental Right to Work will be a very costly process. Again, there is a lot of calculation going on in the press. Yesterday Ram Awadheshji said that ₹36,000 crore will be required if everybody has to get work in the country. No, we are asking for the right to work as a Fundamental Right. And in the budget, a small beginning by way of Employment Guarantee Scheme has been included.

> Technology import is welcome. But it should be only in areas where our own country will benefit, not for consumer durables and not for fancy ideas. In this country, I think the marketing people have taken over.

Last year there was the Jawahar Rozgar Yojana, which was announced with great fanfare. I was one of those who said in the House that the whole idea is employment generation. In the last five years, what we strongly objected to was that the investment in the industrial sector has been made in such a manner that it does not generate employment. In the last five years, industrial employment has shrunk, out of sickness and out of computerization.

Now, the fact remains that most of the foreign technology about which many economists say that the moment you enter foreign collaboration you get upgradation of your own technology—that has not happened in this country. We have seen foreign collaboration working in the private sector in the last twenty years without any research and development. That is just a drain on the foreign exchange. We are against this strategy of industrial development. The right to work stems from this: agro-based industry, village industry. Technology import is welcome. But it should be only in areas where our own country will benefit, not for consumer durables and not for fancy ideas. In this country, I think the marketing people have taken over.

NOT THIS KIND OF GROWTH

By using some slogan, they can always market any product. Pepsi cola has been marketed in this country in the name of Punjab. When you go into details, you will find that Punjab is nowhere, neither in the matter of employment, nor in the matter of farmers' products. So, we are against that kind of growth. I had made three complaints to Shri Chavan last year about his budget. I am happy that Prof. Dandavate has met with those complaints.

Firstly, I had said that the budget must make up the mood of the people. I had complained that the last three or four years' budgets never made the mood of the people on matters such as austerity or control of expenditure or a focus that the rich should be taxed more. This budget contains all those ingredients. The finance minister has restructured the saving mechanism in a way that the rich can take tax shelter, but they will have to save more. Previously, the weightage was in such a way that you could get the same benefit for the same amount of saving, whether you were rich or poor. Now, the rich will have to save more in order to get the same benefit.

The second point is about black money. The budget leaves the matter open and says that on black money, let us have a discussion. But the last three or four years' budgets have been conspicuous by their silence, as if black money does not exist in this country.

The third point is about the public sector. The budget says that we expect higher revenue from the public sector this year. Shri Chavan has said that he does not think that ₹2,100 crore can come. Is it an astrological prediction? I don't think so. I think the public sector is at a stage where all efforts should be made to see that their revenues improve. Last year I had called it a 'course-correcting budget'. I had believed that the last year's budget was a U-turn budget compared to the previous two years.

I had believed that lots of things were done in last year's budget. I did not agree to the transfer of ₹2,300 crore from the oil fund. But apart from that, the basic scheme of the last year's budget was welcome because it was a reversal of what had happened in the previous years.

As I can see, this year's budget has focused on rich people having to give a large share to the exchequer. Take, for instance, the corporate sector. A beginning has been made to simplify the tax structure. What had happened about the investment allowance? We had put investment allowance, which allowed companies to almost escape total taxation by rapid expansion. It was again with public money. Then to counter that, we say: 'No, no. They must pay some tax.' They had to pay a minimum of 30 per cent. Now, all that has been done away [with]. It is a simple thing. Let us not have investment allowance. Let us not allow them to escape taxation. Again, 115J[1] became a bone of contention because of various interpretations. It has been simplified.

> If we want to restructure our economy, we must tighten the belt for five or six years, have a harsher dose of taxation and have simplification. At the same time, you must give relief to the poorer sections of the people.

I am sure that the finance minister will consider further simplification either in the Direct Tax Code or in the next year's budget. All exemptions which complicate the tax law should be removed and the tax rate should be reduced pro tanto. Of course, in the present case, we get even more revenue.

NOT HARSH ENOUGH

Now take the total structure of the budget. The expenses remain

---

[1]115J was the provision for a minimum tax to be collected.

the same. The three items which Shri Chavan mentioned are exactly the three items which I mentioned last year, i.e. defence, interest and subsidy. They account for 60 per cent of the budget. Which finance minister can do anything about it? The general complaint that I have heard from the people is that petrol prices have gone very high or iron and steel prices have gone up, as if the budget is harsh. My frank opinion is that the budget is not harsh enough. If we want to restructure our economy, we must tighten the belt for five or six years, have a harsher dose of taxation and have simplification. At the same time, you must give relief to the poorer sections of the people.

> We should lay down a cardinal rule that any ministry coming with a demand must also bring a request for [a] cut under some other head. The overall budget of a ministry should freeze at the level projected in the budget.

But the taxpayers, the corporate sector and the industrial sector have to be taxed more. We have to look at the tax structure to tax them more with a view to get the revenue. Unfortunately, the taxation is on paper. Even in spite of sharp increases in excise duty, the buoyancy is negligible. It indicates tax evasion. The whole system is structured in a manner that there are leakages and evasions everywhere. We must go far ahead in this sphere of simplification of taxes in a manner that evasion becomes impossible. When Shri Chavan was not here I dealt with the distortions of the economy, on which I am sure he will agree.

On one point I agree with him, and that is the protected deficit of ₹7,205 crore. It will be required by the government to keep a strict watch on the expenditure. Even the finance minister, Prof. Madhu Dandavate, will face the same problem. All ministries come with further demands. I think we should lay down a cardinal rule that any ministry coming with a demand must also bring a request for [a] cut under some other head. The overall budget of a ministry should freeze at the level projected in the budget. Unless the finance minister is very strict on this, it cannot be possible to maintain deficit.

Now the other strong measure required, of course, is on the overall burgeoning government expenditure. That will require a national consensus because there the trade unions will have to be consulted if you have to put a freeze on vacancies. Yesterday, I was tempted to interfere in the Indian Airlines question regarding the 2,000 vacancies. I was tempted to ask if the Indian Airlines can function with 2,000 vacancies—we should examine whether those vacancies need to be filled. But we cannot do it unilaterally. The trade unions are there in the country. There are poorer sections. We must talk to them and see where we can really cut government expenditure.

> The Seventh Plan shows 90 per cent and 10 per cent deficit financing. Now this kind of growth, I don't think should be on the agenda of a country like India. Do you know that the total indebtedness, the total borrowing to GDP ratio in India is over 60 per cent? And people will be surprised to know that the only countries which have a higher ratio than us are Bangladesh, Sri Lanka, Nicaragua and Mauritania.

SOFTER OPTION TO PAY

Here I must mention that in the last five years, even in the higher income groups, the tendency has been to take a soft option and to pay up. I always used to see, five or seven years ago, even in Smt. Gandhi's regime or even before that, the central government employees were up in arms, the public-sector employees were up in arms, the electricity board officials were up in arms, and there used to be a serious struggle going on between the employer and the employee. In the last five years, all that has vanished because of the softer option. There is enough money and we pay. We pay everybody. First, we pay ourselves. If we pay ourselves, we must pay the workers because then you cannot say no.

There is general profligacy, and the result is that the Seventh Plan shows 90 per cent and 10 per cent deficit financing. Now this kind of growth, I don't think should be on the agenda of a country like India. Do you know that the total indebtedness, the total borrowing to GDP ratio in India is over 60 per cent? And people will be surprised to know that the only countries which have a higher ratio than us are Bangladesh, Sri Lanka, Nicaragua and Mauritania. Now the moot question is how this will be corrected.

I don't have to name who are the brilliant NRIs who have come into this country and what havoc they are playing with the economy here. I think their names are printed more often in the newspapers than the finance minister's name. I think this NRI business must be examined afresh.

You will have to find a method of funding this loan. There is no use paying this kind of interest and showing this kind of deficit financing and increasing the money supply by 18 per cent per year. I request the finance minister to please sit with the Reserve Bank and find out an agreeable method to reduce this internal indebtedness.

EXTERNAL DEPOSIT ACCOUNTS

Now, about external debt, there are two very serious matters. One is, apart from it becoming ₹1 lakh crore, the most serious thing is the rate of interest. The average rate of interest, which used to be only 2.1 per cent in the 1970s, is now 5.2 per cent. That is a very high rate of interest for external borrowings, and one of the costliest external borrowings is the non-resident Indian (NRI) account. Unfortunately, again in the last five years in this country the NRI has become a very special person. The moment any policy comes, the NRIs are welcome. I don't have to name who the brilliant NRIs are who have come into this country and what havoc they are playing with the economy here. I think their names are printed more often in the newspapers than the finance minister's name. I think this NRI business must be examined afresh.

I think the finance minister should re-examine whether external deposit accounts bearing such a high rate of interest should have an unlimited scope because the country has to repay that money at a high rate of interest and at the prevailing rate of exchange. Now, I do not have to inform members [of the House] that the exchange rate has undergone a total metamorphosis during the previous regime. Only in the Seventh Five Year Plan period between 1984–85, when the government came with a massive majority of 400 seats; and [in] 1988–89 the exchange rate fluctuation against the dollar from ₹11.89 came to, I think it is about ₹18 now, and pound from ₹14.87 to almost ₹28 or ₹30.

Everything has totally gone out of hand. We will never be able to repay. And we will find that we are only working to repay our NRIs. We should stop this. The total economic situation does not permit you to return this money immediately. But we can put restrictions on further deposits. One demand which we have been making also is that the government should restrict its own borrowing under Article 292 of the Constitution.

Now, my humble request to the finance minister is: at least put a ceiling on the rate of interest on the borrowing. There are Indira Vikas Patras and some other schemes where you are borrowing and the effective rate is more than 14.5 per cent. You have put restrictions on the private corporate sector of 14 per cent. There is no justification for the government borrowing money at such [a] high rate. The government should not borrow money at more than 10 per cent maximum and that itself will restrict the borrowing. If you put restrictions on the rate of interest that you will pay, it will restrict your borrowing. That is the first thing you should do.

We have allowed the public sector to issue bonds, interest-free bonds, and there is no limit on any individual buying. That distorts the picture of taxation. We should not allow it. The public sector has been able to raise its own resources without depending on the government. But in the long run, one has to have a look at it.

AVENUES OF TAX EVASION

There are three particular aspects of this budget, which I strongly support. One is the Gold Control Act. It should be abolished immediately. Shri Chavan was working on allowing import of gold by NRIs. The basic thing is that in India gold prices are all artificial. Smuggling of gold is rampant. One hundred tonnes of gold is being smuggled into the country every year. This Gold Control Act should be abolished and some steps should be taken for import of gold in a partial manner. So, if the prices of gold go down, the lure for smuggling will be reduced.

The second is the gift tax. This is another avenue of tax evasion. Everybody was getting gifts from X, Y and Z and claiming that it was out of love and affection. It was all a method of tax evasion. Gift tax on the donee is much more sensible. Because, after all, why should the donor, who is really giving a gift, further pay to the exchequer? The donee has got the money. So, he should pay. Instead of the Gift Tax Act, this should be covered in the other income under the Income Tax Act.

The third thing is 80M which he has amended, inter-corporate dividend. Again a very progressive step, because it did not make sense that merely because you hold your shares through a company instead of yourself, you can save tax. It was [an] unnecessary tax shelter and I am sure it will mean more payment of tax by those who own companies, but it is a reform which was long overdue.

The two points on which there can be hardship are: removal of 80HH for the backward areas. There, I feel that the finance minister should reconsider how to provide relief. If the provision has been misused and that is why he has changed, I have nothing to say. But backward areas still require incentives. Since you want people to go into backward areas, probably those incentives can continue. On the Cash Compensatory Support (CCS), he has amended certain provisions with a view to simplifying because of different interpretations by different courts. Now, one thing in taxation which I do not agree with is retrospective legislation. If there is litigation, the correct answer is a final judgement of the Supreme Court or a tribunal. Because if by legislation we change the provisions with retrospective effect, it reduces the sanctity of legislation. As a principle, it is better to have a court give a final verdict, which should be applicable to all. But for the future it will not make much difference because export profits are also exempt from tax. Whether CCS is exempt or not, does not make a difference.

I can only say that the economy is full of distortions. It will require at least five consecutive budgets, course-correcting budgets, harsh budgets, to rectify the economy. This budget is a start in that direction. Nobody says that growth has not taken place. But we do not agree with the content of growth or with the cost of growth. We could have achieved the same in a much cheaper way. It should trickle down; in fact, growth should directly go to the lower strata of society. In one sentence, I can sum up to the Opposition. This budget is a prudent budget in difficult times. The difficult times are all of your making. The prudence is that of the finance minister.

SUBSIDY MUST REACH TARGETED GROUPS

Here, Morarka speaks as a minister of state in the Prime Minister's Office in the debate on Price Rise on 10 January 1991. Action has to be taken on two fronts: augmenting supply, if necessary, by imports, and taking stringent action against hoarding. Also, a lot of restructuring needs to be done to ensure that subsidies reach the targeted groups.

As we all know, price rise is a subject which touches the common man and as such, it is one of the most important issues facing the country; in many ways, much more important than the wider issues discussed in the press and with which we are always exercised.

Very valid points have been made by the Honourable Members like Shri S.B. Chavan, who has been finance minister and Shri N.K.P. Salve, who was the chairman of the Ninth Finance Commission. At the outset, let me analyse the price situation as I see it. I would like to say that Shri Salve overreached himself when he said that economic emergency should be declared. It is abundantly clear to everybody that the macroeconomic situation is difficult, the balance of payments position is difficult and the internal budget balancing is difficult and has been for the last two years. It is not a political matter as to which party is in power.

DEMAND AND SUPPLY AND LIQUIDITY

The Ninth Finance Commission headed by Shri Salve has analysed the whole thing in great detail and has given possible solutions. My only submission is, as Shri Salve very rightly said, our credit rating in the international market should be protected. In my opinion, price rise is a combination of two factors. One is demand and supply in particular commodities and the second is liquidity in the economy. As Shri Jagesh Desai rightly pointed out, the money supply increased by 22 per cent. The Sukhamoy Chakravarty Report[1] said that 14 per cent money supply is what our economy can sustain. The previous government also tried to keep the money supply under check. I do not want to cast aspersions on the previous government.

Dandavateji[2], with all his honest intentions, was overtaken by the Gulf crisis and there were other situations which were outside his control. In regard to commodities let us take an item, edible oil. Last year there was a shortage of edible oil. It is true and I am totally with Shri Jagesh Desai that India has an economy where even a small shortage reflects in a big manner because of the hoarding that takes place. But at the same time, if the shortages are large, then no amount of this tactic can solve the problem.

> We have to act on both fronts. We must augment the supply, by imports, if necessary, if there is no other remedy, and by ensuring de-hoarding with stringent action against people who have this tendency of making profit out of the country's misery.

WHY SHOULD ONION PRICES GO UP?

Both actions have to be taken simultaneously. There are other factors affecting the common man; take, for example, onions. Why should

---

[1] The Sukhamoy Chakravarty Committee was appointed in 1985 by the Reserve Bank of India to review the working of the monetary system.
[2] Madhu Dandavate was finance minister in the V.P. Singh cabinet.

the price of onions go up? You have no way of importing onions. But problems arise because of your transport bottlenecks. It is not strictly the Gulf crisis or the petroleum prices. There are a lot of other problems. There are regional pockets where the prices shoot up because of transport bottlenecks. The government must act. Hoarding exists across the board and nobody denies that. So, on these items of the common man, immediate action by the respective state governments and by the central government should be taken for de-hoarding as well as for augmenting supplies, wherever it is possible.

On the larger issue, on the liquidity in the economy, the long-term fiscal policy was announced in 1985 and we made an analysis of that. We found that the returns that were expected from the public-sector units did not come about and, therefore, there were gaps. The Seventh Plan was the first plan where all the targets were fully met. That fact we cannot obliterate. It has also been mentioned by the Ninth Finance Commission. In fact, in key sectors, the targets were overshot and now, the imbalances that have taken place are because of the fact that the revenues did not come about and borrowings had to be resorted to, and the repayment of borrowings had to be phased out because the interest payment has formed a significant part of our annual budget.

On subsidies, I do not know how much you can cut. But certainly, there is a lot of restructuring that can take place to ensure that the subsidy reaches the targeted groups because the government will be spending a lot of money on subsidies, but the targeted groups may not be getting them.

Now, 'austerity' is the key word which the prime minister[3] has given as soon as he assumed office. So, all efforts will be made in the budget to cut unnecessary expenditure. There are expenditures

---

[3]Chandra Shekhar

like defence expenditure, subsidies and interest payments which, till now, have been accepted.

REDUCING THE COMMON MAN'S MISERY

On subsidies, I do not know how much you can cut. But certainly, there is a lot of restructuring that can take place to ensure that the subsidy reaches the targeted groups because the government must be spending a lot of money on subsidies, but the targeted groups may not be getting it.

Recently, there was a statement by the deputy prime minister[1] to the effect that the food subsidy and the fertilizer subsidy should be restructured in such a manner that the farmers can get a better advantage. The consumer can get immediate relief only after the prices come down in the key items which touch him, and that can be done by the short-term measure of de-hoarding and seeing that supply lines are augmented. One unfortunate decision which the previous government took was this: they said that they could not afford to augment the supply of edible oils because of the foreign exchange constraints. Foreign exchange is in a difficult situation along with the balance of payments. But the government also should consider that it is the common man who is involved here and edible oil is an item used by the common man.

Even if the foreign exchange constraint was there, some methods should have been found to see that we were able to augment our supplies of edible oil in the short term and to see that the next year's crop was better. This is a sort of holding operation. I am afraid the price situation in respect of edible oils cannot come under control only by a de-hoarding operation. The finance minister[2] is fully seized of the matter.

I did not agree with this one decision of the previous

---

[1]Chaudhary Devi Lal
[2]Yashwant Sinha

government. It was unfortunate. They were saying: 'No. Under no conditions would we import edible oils.' I do not think that this government is committed to any such dogmatic approach. Everything possible will be done to see that the common man's misery is reduced. Nothing is ruled out.

OVERVIEW OF THE ECONOMY

Speaking on the Finance Bill, 1989, on 8 May 1989, Morarka points out that most of the policies in the past four years were geared towards industrialization. However, the bulk of the growth was accounted for by public-sector investments. 'So where is the result of the liberalization, foreign collaboration and foreign investment?' he wants to know. Besides, 40 per cent of the 9 per cent growth was in the services sector, which is not productive at all. Giving a lucid picture of the economy, Morarka says about rural unemployment, 'The unemployment in rural areas cannot be measured. If there is any measurement, [...] it is the social tensions that are created: [...] communal troubles, linguistic troubles, etc., which all arise out of idle, educated youth who find their dreams shattered.'

In the budget discussion in both the Houses of Parliament and thereafter, there have been general comments from both the sides— the Opposition saying that the economy is in trouble, and the ruling party countering it, saying that most of the problems brought to notice are because the country is in a phase of immense development.

I would like to give a few economic indicators of the Seventh Plan period, which roughly coincides with the tenure of this government. We are in the last year of the Seventh Plan and this is the final year before the elections. While the GDP has gone up by 9 per cent and everybody is very happy, the other factors have gone up much more adversely in relation to the real development.

The GDP from 1984–85 to 1988–89, which is the five-year

period which represents this government and the Seventh Plan, has gone up from ₹206,732 crore to ₹293,306 crore at current prices, which shows an increase of 41.88 per cent. But at 1980–81 prices, at constant prices, the GDP has gone up from ₹148,955 crore to ₹170,363 crore. The increase at constant prices in the GDP over the five-year period is 14.37 per cent. The per capita income during this period has gone up from ₹1,791 to ₹1,918. It is an increase of 7.09 per cent.

THE COST OF DEVELOPMENT

Taking this as the base, that this is the degree of development that has taken place in the last five years, let us examine at what cost we have made this development: the money supply, which is the first thing which is an indicator, has gone up during the same period from ₹101,957 crore to ₹189,885 crore. It is an increase of 86.24 per cent. This is another indicator that much of this development has taken place by deficit financing. The money supply in the economy has gone up by 86 per cent for a growth of only 14 per cent. The foreign exchange reserves during the period have depleted from ₹7,243 crore to ₹6,308 crore. This is a steep decline.

About the balance of payments, the current account deficit, which used to be ₹2,852 crore, is now ₹7,500 crore. It has gone up three times. The balance of trade which is another indicator, the difference between import and export which used to be ₹5,390 crore, is ₹7,000 crore now. The exchange rate, which determines the strength of your currency abroad, has depleted by 51 per cent, with a further decline this year. All these indicators will make it clear to any objective persons that the economy is in trouble.

We may have developed. Nobody is disputing that development has taken place in five years. Agricultural production has gone up, industrial production has gone up, but just as population goes up, just as prices go up, a certain increase will be there. We cannot go on taking the credit. The question is, how does it relate to percentages? What we find is while the various indices of GDP and GNP have gone up, the one index which affects the common man is the price index. And even after this budget there was a briefing by the finance ministry, which said that there will be a minimal effect on inflation.

Ever since the budget, in the last two and a half months, the wholesale price index is shooting up. Again, I don't want to quote too many figures, but if you take the selected economic indicators announced by the Reserve Bank, we find that the wholesale price index for a full year has gone up by 5.9 per cent, out of which food articles is 7.4 per cent and foodgrains 9.2 per cent.

POWER AND EGO

Shri Jaswant Singh, who is a member of this House, got policies of ₹50,000 each in the names of his children. The tax deducted at source amounted to ₹256. He was late by four days in depositing this amount.

A prosecution has been launched against him and a non-bailable warrant of arrest [was] issued. The income tax officer said, 'Why don't you admit your mistake and settle it?' Mr Singh said, 'No, you proceed according to the law.' A police officer went to his house to arrest him and asked whether Mr Singh was at home. Mr Singh said, 'Yes, I am here.' The embarrassed police officer told another member of the household, 'Why don't you tell me that Mr Jaswant Singh is not here?' The latter said, 'Why should he say that I am not here? You can arrest me.'

So Mr Singh was produced before the magistrate for an offence of ₹256. And it does not end there. The magistrate agreed to release him on bail for ₹20,000. If this is not a mockery of the law, what is it? Most prosecutions fall under this category. It is the parking offences that are being prosecuted, not the dacoits. I sincerely request you, please review this whole procedure. Let us have a better tax compliance. Let us stop this petty fogging. Only the bureaucracy is having a heyday. They have absolutely no interest either in revenue collection or in any honest implementation of the tax laws, only an interest in power and ego.

MAJORITY SPENDS 70 PER CENT OF SALARY ON FOOD

Unfortunately, the weightage for foodgrains in calculating the index is only 12 per cent. So, it does not give a correct picture. For the vast majority of the country foodgrains is the main thing. They are spending 70 per cent of their salary on food. We have seen during the last one year also, inflation has been there.

This year's budget, though it makes a feeble attempt at curbing the deficit financing... Going from the past five-year record, the actual deficit financing at the end of the year is more than what is projected. I am afraid that in spite of the very large revenue mobilization effort made in the budget, we are still going to fall short. We are going to have deficit financing and it will be reflected in the inflation. Unless we control inflation, the other parameters cannot be controlled.

The first problem, of course, is that the common man is immediately affected. The second problem is, all the consumer price indices go up and you have to increase DA (dearness allowance) of all the government servants, the state government servants and everybody, which again gives rise to price rise. The third thing is that the state budgets go out of control. Some of my friends may not like what I am saying, but if we compare the budget over the last few years, the Centre's transfers to the states have gone up, though states are always complaining of paucity of resources. Between the Centre and states, out of the total revenues, the Centre used to retain 76 per cent and transfer about 22 per cent. Now it is 65:35.

But in spite of these larger transfers to the states, the states' economies are in trouble because of rising inflation. The price stability is something which is the responsibility of the central government. Unless the central government is able to keep plan prices stable, no State Plan and no Central Plan will work. And while the central government may find it a little easier, because the uncovered gap can always be made up by deficit financing by the Reserve Bank, the states can be squeezed. And they resort to overdrafts, to which there is a limit. The central government very prudently tries to put a check on it. But the net result is, development effort suffers because first, the money will have to be paid for salaries to meet their raised expenditure.

That is exactly what is happening in the economy today. What did the finance minister inherit before he tried to prepare this budget? He found this is the fifth year of the plan. The economy was recovering from drought. There was an expected growth of 9 to 10 per cent. It has been proved true. The budget deficit is much higher than [the] ₹7,484 crore projected last year. The trade deficit is much higher than what we had thought and the debt service has reached 25 per cent of the current earnings.

The savings as percentage of GDP have gone down. With all this, a layman can see for himself that 40 per cent of the people are still living below the poverty line. The government has taken a lot of measures. Even in this budget we have announced a lot of measures. Expenditure on expensive hotels, foreign travels, personal transport and durable consumer goods has increased. This is a further distortion in the economy and from where does this money come? It largely comes in the last four years from whatever taxation relief you have given to the middle class.

Now, I find a very strange statement coming from the finance minister this year—though I welcome this—but it is this: the government will not increase kit consumer culture. Now, who introduced this kit consumer culture? It was unknown to this country before this government came. This import of VCRs, TVs, Maruti cars and this kit consumer culture has been introduced by this government.

CREATING PROBLEMS

I am reminded of a joke. A friend got married and after one year somebody asked him: 'How is your marriage doing? How is your wife?' He replied: 'My wife is very good. She is helping me to solve all my problems which would not have been there had I not married her.' Similarly, in this budget, the finance minister is trying to make a valiant effort to solve problems created by this very government in the last four years.

WHAT IS THE 'DEBT TRAP'?

The basic development process in the country is still untouched. What we are trying to do is to undo the efforts of the past four years. It is a U-turn. Speaking for myself, for my party, we welcome this. But the earlier we stop this 'kit consumer culture', the earlier we stop this drain on foreign exchange, the earlier we make programmes for poverty alleviation, for giving more employment, the better it is. This government cannot escape the blame for the morass in which we are.

Today, the prices have reached a certain position from where they will go on increasing. If deficit financing has reached an all-time high, which is more than what prudence permits, if internal debt position is becoming alarming and the balance of payments is totally out of gear, the total responsibility [of] one [of] these will have to be taken for wrong policies pursued, especially in the last four years.

Another statement of the finance minister is, 'The balance of payments position is bad but not alarming.' We are discussing finance and statistics. No one can say what is the level above which this is alarming. I would like to know from the finance minister in his reply about what is the benchmark beyond which it becomes alarming. The 'debt trap' is a word which is frequently talked about but not understood. What is the 'debt trap'?

Every time the government will say we are not going towards the 'debt trap'. The thing is, during a particular year we are borrowing about ₹5,000 crore from abroad. ₹3,000-odd crore are going into repayment of old loans and the interest. So the net inflow is only ₹2,000 crore, which means 60 per cent of fresh borrowings are being used for repayment and for servicing. Only 40 per cent can be used today. As time goes by this will become more adverse because even on the existing loans, the interest goes higher and higher because the old loans mature, which we have to pay, and the new loans are contracted at a higher interest rate.

So, for the same level of borrowing the interest charges are higher. Now, if the 60 per cent becomes 80 per cent and 80 per cent becomes 100 per cent, when we reach a stage when we have to borrow and repay the entire money—that is the debt trap. I do not understand anybody who therefore says, 'We are not going towards a debt trap.' A figure which was only 25 per cent a few years ago…if it reached 60, I think we are speedily going towards the debt trap and action has to be taken to halt this.

SERVICES SECTOR, WHICH IS GROWING, IS UNPRODUCTIVE

Taking it absolutely in another perspective, what is the result of all the policies that we have pursued? This 9 per cent growth which we have achieved, 40 per cent of it is in the services sector. This is another feature which is very disturbing because in 1950–51, rather the First Plan period, 1951–56, 60 per cent of growth was in the agricultural sector, 25 per cent in the industrial sector and 15 per cent in the services sector. In this Seventh Plan period, 1985–88, while this government is in office, agriculture growth has come down to 33 per cent, industry has gone up to 27 per cent and services have gone up to 40 per cent.

In a developing country like India, the services sector is not a productive sector. It represents defence, public administration, banking, insurance, transport and communications. In Western countries, the concept of the services sector is quite different. With automation in agriculture, [a] larger part of the agricultural employment shifts into the agricultural sector. It is not so in India. If the services sector accounts for 40 per cent then our real growth, productive growth, is much less and out of the productive growth in agriculture and industry, it is the agricultural sector which has shown this growth; because of the good monsoons we have had a bumper harvest.

I do not want to make comparison of the drought years and [rather], let us make peak-to-peak comparison. In 1983–84 which is the last peak, the foodgrains' production was 153 million tonnes. This year, it is 166 million tonnes or maybe 170 million tonnes. That means over five years, the growth has been of the order of 8.5 per cent to 9 per cent, which is an average growth of only 1.5 per cent per year and our population is growing by a higher percentage than that. So, our food production is at a stage where we should feel, by no means, very satisfied. It is good we do not have to import foodgrains. But with the ever-increasing population, our food production will have to keep up this pace.

Most of our policies in the last four years have been geared to increasing industrialization and even within industry, what is the growth area? The growth areas are still power generation and petroleum refining. The bulk of our industrial growth is accounted for by public-sector investments. So, where is the result of the liberalization policy, privatization policy, foreign collaboration and foreign investment? The sum total of all those high-profile policies announced with great fanfare is very little and, of course, I must compliment the minister that he himself has realized it and therefore, in this budget, we see there is a break on TVs and the so-called fuel-efficient cars and all these consumer durables. In the last four years, there has been a massive drain not only of foreign exchange resources but internal resources towards the area of industry or that area of economy from which the return is not commensurate.

WHY SURCHARGE TO FINANCE JAWAHAR ROZGAR YOJANA?

In a country like ours, our thrust has to be on rural employment, rural-oriented programmes. Since there will be a separate discussion on the Jawahar Rozgar Yojana, I do not want to take the time of the House on that. But ₹500 crore was announced and here I want to go on record to correct an impression: when I made my budget speech, I referred to the long-term fiscal policy and I said, a time has come to have another long-term fiscal policy. The finance minister was in a hurry. He was going to Washington on that day. He was not very attentive to my speech. In his reply, he said that Mr Birla and Mr Morarka have referred to the long-term fiscal policy and we have to take cognizance of all classes of people etc., etc.

I went through the record and I found that Mr Birla had objected to this 8 per cent surcharge on incomes above ₹50,000. That was not my point. I want to go on record that my party and I are in favour of progressive system of taxation. We have absolutely no objection if the higher income groups are taxed higher. So, if in principle, people getting an income above ₹50,000 are charged 8 per cent surcharge, etc., and that money is used for employment programmes, we have no objection.

Our objection is [that] it is a surcharge. Now, surcharge has two deficiencies. One is, it is not shared with the states. So, this 8 per cent which you get will all remain with the central government. It is not fair because it will come from the higher income groups. Even if it was a normal increase in taxation it would have been shared by the states. Why surcharge? The last one was a surcharge on drought, which was a temporary thing. Is this Rozgar Yojana going to be temporary?

> You will call it economic strategy. We will call it election gimmicks.

Let us seriously think. You are going to start a Rozgar Yojana. You are not going to see the people once employed off after one year. It is a permanent employment programme. So, surcharge will not help us. What we want is a permanent source of revenue. It would be much more prudent to increase the tax level. In that case, it would have been shared with the states and there would be no question of its being withdrawn after one or two years. If it is the philosophy of the government that the high-income group must pay and that money should be earmarked to create employment, it is fine. But let us do it in a straight way.

The second part is the implementation of it. Again, if the states had shared it, part of the implementation would be done by the states. The prime minister announced recently that all the old schemes have been merged and the Jawahar Rozgar Yojana would have an outlay of ₹2,100 crore. The additional outlay is only ₹500 crore, by whatever name you call it. The people who have been employed under the Integrated Rural Development Programme, National Rural Employment Programme, etc., will continue to be so employed. Additional employment will be created only to the extent of ₹500 crore. By whatever method you use, ₹500 crore for 300 working days cannot create employment for more than four or five lakh people per year.

I am assuming that there are no leakages, no corruption and no misuse of money. The prime minister himself is on record as saying that only ten paise out of every one rupee of the poverty programmes reaches the poor. If that is the ratio, what will happen? Even assuming that everything is implemented according to schedule, additional employment generation will hardly be [for] four or five lakh people. So, it is hardly touching the fringe of the problem. Now, the unemployed on the employment exchange register were of the order of 28,500,000 in 1984–85 when this government came to power and according to the latest records, the number of persons on the live registers is of the order of 3 crore.

THIS IS SUICIDE

There has been an increase of 65 lakh people in five years on the live register. Mind you, this is not the measure of unemployment in this country. This is only the fringe of the problem. I want to quote Adam Smith from *Supermoney*, used in a different context. Though used in a different context, I quote it in connection with the statistics saying, 'This is the development. This is what we have done. This is the employment we have created.' The fallacy is, I will quote: 'The first step is to measure whatever can be easily measured. This is okay as far as it goes. The second step is to disregard that which cannot be measured or give it an arbitrary quantitative value. This is artificial and misleading. The third step is to presume that what cannot be measured easily is not very important. This is blindness. The fourth step is to say that what cannot be easily measured really does not exist. This is suicide.'

Unfortunately, in our whole system of administration that we have built up, we have got used to using certain indices and we stick to those indices. Over the years we find that those indices are getting further away from reality. The unemployment in rural areas cannot be measured. If there is any measurement of the unemployment in rural areas, it is the social tensions that are created: it is the so-called communal troubles, linguistic troubles, etc., which all arise out of idle, educated youth who find their dreams shattered. If there is any measurement, it is that.

Everybody is aware that with each year, social tensions are accentuating. Again, taking a balanced view, not talking politics, these programmes are welcome. But, what do we see? The outlays on agriculture, rural development, irrigation and flood control are shown at different places in the budget. This is the gamut of what we are giving as a package to rural areas. What does the total outlay, the package, show?

In 1987–88, it formed 12 per cent. In 1988–89, according to the revised estimates, it is 10.8 per cent. And in 1989–90, including the ₹500 crore, it is 9.2 per cent. Over three years, the total bill on rural areas has gone down from 12 per cent to 9.2 per cent, in spite of our Jawahar Rozgar Yojana and our concern for poverty alleviation and creating employment. This is a serious thing. I can understand the defence budget being slashed and the subsidies going up. But I do not understand why the total bill on rural areas should go down. This way, we can never create employment opportunities. On this subject I would like to discuss our method of financing our plans. I want to draw the attention of the finance minister, though he knows much more than I do—in the Fifth Plan period, out of the total plan outlay, 52 per cent was financed by our own resources, 33.2 per cent was financed by domestic borrowings and 14.8 per cent by external borrowings.

In the Sixth Plan, 1980–85, the share of our own resources came down from 52 per cent to 36.7 per cent, domestic borrowings increased from 33 per cent to 50.6 per cent and the share of external borrowings came down to 7.7 per cent. But what is happening in the Seventh Plan period, 1984–89? In the entire outlay the share of our own resources is zero, negligible, nil; it has been financed by domestic borrowings of 90 per cent and external borrowings of 10 per cent. We have reached a stage where all the revenues that we collect are being used for our own expenses and there is no money for development.

Coming to long-term fiscal policies, it was found that balance from current revenues will be negative. The entire Seventh Plan average has become negative. In regard to the non-developmental expenditure, one of the figures which are hidden in the budget proposals and which the common man really does not get to see is that the non-developmental expenditure as a percentage of the GNP—again, if I say this in thousands of crores or lakhs of crores, Prof. Thakur will get up and rebut it, saying that if growth goes up, expenditure will go up. I am giving it as a percentage of the GNP so that he will have no quarrel with me. In 1960–61 it was 6.6 per cent of the GNP; in 1970–71 it was 9.1 per cent of the GNP. In

1980–81 it was again 9.1 per cent. Between 1970 and 1980 the government could contain its expenditure. But in 1988–89 it was 12.7 per cent of the GNP. That means, between 1980 and 1988, in these eight years, the non-developmental expenditure went up by 3.6 per cent of the GNP from 9.1 per cent to 12.7 per cent.

UNHEALTHY SIGN

Ours is a resource-scarce country. We also understand that in a democratic system development takes place slowly. But how come our expenditure outstrips our growth? That is something which should never happen. In fact, Indians are known to live frugally. We are a government, we are a people, who can do with less expenditure and more production. But here is a situation where non-developmental expenditure as a percentage of GNP goes up to a staggering 12.7 per cent.

Between 1960 and 1988 it has doubled, more than doubled. This doubling is not a healthy sign at all. That is why we have to borrow money. Our balance from the current revenues is negative. And developmental expenditure, which used to be 17.9 per cent in 1980–81, has just gone up to 20 per cent. That means that for development purposes, we can give only 3 per cent of the GNP and the non-developmental expenditure has outstripped. This is a very unhealthy sign and I want the finance minister to pay special attention to it.

Some of the disquieting features of the financial position have been very well brought out by the economic survey. It has lucidly mentioned the problems of balance of payments and internal debt and deficit financing. The Ninth Finance Commission has made some very useful suggestions, which should be implemented without delay. Again, rising above politics, I would like to mention that there are a number of state governments which are being ruled by the Opposition parties and their finance is as equal as that of the central government. There are two things: ultimately, the stability of the price, the stability of the currency, depends upon the central government and the responsibility of the central government cannot be on par with the state governments.

While the state governments have a direct link with the anti-poverty programmes, the central government has no such link and, therefore, I am a bit pained—I am not saying this for politics. I do not have any objection if the Congress (I)-ruled states also do the same thing.

But the central government should not start distributing saris to destitute women; I do not think it is a healthy thing to do. Please do not mistake me. Poverty elimination is very important. But that can be left to the state government, for these kinds of programmes are not only populist, but very difficult from the financial prudence point of view. Let the central government not enter into this. There is nothing much new and already our coffers are empty and we will not be able to meet these kind of demands.

PROFLIGACY AND SQUANDERING OF MONEY

Finally, I come to what is the solution to all these problems and what has been attempted in the budget. Now, in the budget, as I have seen it, the only attempt which is there, which is needed and to which we respond positively, is that the consumer culture is sought to be restrained and the higher income groups have been made to pay a little more and some sort of programme has been made for the poor, though with the reservations which I have mentioned, which will be discussed separately. We do not see any attempt to curb expenditure. Profligacy is at its peak and all the government departments are squandering money, are wasting money, and even the common man can see [that]. An atmosphere of austerity has not been brought about in the budget.

Second, there is no plan to show how the debt position will be controlled. Of course, internal debt follows from deficit financing and the minister of finance knows it. There is no internal debt without deficit financing because it is towards the Reserve Bank, because they print notes and give them to us. That is internal debt. But what about the external debt? Now, there is a lot of talk of exports in this House. The finance minister has said that the time has come now not to give additional incentives to exports but to see that the procedures are simplified and red-tape is cut. I doubt this. Because, what is the buoyancy of exports which you have seen in the last few years? It is only in gems, jewellery, garments, etc.

Take the high-tech areas. In the industries which have come up and which have taken a lot of foreign exchange on the basis that they are going to make internationally competitive products—their production is dismally low, their export effort is dismally low and there is more than one figure to show that top industrial houses or the industries which have come up with high technology and started with export potential have failed to materialize. And it is a tragedy—and I am personally very much concerned—to see the statement from one of the captains of industry, when he was confronted by the commerce minister as to why the big houses are not exporting, he said that they cannot be expected to compete with tailors and cobblers.

BIG INDUSTRIES NOT OBLIGED TO EARN FOREIGN EXCHANGE?

I do not understand that this country is a country of tailors and cobblers. I do not understand the social philosophy. Are we to understand that big industries can use the foreign exchange of the country and then they have no obligation to export and earn foreign exchange? I do not think this is acceptable. This is totally contrary to the economic consensus accepted by this country.

Nehru's Industrial Policy Resolution and all other policies towards the socialist pattern of society are totally negated by this kind of approach. It is bad enough that we are encouraging Pepsi cola, Coca Cola and all other foreign exchange drinks on the country. But if the captains of industry within India take this attitude, I think the future of exports is not very bright.

Gems and jewellery have shown an export of ₹2,000 crore. It is import-based export, as you know, it is not added value. I think time has come when the government must scrutinize very carefully, what are the subsidies, what is the return we are getting, because in the years to come the balance of payments will become more difficult. I do not think that a change in government or a change of finance minister can help that situation, because these are already contracted.

The International Monetary Fund's conditions are bad enough. I do not think our country can afford to borrow at commercial rates in the international market. But in the last few years we have seen that big companies have borrowed at market rate. They may be private companies. But international obligations have to be met by the country. I do not think that you should allow prudence to take a holiday when dealing with foreign exchange. Our currency is under pressure. But if our export effort is not taken as a war effort, I do not think exports will go up overnight. More than that, imports should be curbed mercilessly.

All non-essential items should be stopped immediately. Once we restore this balance of payments position—which the finance minister says is not alarming—in six months it will be alarming. Before that happens, I think immediate steps should be taken to curb imports and push exports.

We can generate revenue either from taxation or from the public sector. Government handouts make us believe that the public sector is doing very well, having earned ₹2,183 crore last year. I went through the figures in the Public Sector Survey placed on the table of the House. Out of the central government companies, 115 companies have made profits totalling ₹3,900 crore. However, 102 companies have made losses totalling ₹1,700 crore. So the net is only ₹2,183 crore.

It may be pointed out that the petroleum sector has made a profit of ₹2,200 crore, which means if we exclude the petroleum sector, the others have lost. A loss of ₹1,700 crore in a single year is something we cannot afford. On the profit side, who is making it? ₹2,200 crore: petroleum sector; ₹336 crore: MTNL and Videsh Sanchar Nigam: ₹302 crore; National Thermal Power Corporation (NTPC): ₹75 crore; International Airports Authority and Indian Airlines: ₹50 crores; STC and MMTC: ₹110 crore, and this also includes subsidies. Most of the areas are monopoly areas where the consumer is paying a high price. But profit is there, though this credit cannot go to the managers of the public sector.

But who is losing money? The Indian Iron and Steel: ₹116 crore; National Textile Corporation (NTC): ₹200 crore; Scooters India: ₹27 crore—the scooter companies in India are making bumper profit, but here we have got one scooter company which is losing ₹27 crore; Cement Corporation: ₹32 crore [when] every cement company in India is making profit. Fertilizer Corporation of India and Hindustan Fertilizers made a loss of ₹150 crore.

PRIVATIZATION SHOULD BE ABOLISHED

I want to make it very clear—privatization should be abolished. It is totally irrelevant to India. There is a lot of talk in the press about privatization. Where is privatization in India? Do you mean anybody will buy this company in the private sector? Even if he does, how does he pay? He will take a loan from the Industrial Development Bank of India (IDBI) and pay! Privatization in India is not a concept which has much promise. But what can be done surely is to have good management of the public sector. We must put people of proven competence in the public sector, people who can manage the units.

I do not want to mention names because that will be going against the traditions of this House. Who are the public-sector managers who get promoted? Not those who manage their companies well but only those who can manage the bosses well.

We have managers who have landed companies into trouble and yet who have got better companies to look after. This will not help us because already forty years have passed and the public sector, as you know, has ₹70,000 crore investment. There is no escape but to put good people who can produce good results. And I am not one to believe that only private enterprises can make profit. Take Tata Iron and Steel Company. It is not being managed by the Tatas, but by professionals for a salary. If the Tatas can get good managers for a salary why cannot the government? Only, you have to give them the right environment to work.

Unfortunately, I see most of the efforts of the public sector are turned to trivial things, not on the long-term things. Even the steel plant modernization is being done largely on external aid. In Heavy Engneering Corporation (HEC) and Metallurgical and Engineering Consultants Ltd (MECON) large capacities have been created in this country but which we cannot use and we are going for foreign aid. The reply of the steel minister—I can predict—will be, 'We are short of resources; so we accept foreign aid.' We are converting an internal deficit into an external deficit. If HEC and MECON are loaded fully with orders, probably the deficit will be more. But at least their capacity utilization is there, employment is there. By keeping them idle and by importing you are converting the internal deficit into an external deficit. It does not help us.

I want the finance minister to look into this aspect. But he must do something for the steel sector, coal sector, textile sector and fertilizer sector. These are the main areas which are losing about ₹1,000 crore between themselves.

Finally on the revenue side, on specific proposals I have moved some amendments also, which may come up for discussion tomorrow. One is for the lower income group (₹18,000–25,000). The finance minister has reduced the tax rate from 25 per cent to 20 per cent. There has been an overwhelming demand for increasing the exemption limit. I feel that this 20 per cent should be reduced to 10 per cent for two reasons.

One, it would give some relief in these inflationary days. More important than that is, up to ₹18,000 when a man does not have to pay tax, the moment he steps into ₹20,000, on ₹2,000 if he has to pay 20 per cent. That means for ₹7,000—on an income of ₹25,000—he has to pay ₹1,400 a year, which to him is a big amount. At the entry point the tax should be minimal. The idea should be to widen the tax base. The propensity to evade taxes starts from the higher brackets progressively. We have had to reduce taxes for better compliance.

The other amendment I have suggested is for retiring employees. For retiring government employees you have created a scheme, which is very good. It should be extended to public-sector employees, even to private-sector employees. Why should all employees not be benefited by that scheme? After all, that scheme is only a savings scheme.

The final point is on tax evasion. Over the years we have seen that there are umpteen reports about a parallel economy in this country. I have got figures from the finance ministry on searches and seizures and while I am happy to see that in 1988–89, 7,505 searches were conducted, the average seizure has gone up to ₹203,000, which is a very healthy sign. But considering the overall economic framework, the average seizure should be above ₹5 lakh or ₹10 lakh, and that is not difficult. The number of searches should reduce.

The department should do its homework and really attack the people who are evading tax. Just because there is a department and it has to do some work, does not mean that it has to search and seize. There should be a minimum standard of information. Otherwise, cost of this is much more than the benefit we can derive. No search and seizure process is ever completed except where the assessee is bullied into a settlement.

ENHANCING REVENUE OF THE STATES

A touchy issue if there was one, Centre–state relations. On 12 May 1989, in this debate, Morarka pleads for the states, who he says do not have the same flexibility to raise revenue as does the Centre. 'After all, the aim of the Centre and the states is the same: collection of revenue in the least painful way,' he points out.

The two bills before the House—the Union Duties of Excise (Distribution) Amendment Bill, 1989 and the Additional Duties of Excise (Goods of Special Importance) Amendment Bill, 1989—have been brought in pursuance of the recommendations of the Ninth Finance Commission. At the outset, I have to say that over the years the state governments have been finding a resource crunch. The Ninth Finance Commission has said in its report that its second report will give deeper thought to the proposals made by different states. Before I go into the detailed demands made by the states and the suggestions they have made to the Ninth Finance Commission, I would like to say a few words on the overall financial picture and the present resource crunch which is being faced by the states and, in fact, also by the Centre.

It is the Seventh Plan period now and, in fact, it is the final year of the Seventh Five Year Plan period, and the Ninth Finance Commission has said that it does not want to make far-reaching recommendations because it does not want any drastic change in the financial pattern in the final year of the Seventh Plan. The fact remains, however, that the Seventh Plan period itself has seen a sea change in the fiscal scenario of the country. The total plan outlay has been met by borrowings and I do not want to go into the facts and figures because they have already been discussed during the debate on the budget and the Finance Bill. But the fact remains that the central government has relied more heavily on deficit financing, that is, internal borrowings as well as external borrowings, in financing the plan. At the same time, the resource generation by way of administered prices and increase in indirect taxes has been phenomenal.

> So, why the state governments are at the receiving end is due to two factors. One is that the revenue sources are limited and the second is that price stability is not in their hands.

If we take an overview of the last five years, and the ratio between the direct taxes and the indirect taxes, we will see that the indirect taxes have contributed 87 per cent of the total resource generation from taxes. Not only that, what we find is that the sales tax has been sharply increased by the various states. The sales tax on goods, which used to be about 2 or 5 per cent, is 8 to 15 per cent, and the basic reason for this is that the main source of revenue for the state governments is the sales tax. Now, as per the old formula, out of the basic excise duty, only 40 per cent is the share of the states.

Taking an overall picture, the finance minister[1] must appreciate that the time has come when, because of the increased DA—yesterday also we announced another DA instalment for the central government employees, and the state governments will have to follow now—and because of the increased pressure of revenue expenditure, resource generation has become crucial.

---

[1]Shri S.B. Chavan

As far as the central government is concerned, they have got many sources of funds including deficit financing, including external debt, whereas the states do not have that sort of flexibility in raising revenues. One inequity is that the central government can generate its own money by methods which may not be acceptable or which may not be prudent, but they can get the money. But the state governments cannot. The second thing is that price instability takes place, which further damages the budgets of the state governments. So, why the state governments are at the receiving end is due to two factors. One is that the revenue sources are limited and the second is that price stability is not in their hands.

STATES UNABLE TO EVEN MEET REVENUE EXPENDITURE

I find that most of the state governments are unable to meet even the revenue expenditure fully, so much so that the development of the state has really taken a back seat. It is a very serious matter which only the central finance ministry can do something about in the long run. I think that the time has come when the finance minister should call a conference of the state finance ministers, the finance ministry and the various other departments and arrive at [a] certain basic parameter, which all state governments must follow.

I will come to some of the specific points which arise out of these two bills. The first point to note is that these two bills relate to the share allocation of the states only for the year 1989–90. The Ninth Finance Commission has reserved its right. In their second report, they may change the share percentages. I would expect the government to assure us that the moment a report is received they will again amend these percentages to fall in line with the recommendations of the Ninth Finance Commission, which should come by the end of this year.

One of the observations made by the Ninth Finance Commission which directly affects the states is the business of levying cess. The excise duty is in the divisible pool. Take this special cess, which you impose on crude oil. If the cess on crude oil was in the divisible pool, it would make a significant difference to the revenue of certain states. Now for Gujarat, the matter has been raised sometimes in this House. For Maharashtra also, the matter has been raised for the Bombay High. But on certain items there is excise duty as well as cess, such as tea, sugar, bidi, textiles, paper, jute and automobiles. But it is only the excise duty which is shared and not the cess. Then there are certain items where there is cess of a particular type, like iron ore and coal.

POOR RICH STATES

State governments like Bihar, Bengal and others which have coal find that they are unable to share the cess on coal. These are the various factors which were brought before the Ninth Finance Commission and it observed that to the extent possible the government should try to reduce the cess. But they have not opined that cess should be brought under the divisible pool. I must point out here that in the long-term fiscal policy which your government presented in 1985, they did talk of either abolishing the cess or reducing it significantly. That has not been pursued. I have to request that during this year the finance ministry should consider either to bring the cess into the divisible pool or to reduce the cess and the additional duties, so that they do not make a significant dent in the revenues of the states.

The second suggestion is on administered prices. Here the finance commission has made a clear recommendation. Their recommendation is: 'If the purpose of revising administered prices is to raise resources for the government, it should be done through increase in excise duties so that the states also get a share of the proceeds thereof notwithstanding the fact that the extent of increase would be higher in such cases.'

It appears now that when the Ninth Finance Commission was discussing this matter, the union finance ministry had taken the stand that this are not feasible because if the administered prices are increased by way of excise and thereby they have to share them with the states, then the increases will have to be much higher, which is natural. In spite of that the finance commission has said that they are unable to accept this argument and in spite of the stand of the finance ministry, the Ninth Finance Commission has recommended that whenever administered prices are to be increased, that should be done by way of excise duties as a source of revenue. Of course, if the administered prices are increased for meeting the cost of a product, that is a different matter. But if it is for the resources of the central government, it should be divisible so that the states also get their due share.

The next question is that of the basic excise duty states share. Now, the Eighth Finance Commission had fixed the share at 40 per cent [with] another 5 per cent to be distributed among the deficit states. The Ninth Finance Commission, for 1989–90, has stuck to that formula on the ground that being the final year of the Seventh Plan, they did not want to change the pattern drastically. But various states have urged that this 45 per cent should now be increased to 50 per cent. Some states have demanded even 60 per cent. But I think the time has come when, if we are not reducing the cess or merging it with excise duty, then the share of the basic excise duty should be increased to 50 per cent. Perhaps we will have to await the final recommendation of the Ninth Finance Commission.

Excise has become the main source of revenue for the Centre and sales tax has become the main source for the states. A host of items are still being subjected to sales tax in the states.

I do hope that the finance ministry will consider that this share should be increased. Another question is the additional duties in lieu of textile, tobacco and sugar. As you know, this was done long ago. The idea was that it is simpler to collect this duty; sales tax for simpler administration and collection. But what has happened over the years, as we see, is that there has been no simplicity. Excise has become the main source of revenue for the Centre and sales tax has become the main source for the states. A host of items are still being subjected to sales tax in the states. Many states have come up with the suggestion that these three items should also now go back to the states. I am not saying this should happen. This excise in lieu of sales tax is in the nature of a tax rental arrangement. It is time to review this arrangement. This arrangement was arrived at by the National Development Council in 1956 or so. Probably there should be another meeting of the National Development Council to reconsider what changes are required to make this acceptable to the states in the new scenario. And one of the comments of the finance commission is very important:

'We hope that by the time we are to finalize our views on the merger issue for our second report, the apprehensions and misgivings of the state governments relating to the tax rental arrangement would have been redressed. This would help create an atmosphere conducive to an objective and dispassionate approach to the question.'

SAME AIM: COLLECTION OF REVENUE

What I want to say is that after all, the aim of the Centre and the states is the same: collection of revenue in the least painful way. Development processes are going on, which are not contradictory. The Centre wants projects and the states also want projects. But if a stage has come when the states have this misgiving that they have been deprived of their due share, there is a suggestion to merge the additional duty with the basic duty. The Centre insists [that] this threshold limit of 45 per cent should not go up. The states feel that it should go up. I think time has come when these matters should be sorted out amicably. The Ninth Finance Commission has said, if this is done before the final report, it would go a long way in having a consensus in the proportionate sharing of the revenue.

The finance commission has pointed out that they are very much concerned on two issues which the states have raised. One of them relates to numerous exemptions issued by the central government in respect of goods which would otherwise have attracted additional duties of excise. The central government has powers to exempt.

The other matter relates to undue expansion in the coverage of additional duties of excise. As a result, the list of items on which the states may levy sales tax is becoming restricted. There may not be technically any restriction and there are a lot of items where the states also can levy sales tax in spite of excise. In taxing an item beyond a certain limit the law of diminishing returns sets in. So if the Centre goes on expanding its list of additional excise dutiable items, the state list where they can get some sales tax goes on getting restricted. This is basically a revenue problem for the states. The Centre has not demonstrated its earnestness to sort out these issues, which makes the states apprehensive.

Now, the finance commission has said—I quote: 'We recommend that the Standing Review Committee may meet urgently to resolve these issues. The report of the committee in this regard may be made available to us by the end of October 1988 to enable us to consider the matter in our second report.' I do not know what has happened. I would like to be enlightened by the minister on this. A number of formulae were tested from the First Finance Commission onwards as the basis for sharing the revenue inter se among the states—whether it should be on the basis of population or area or consumption. A consensus was evolved that basically, the sharing has to be on the basis of consumption. But various finance commissions, the Sixth and Eighth Finance Commissions especially, found that accurate data on consumption is not available.

MORE POPULATION UNDER BPL

The National Sample Survey, too, in the thirty-eighth round has done a lot of work, but accurate data is not available. So, the Eighth

Finance Commission gave the state domestic product (SDP) and the population equal weightage, which really means the per capita domestic product. The Ninth Finance Commission has also followed the same formula but with one refinement, and that is, for states where there are more percentages of people below the poverty line, they have tried to give a small weightage in their favour.

I feel that though we are in a resource crunch, there are states in the country where backwardness is much more and something will have to be done to see that those particular backward areas—adivasi areas or tribal areas or very backward areas—get some extra money. Though we have got grants-in-aid, I feel that when the final formula for devolution of resources to the states is worked out by the Ninth Finance Commission, there should be a provision to give weightage to people living below the poverty line. Again, data on that is not accurately available. But I do hope the finance ministry will do something to generate that sort of data.

I basically support the recommendations of the Ninth Finance Commission and I do hope the government will take into consideration the feelings of the House, part of which I have expressed, and I am sure my other friends will do the same. And I do hope that the finance minister will consider these matters sympathetically to make it more rational.

ALLOW DUTY-PAID GOLD INTO THE COUNTRY

Pointing out that anti-smuggling operations were not able to seize even 4 per cent of the gold actually entering the country illegally, Morarka suggests officially allowing people to pay duty and bring in gold. Implement the Rangarajan Committee's recommendation on import of gold, he argues in this debate on 28 May 1990. Incidentally, according to the All India Gems and Jewellery Trade Federation quoted in the media, 950 tonnes of gold was imported in 2012, and 250 tonnes of this was smuggled in.

I wish to draw the attention of the finance minister[1]—unfortunately, he is not present here—to the menace of gold smuggling, which has reached threatening proportions now. The government appointed a high-power committee under the deputy governor of the Reserve Bank of India (RBI), Shri Rangarajan, which has submitted a report to bring changes in the Gold Control Act.

The recommendations of this committee are very mild. My first request to the finance minister is to immediately implement the recommendations of the Rangarajan Committee. According to the government's own estimates, the annual demand of gold in the country is of the order of 150 tonnes. Our own production from the two gold mines is 1.7 tonnes. According to international studies,

---

[1]Prof. Madhu Dandavate

the gold being smuggled into the country is between 90 and 100 tonnes, which is estimated at about ₹3,000 crore. And the total seizure, in spite of the anti-smuggling operations, was 2.26 tonnes last year. In the first half of this year they have seized 1.9 tonnes.

This does not amount to even 3 per cent or 4 per cent of the total smuggling that is taking place today. Interrelated with gold smuggling is the smuggling out of drugs and hashish and other things. So this problem of gold smuggling is interrelated with the entire economy of the country. My suggestion to the finance minister is to take an entirely new look at the government's gold policy. Returning Indians from abroad should be allowed to get in primary gold as a dutiable item officially. Let them pay duty and get gold in the country. Non-resident Indians should be allowed to send gold to India, provided it is done through official channels—duty-paid gold—where no foreign exchange is involved.

Unless the availability is officially increased, this problem cannot be controlled by merely increasing anti-smuggling or coastal customs vigilance, etc., because the basic problem of demand and supply will remain. And this has a far-reaching impact on all other economic parameters. My request to the finance minister is, if necessary, to call a small committee of experts and immediately act on the Rangarajan Committee report to stop gold smuggling.

> **Returning Indians from abroad should be allowed to get in primary gold as a dutiable item officially. Let them pay duty and get gold into the country. Non-resident Indians should be allowed to send gold to India, provided it is done through official channels—duty-paid gold—where no foreign exchange is involved.**

BE BOLD IN TACKLING GOLD SMUGGLING

Gold first came under control after the Chinese aggression, in January 1963, as part of the Defence of India Rules, and the present Gold (Control) Act, which we are seeking to repeal, was enacted in 1968. As per the Objects and Reasons of the Bill at that time, the purpose was to restrict the circulation of smuggled gold by putting restrictions on the holding of primary gold, and the idea was that smuggling would be controlled and would go down. The making of new jewellery was restricted to only fourteen carats so that smuggled gold, if used in making of jewellery, could be detected. That was the purpose of the act.

In most of the acts in India, unfortunately, the implementation is not reviewed. If it was done in this case, for instance, this act should have been repealed probably within two or three years of its enactment. Shri N.K.P. Salve very rightly pointed out ab initio the purpose was very doubtful in 1968 itself.

MERELY REPEALING LAW WILL NOT BRING DOWN PRICES

It requires a lot of courage in this country to undo something which has been done, something which everybody agrees is wrong, something which is going on for the last twenty-two years; still, it requires a lot of courage in this country to come forward and repeal it. Therefore, I want to place on record my heartiest congratulations to the finance minister. When he made a mention of this in his budget speech I know of many responsible persons who said that this is only a part of the budget speech, it will not be done, you just wait and see, sessions will come and go but the Gold (Control) Act will not be repealed. Therefore, I am a very happy person that all these Cassandras have been proved wrong.

I may clarify that nobody should be under the impression that the repeal of this act would bring down the prices. It cannot, because availability of gold will not go up merely by repealing this act. Other complementary measures will have to be taken. I have a few suggestions to make for the consideration of the finance minister. The Rangarajan Committee report is pending with the government. The previous government was considering it. I had made a special mention when Shri Shankarrao Chavan was the finance minister. I do not know where it got held up. I was told that probably the cabinet was considering it.

The Rangarajan Committee had recommended that inter alia 100 grams of gold per person should be allowed to be imported by returning non-resident Indians. I feel this limit is too low. He should think of 200- or 500-gram limit seeing other considerations, but you will have to give a substantial concession for bringing gold into the country by legal means. Today the statistics are very clear. One hundred to 150 tonnes of gold are being smuggled into the country every year.

GOLD SMUGGLING LINKED TO LURE OF PROFITS

Seizures, as reported in the press or on the TV, are about 5 tonnes and the total production in the country is 2 tonnes. So, 2 tonnes is the production, 5 tonnes seized and 100 to 150 tonnes are still smuggled into the country without payment of duty. Our great economists and even the finance ministry mandarins will tell us, 'Don't allow import of gold, the balance of payments position will go wrong, the foreign exchange will not come.'

I am not an economist; 100 to 150 tonnes of gold which is coming to the country today is being paid for. It is not coming free. It is being paid for through illegal channels. There are hawala transactions galore: you know the situation. For twenty-two years we have seen that our stopping gold does not stop gold. Our putting restrictions do not work. It is much better to give a little flexibility and let the water find its own level. Gold smuggling will come down the day the lure of profit is reduced, which means the prices in the Indian market must come down. This will not happen unless gold comes in through legal channels. So, I submit for the consideration of the finance minister, apart from the Rangarajan Committee's report with scaling up the allowance from 100 grams to a higher quantity, two or three suggestions.

There is the foreign currency NRI account, which has got a deposit of 8,000 to 10,000 crore rupees and the annual interest that we are paying in foreign exchange is about ₹800 to ₹1,000 crore. If against that interest of ₹800 to ₹1,000 crore, you allow them to import gold, many of them will do that because gold is profitable. That is not your foreign exchange. Your balance of payments is not touched. In any case, you have to pay in foreign exchange. You allow them to import gold against that amount. I think 30 to 40 tonnes of gold can be imported against that amount.

HAWALA RATES WILL BE REDUCED

Similarly, the non-residents' [Indians] external account is there. For the last three years, the figure is constant. Every year you are getting about ₹3,000 crore in that account. The figure is not going up. Why? Because money is coming through hawala transactions. Everybody knows there is a premium of about 25 per cent between the official rate of foreign exchange and the hawala rate. If you allow gold to be imported, the water will find its own level, the hawala rates will go down, the gold prices will go down and people can make some profit. Of course, we have to find a balance. I do not say that we should allow these people to make fat profits. It should not be allowed for black-marketeering in gold. But a little opening, a little flexibility, I feel, will reduce a lot of these things.

> Gold smuggling will come down the day the lure of profit is reduced, which means the prices in the Indian market must come down. This will not happen unless gold comes in through legal channels.

Our coast is very big. Our borders are very big. It would be impossible to police the entire border or the entire coast to stop gold smuggling. We have been doing it for the last twenty years. We can have separate figures to see how much money we have invested in vessels, faster vessels and all sorts of modern gadgets that are available for intercepting gold smuggling. All these have limitations. Ultimately, in economics, unless the lure is reduced, your policing will not be effective. Over the last twenty years, we have seen smuggling has proliferated beyond all expectations and calculations.

It is high time that concomitant with the assurances that the finance minister has given, he should come forward with bold measures to attack the menace of gold smuggling. In answer to a question a few days ago, Shri Anil Shastri, the deputy finance minister, told the House that the annual demand of gold in the country is about 150 tonnes. He did not want to admit that it was met through smuggling. But he did say that that is the demand and the production is only 2 tonnes and the seizure is 5 tonnes. The rest, he said, was met by recycling.

SMUGGLING OF GOLD IS RAMPANT

I do not agree. Smuggling is rampant, it is obvious to everybody. The deputy finance minister did not commit on the Rangarajan Committee report. He only said that presently NRIs are allowed to bring some gold, which they are doing. But I feel there is nothing wrong if we allow all visitors abroad to get some gold back on payment of small duty. Duty element is important. I am not suggesting import of gold without duty.

> Gold prices have a bearing on a lot of other things, like foreign exchange, black market in foreign currency, hawala rates, etc.

But the duty element can be such that the import is legalized; at the same time, there is stability of prices in the market. These are some of the suggestions which I am leaving with the finance minister. I just want to say that abolition of Gold Control Act in any case will be welcomed all over the country by thousands of people because we all know that even today the restriction is on holding primary gold. I know of people who buy primary gold and get it converted into jewellery the same evening—and there is no restriction of holding jewellery.

In any case, this act has been followed more in the breach than in observance. So, it being repealed is welcome. The other measures, complementary measures, should be announced soon. Otherwise, today in the public the general impression is what Prof. Thakur has just now said, that by repealing this act the prices will go down. But actually, the prices will flare up after the bill is passed and there is no restriction on holding gold. So there is the danger that prices will flare up.

The deputy finance minister said that gold is not an essential commodity and so he tried to say that government is not so much worried about the price of gold. Gold prices have a bearing on a lot of other things, like foreign exchange, black market in foreign currency, hawala rates, etc., So, I feel that the finance minister should seriously look into this matter at his level only because, I can assure him that a lot of economists and bureaucrats are going to say 'No'. He will have to take saner counsel from members across the floor, come to some firm conclusions and take some very bold and dynamic decisions.

CONGRESS SHOULD STAY AWAY FROM KASHMIR

Pointing out the Congress's double standards vis-à-vis itself and the role of the V.P. Singh government in Kashmir, Morarka asks it to stay away from that state. The hypocrisy especially shows in the attitude towards Dr Farooq Abdullah and the governor, Jagmohan. He says in this Discussion on the J & K Situation on 14 March 1990, that the Congress should stop fishing in troubled waters and Kashmir is indeed a troubled state—with much of the trouble having been fomented by the Congress itself.

At the outset, I wish to agree with Shri P. Shiv Shanker that Kashmir is a national problem and should be tackled in a spirit of not trying to score points against each other. Much of what he has said reflects the national ethos on Kashmir and when he says that the problems we see there today are because of the growing trend of fundamentalism and narrow outlook, we in the Janata Dal cannot agree more.

Before I go into some of the historic reasons why Kashmir has come to acquire a special position and the problem has lingered for so long, I would straightway say where we disagree with Shri Shiv Shanker. I do not understand how the Congress party, in its introspective mood, with its full sense of responsibility, can run away from the fact that in 1984 they committed the Himalayan blunder of dismissing the Farooq government, of engineering defections and of forming a government with the breakaway group, which is the source of all the problems that Kashmir is facing today.

A MUSLIM-MAJORITY STATE THAT DECIDED ON INDIA

Not that before 1984 there were no problems in Kashmir. Kashmir has had a chequered history. There are certain relevant dates which the House should take note of. It was only in October 1947 that the Instrument of Accession was signed. It was signed much later in comparison to the other princely states. It was a fitting tribute, if there should be one, to the secular and democratic character of India. When the princely states were allowed to merge with one of the two dominions, in spite of the best efforts of Pakistan, in spite of all the temptations given, here is a Muslim-majority state which decided to stay with India. I am quite sure that had India, on that day, talked of a Hindu Rashtra or a theocratic state, Kashmir would not have decided to stay with India.

Kashmir decided to stay with India because India declared that it would be a democratic and secular state. And mind you, the accession of Kashmir to India was not only the wish of the maharaja, but it had the popular support inasmuch as Sheikh Abdullah, who was leading the National Conference, which was undoubtedly representing the masses of the people of Kashmir, was behind, in full support to the accession of Kashmir to India. The events of 1953 broke the heart of Jawaharlal Nehru and all secular Indians. Action had to be taken to preserve whatever was achieved, but not before long; Jawaharlal Nehru, before his death, started a dialogue with Sheikh Abdullah in March 1964 to bring back normalcy. The sudden passing away of Panditji again put things in reverse gear.

If you tinker with Article 370—that is what Pakistan's trap is, they want you to interfere with Article 370—the Kashmir issue becomes wide open.

However—though it is not for us to go into the internal affairs of another country—the fact that there were events in Pakistan which took place and it broke into two had a big bearing on the 1975 accord of Sheikh Abdullah with Indira Gandhi, whereby Sheikh Saheb again became the chief minister of Kashmir in February 1975. I wish to state for the record, let there be no mistake that whatever might have happened earlier, from February 1975, nobody could even question the integration of Kashmir with India. The same Pakistan which in the United Nations (UN) used to say that till Sheikh Abdullah, who was the conscience of the Kashmiri people, was in jail, elections in Kashmir had no meaning, the same Pakistan which used to say that Sheikh Abdullah was the only authentic voice of the people of Kashmir, had no voice to even talk after February 1975, because it was the same Sheikh Abdullah for whom they stood and the same Sheikh Abdullah, the Lion of Kashmir, whom they would accept as the authentic voice of the Kashmiri people, again affirmed the accession of Kashmir to India as final.

ISSUE OF PLEBISCITE IS DEAD

Then all doubts of an imaginary character being raised by Pakistan were finished. I totally agree with Shiv Shankerji that the very issue of plebiscite is dead and gone because the elementary condition, at that time, for plebiscite was that Pakistan would withdraw its troops from the Occupied Kashmir. Having failed in that elementary task, Pakistan has no business to talk of plebiscite. What Pakistan is talking today is humbug.

> The problem is whether the population of Kashmir is emotionally integrated with us. That is the crux of the problem. We are concentrating on geography. History is more important than geography.

I do not think, cutting across party lines, that there should be any doubt about a few facts. Kashmir's accession to India is final. The question of reopening the Kashmir issue or internationalizing it has no relevance or meaning. The other question is about Article 370. Once again I want to make it clear on behalf of our party—the prime minister[1] has said it in the other House yesterday—that we stand by Article 370. Whoever may be demanding the abrogation of Article 370, it is only emotional; it is academic and abstract; it is not historical or practical.

Let us even assume that there is a government which amends the Constitution. Even then, Article 370 cannot be removed without the assembly of Jammu and Kashmir amending the Constitution of Jammu and Kashmir. I think there is total, all-round ignorance when we say that we can do things. There is an Instrument of Accession, which is based on certain conditions. What happens if you remove those conditions? If you tinker with Article 370— that is what Pakistan's trap is, they want you to interfere with Article 370—the Kashmir issue becomes wide open. The question of tinkering with Article 370 does not arise.

Now, the other aspect of Article 370, which people do not understand is, over the years, there have been a number of Jammu and Kashmir Constitution Orders whereby the Supreme Court's jurisdiction has been extended to Kashmir, the writ jurisdiction of the High Court has been extended to Kashmir. The appointment of High Court judges in Kashmir till 1957 was done there. After 1957, this is done by the president of India in consultation with the Chief Justice of India. From 1959 onwards, the election commission has got jurisdiction in Kashmir.

The process of integration with respect to the various subjects is gradual and with the willing cooperation of the people of Kashmir. After all, what is the Kashmir problem? Is it land or the people? If it is land, it is very easy. Nobody can take an inch of our land. But that is not the problem. The problem is whether the population

---

[1]Shri V.P. Singh

of Kashmir is emotionally integrated with us. That is the crux of
the problem. We are concentrating on geography. History is more
important than geography.

There is no use keeping a country intact in a particular
geographical shape when the people are not willing. It will be
unethical and immoral to hold the people against their will. The
question is, in the last forty-two years, what has been done towards
that end? I have no doubt in my mind that after 1975, when we
obliterated all the mistakes of the past, we made a grave error in
1984 and pushed the clock back for the rest of its life.

SECULAR KASHMIR

I do not understand how a party like the Congress party, which
was ruling the country and most of the states, could fall a prey
to getting into part-share in a government and appointing three
ministers. For achieving that very little, it has paid a very high
price, not only for the Congress party but for the country as a
whole. Every day people come and say that Pakistani flags have
been hoisted there. We must understand the history of Kashmir.
Kashmir was the only place where communal riots had never taken
place. Kashmir was secular not only in practice but even in their
Constitution. I will read a portion of the Jammu and Kashmir
Constitution which is very significant. Section 25 of the Jammu
and Kashmir Constitution reads:

'The State shall combat ignorance, superstition, fanaticism,
communalism, racialism, cultural backwardness and shall seek to
foster brotherhood and equality from all communities under the
aegis of a secular State.'

What went wrong? It was in 1986 that for the first time in the
history of Kashmir, communal riots took place when Shri G.M.
Shah was the chief minister. Shri Jagmohan appointed by you is
a good governor and Shri Jagmohan appointed by us is a bad
governor! When Dr Farooq Abdullah got the mandate, he was

anti-national and unpatriotic. When he made an accord with you, he was a symbol of patriotism!

I have no comment on Shri Jagmohan except to borrow what Shri Rajiv Gandhi said in the other House and what is said today: that he is the same man who ordered the bulldozing of the Turkman Gate houses. I agree. Only one thing, I think, I will have to concede to them. What they mean is that Jagmohan is fit for this kind of operation. What kind of operation did they want done? They wanted to bulldoze the Farooq ministry. They wanted to come to power by these means, for which they felt Shri Jagmohan was fit. I respect the opinion of somebody who says that Shri Jagmohan should not have been sent. However, under our Constitution, the selection of a person cannot become the subject of a parliamentary debate.

I would say that the governor has been appointed on 19 January 1990. If I am to believe what the Congress party is saying, I must also be able to believe that everything was hunky-dory in the state of Jammu and Kashmir till 2 December 1989, that the moment Shri V.P. Singh took over as prime minister there has been a rapid deterioration, to the extent that the masses have become anti-national, that they abducted the home minister's daughter and lakhs of people came out on the streets who one week ago were very patriotic, all by sending Shri Jagmohan. Am I to believe that?

Even a Standard III student knows that communal harmony or communal discord cannot be created in matter of a day or a week. It takes years and years to bring communal harmony. And, what has really happened in Kashmir is that a series of mistakes and blunders have been committed by the authorities, which have led to the current situation. We are all Indians. It is in our interests to see that Kashmir not only remains an integral part of India, but also we should win back the people there, we should win the confidence of the people there today.

COMMUNAL VS SECULAR RIGGING?

In the 1987 election, 32 per cent of the electorate had voted for the Muslim United Front. At least after that you should have formed a committee, like the National Front formed an all-party committee. But if you do not want to learn the lessons of history, if you are only interested that your three ministers should be there to do your bidding, I do not understand what you are trying to do.

Kashmir is not Andhra. In Andhra the same thing was done. The Opposition parties took a united stand and rebuffed the attempts. In Kashmir our hands are tied because it is a sensitive state, it is a border state. In 1987 we could have done the same thing. Then we would have had to support the Muslim United Front, which we did not want to do. Now if you are claiming that there is a difference between communal rigging and secular rigging, I have nothing to say.

> [...] if we try to keep this country together with the help of the police and the army, all of us, in all parties, will be rendering ourselves irrelevant. Our relevance is that we should be able to harmonize the aspirations of the people with national aspirations.

The facts are that the population of the place got alienated from the Government of Kashmir, from the Government of India. Who is responsible is a matter of detail. Certainly the Opposition cannot be responsible, at least not before 2 December; we were in the Opposition then. Today, you cannot be responsible. Today, to say that the entire deterioration has taken place in the last three months, that Kashmir has come to the brink of breaking away because of the misdeeds of this government, is something one cannot accept. You can say that the governor's appointment is wrong. You are entitled to say that.

We have responded to that by having an all-party committee.

We ourselves wanted it. In fact, let us not mistake ourselves, if we try to keep this country together with the help of the police and the army, all of us, in all parties, will be rendering ourselves irrelevant. Our relevance is that we should be able to harmonize the aspirations of the people with national aspirations. Whether it is Janata Dal, whether it is Congress, whether it is National Front, if we recognize that this is the problem, if we recognize that all of us work together, fine!

WHAT IS AN 'OPEN' GOVERNMENT?

You also complain that this governor is not the best governor. You are shying away from the demand of the recall of the governor. That is a surprise to me. If that is your demand, please make it. Whether the government will do it or not, it is the government's outlook.

I want to make two more points. 'Open Government', 'Open Government'—I heard this so many times that my mind shut down. 'Open Government' does not mean that we can go beyond the Constitution. 'Open' means openness within the Constitution. We have a Constitution.

We have collective responsibility of the cabinet. There is a home minister responsible for the overall domestic affairs in the country. It was said by the all-party committee that Kashmir needed intensive, concentrated treatment because of the problems that are there today, and it was necessary that a specific minister should be allotted this task. He can be in regular touch with the governor, with the administration of the state and coordinate with the Centre.

It does not mean that he is either super-imposed on the home minister or he is working under the home minister, as some members pointed out. He is a cabinet colleague. There is the collective responsibility of the cabinet. The Kashmir problem, we have already decided, is even beyond the cabinet. It is a national problem. All of us are together in this. I am sure Shri George Fernandes will get all the cooperation and assistance from the Opposition. So I do not think we should try and divide or try to score small points on this. There is a minister for Kashmir affairs.

Their government appointed—unprecedentedly—a minister for West Bengal affairs, for reasons which I entirely disagree with. That is to facilitate their party to get into power, which they did. At that time nobody asked whether Shri Siddarth Shanker Ray was above the home minister or below the home minister. There are things which you must take more seriously. Kashmir is an affair we cannot tinker with. The home minister is very much there. The minister of Kashmir affairs is also there. An all-party committee will work. And there need be no fear on this account.

Dr Farooq Abdullah is a personal friend of mine. He made a statement that the Janata Dal should clarify its policy on Article 370. When has the Janata Dal been ambiguous about Article 370? Most of the Janata Dal leaders, whether it is Shri V.P. Singh, Shri Devi Lal, Shri Chandra Shekhar, Shri Charan Singh's son Shri Ajit Singh—they all had the ethos of the freedom struggle with them. They were at the feet of Mahatma Gandhi and with Jawaharlal Nehru. They were the colleagues of Jawaharlal Nehru. They were the colleagues of Indira Gandhi.

The basic ethos of developing India into a multi-lingual, multi-religious society is fully accepted. 'Democracy–Secularism–Socialism', I think, are acceptable to the Congress and us. The National Front's avowed policy is to maintain a multi-lingual, multi-religious and multi-ethnic society in India and to harmonize its unity in diversity. That is what we have been taught by Mahatma Gandhi.

> The federal character of India is being destroyed by the machinations of the Congress party at the Centre and Kashmir is a living example of it.

THE CONGRESS TOUCH TURNS GOLD INTO MUD

We have no business to run away from it. It is all enshrined in the Constitution. I will be very happy if anybody here from the Opposition stands up and says: here is where Janata Dal has gone wrong. But the shoe is on the other leg. A party which has overseen Meerut and Bhagalpur has turned round to us and said: 'You are allying with communal forces.' I am amazed. I don't understand it. I have stated during my speech on the President's Address last time—my friend Shri Deba Prasad Ray was annoyed with me—that the federal character of India is being destroyed by the machinations of the Congress party at the Centre and Kashmir is a living example of it. By dismissing Farooq Abdullah it committed one blunder. Then, by aligning with Farooq Abdullah and by tempting him into the government, you have destroyed the heritage of Sheikh Abdullah which he inherited. It is a loss to Farooq Abdullah. It is a loss to the country.

People used to say that if Mahatma Gandhi touches mud it turns into gold. He put his hand on Pandit Jawaharlal Nehru, Sardar Patel and a heap of leaders who grew at his feet. It is true of the Congress party in reverse. They touch gold and it becomes mud. Farooq Abdullah was accepted by the people of Kashmir as a true legatee of Sheikh Abdullah. Sheikh Abdullah has a history since 1931. He fought for the freedom of India. He fought for Kashmiri aspirations. And what happened? The moment you touched him, you finished Farooq Abdullah and you have finished Kashmir and you have brought about this problem.

It was made out that our problem started after 2 December 1989. I fail to understand what has happened after 2 December 1989, except that a particular person has been made governor, about whom opinion may be divided.

THE KIDNAP EPISODE

Much has been said on the kidnapping episode. Shri Shiv Shanker said that the girl had been kidnapped and the message went out that it was a weak government. I do not think so. It is a personal and sensitive point. She is the home minister's daughter. I do not want to say anything. I strongly object to what my friend, Smt. Jayanthi Natarajan, has said. The home minister had no role in the decision-making or in the process of getting Miss Rubaiya[1] released. Let me put it on record. This is one of the points my friends don't understand. What Farooq Abdullah has been saying is that Miss Rubaiya could have been released by much less or she could have been released by releasing one terrorist instead of five terrorists. We are not in a baniya shop. We are running the affairs of the state. What is this logic that it is too costly and that it could have been done cheaper? I don't understand it.

I can say with all emphasis at my command that the ethos of the freedom struggle says that the life of an innocent girl is more important than the lives of five useless terrorists. I can understand the anxiety of the members to capitalize on the Rubaiya episode because after this government has come to power that is the only thing which has taken place, which can be pointed out against this government. So, I fully appreciate the lack of other points due to which the Rubaiya episode becomes important.

CONTRADICTORY CRITICISM

I want to make it clear that this government does not underestimate the significance of the Rubaiya episode. That episode has taught us a lot of things. For us, just like for the rest of the country, it was an absolute shock that the release of the terrorists could have brought millions of people on to the streets. I am reminded of what John Kennedy said when he came to power. People asked him: 'How do you find things?' He said, 'Unfortunately, things are as bad as we were saying they were.'

_____

[1]Daughter of Mufti Mohammed Sayeed, then home minister of India, was kidnapped on 8 December 1989 and the ransom demanded was the release of five imprisoned terrorists. The V.P. Singh government accepted the demand.

That is what has happened. We knew things in Kashmir are bad. But not for one moment did we imagine that this is what they have brought Kashmir to.

Now they are saying that this incident has given a message to the terrorists that it is a weak government. I do not understand this. On the one side they say that the message is that it is a weak government. On the other hand, they say, by sending Jagmohan you are sending a bull into a China shop. Now, which is correct? Both cannot be correct. So, it is certainly not a weak government. As far [as] Pakistan is concerned, day in and day out the prime minister has made it clear, and I repeat for the sake of the record, that Pakistan can forget about Kashmir, and if they try any military adventure, they will get a fitting reply. I am sure the whole country is one on that.

> If your government has an experience of terrorism in Punjab, and for the last two years in Kashmir, and if you expect us to stop terrorism in three months, we are flattered by your confidence in us.

As far as the terrorists are concerned, let us not run away from the problem. If the terrorists are Indian citizens, it is our problem; it is not Pakistan's problem. Pakistan may be sending people across the border. Pakistan is fishing in troubled waters. They are doing that in Punjab also. I want to make this clear. In Punjab, there is no Article 370. Still, we are having problems in Punjab. As far as the Rubaiya episode is concerned, the government cannot allow innocent people to be kidnapped or their lives to be put in danger. It is not merely to score a point over the Opposition. No. It is a national problem. Things will be done with maturity. We will see to it and we have taken all possible precautions to see that terrorism is controlled and contained. But if your government has an experience of terrorism in Punjab, and for the last two years in Kashmir, and if you expect us to stop terrorism in three months, we are flattered by your confidence in us. We will never be able to do things in three months which could not be done by you for so many years.

You sent a governor to Punjab and said that he would bring terrorists under control in three months. Let us not go into it. It is a problem which has to be tackled on a national footing. The key thing is to win the confidence of the Kashmiri people. They must feel that India is a country which honours its commitments, the Constitution is supreme, elections are fair and whoever is elected will be allowed to rule and no underhand methods will be used to dislodge him or create defections.

I suggest, as a concrete measure, Congress (I) should get away from Kashmir. Let Farooq Abdullah do his politicking there. You get out of Kashmir. That will create a lot of confidence in the Kashmiri people, and we will be able to win back their confidence that at least an anti-democratic force is outside the democratic polity of the state.

By all means, if you disagree with the government, say so. But please do not fish in troubled waters, and Kashmir is troubled.

THE BUDGET IS NO MORE SACROSANCT

In this speech delivered on 5 May 1988 on the Financial Bill, 1988, Morarka expresses his anguish at the fact that taxes are introduced just before the budget. He touches upon every significant aspect—higher taxation ostensibly aimed at the rich but which ultimately hits the poor, the inflationary spiral, lack of attention to how the taxes are spent, the government's inability to curb expenditure while taxation has reached a saturation point, the need to make managing directors of public-sector units accountable, and questions the taxman's penchant for assuming that the highest taxpayer is necessarily the biggest tax evader. As he observes, 'But the law should be made in such a way that the honest get priority over the dishonest. If the law makes it cheaper not to pay taxes, who will pay taxes? Not paying tax should become a costly thing.'

The Finance Bill, which is before this House, is woefully inadequate to achieve the objectives for which it has been presented, and the budget which it reflects, leaves much to be desired.

For many, many years, the budget and the Finance Bill were extremely important documents, which not only served the purpose of giving the revenue and the expenditure of the government, as also the taxation or the changes in the taxation structure, but it was a very important indication of the social philosophy for the next year. I speak with considerable anguish that over the years, we have seen that the budget is no more sacrosanct, the government levies taxes many times and this year in particular, we have seen that a very heavy dose of taxation has been levied just a month before the budget, in the shape of not only administered prices but also levies on petroleum and posts and telegraphs.

DEFICITS ARE RUINING THE ECONOMY

This is a very vital change in the management of the economy of this country. While the Opposition protests every time there is a taxation burden, it is really the common man, the small man, who suffers. The inflationary spiral is generated every time commodities of daily use are taxed, which leads to a cascading affect, and the budget estimates, together with the Finance Bill, leave very little scope to take any corrective measure, which we may suggest or which even if the government desires, they would not be able to do.

The first point I want to raise about these proposals is the increasing deficits. These kinds of deficits are ruining the economy. The effect of deficit of ₹8,000 crore or ₹9,000 crore cannot be understood in a matter of weeks or in a matter of months. The budget or the Finance Bill is [up] for discussion for a few months. After this House passes it, after the presidential assent, it becomes law. But the population of the country will have to suffer the effects of it not only for this year but for years to come. And therefore I feel that the first attention of the finance minister should be on restricting the deficit to the minimum figure possible. Now that the deficit has already been proposed at that level, I have got two requests to make.

One is that no fresh taxation proposals should be brought during the year and the other is that the deficit should not be allowed to increase. Both these things may appear contradictory. But actually they are not so, because there is one way in which the deficit can be contained without raising fresh taxes and that is by controlling government expenditure.

We see that even the person who is taxed is more worried about the rates of taxes and is trying to see that he is taxed less. But there is much less attention on how that money is spent. I feel that while there may be certain items of expenditure like defence or food or fertilizer subsidies on which it may not be prudent for us to suggest to cut down, though we do feel that economies are possible, we do not feel that the money spent on defence is spent in an optimum way. When we talk of defence expenditure, we link it to the security of the country. We will be told that the best is being done. Apart from defence, apart from fertilizer subsidies, there is a large component of non-developmental expenditure.

Even if the government makes a small effort in avoiding wasteful expenditure, the common man can be saved from the crushing burden of additional taxes.

The budget is no more sacrosanct, the government levies taxes many times and this year, we have seen that a very heavy dose of taxation has been levied just a month before the budget.

ULTIMATELY, ALL TAXATION HITS THE WORKING CLASS

It is a well-known thesis of economics that ultimately, all taxation hits the working class. We may say that we are taxing the rich. We may say that we are taxing the higher income brackets. We have patterned most of our taxation laws as per the study of Prof. Nicholas Kaldor who came to India in 1956. Even in thirty-two years we have found that most of the burden is shifted to the common man. The upper classes do not feel the burden. It is the fixed income group, the poorer class, which bears the burden of each rupee. My humble request to the finance minister is that the minimum the government owes to the common man, during this year, is to see that the deficit is contained as projected and no new taxation proposals are brought during the year.

I come to the interesting aspect of inflation—this matter is far more serious than party politics. It is the country's money. From 1980 till now the Janata Party has not come to power. It is the Congress government. Let us just see the figures of these eight years. These eight years' figures tell us the story of what is happening. Inflation is one thing which hits the common man first. When banks were nationalized by Smt. Indira Gandhi in 1969, the total bank deposits (of all the banks) in the country were ₹4,338 crore. By 1980, in eleven years, these deposits reached ₹31,759 crore from ₹4,338 crore. From 1980 to 1987, the figure of ₹31,759 crore has reached ₹102,127 crore. By the total deposits with the nationalized banks, the common man may feel the country is becoming rich. It is not so.

What is this ₹102,000 crore? It is the money in circulation. How did the money in circulation increase so much? This is what is causing inflation. These figures the common man normally does not get to read. But the fact of the matter is that this kind of increase in bank deposits—and there is a corresponding figure of money supply which is given by the Reserve Bank—the money supply in 1969 was ₹5,779 crore; it increased to ₹20,000 crore in 1980. But between 1980 and now the figure has risen from ₹20,000 crore to ₹51,000 crore as compared to ₹5,779 crore when the banks were nationalized—this kind of increase in money supply will inevitably lead to inflation. And, as the finance minister is well aware, inflation ultimately hits the common man.

On the non-development expenditure—there are the figures again—between 1980 and 1987—I am not talking of the period before that—the non-plan expenditure was ₹3,112 crore and in the budget which we are discussing, in this Finance Bill, it is ₹9,091 crore. And it does not mean that all the plan expenditure is non-inflationary. Part of the plan expenditure is also inflationary because the projects we are setting up take a long time to complete. We have put up so many projects like the Visakhapatnam Steel Plan, the Salem Steel Plant, and so on. The Visakhapatnam Steel Plant has not yet come into production. So part of it is, therefore, inflationary investment. In this non-plan expenditure of ₹9,092 crore, a cut of, say, 20 per cent will take care of any additional burden that the common man may have to face during the year. This is something which is easier said than done. It requires strong action on the part of the government. The finance minister will have to be very brutal with his fellow ministries in cutting the expenses.

BORROWING MONEY FOR DAILY EXPENDITURE

I go on to another interesting aspect of the Finance Bill under the budget. And that is for the last two years, especially in this year's budget, out of the money raised on capital account, we are using it for revenue expenditure. This is the most serious thing. Twenty, twenty-five years ago under Dr C.D. Deshmukh, Shri T.T. Krishnamachari, there used to be surplus on revenue account and deficit on capital account, and it was justified on the ground that they needed money to put up steel plants, dams, factories and so on for the development of the country.

I can understand it as legitimate and we had to borrow money for that. But now a stage has come when you have to borrow money to meet our daily expenditure. If we have to borrow money to run our households, I don't think we will be able to last long. This is the country's budget and if this deficit increases year after year, it is not going to give us any hope for the future. Then what is the method by which the government meets this deficit when they are not able to curb expenditure and when taxation has reached the saturation point?

There are only two methods: one, by printing currency notes, by which the money supply goes up; the other is market borrowings. Forty years ago in the United Kingdom, when budget-making was done, the chancellor of the exchequer gave a thesis that the expenditure of war, which was a very major expenditure, an unexpected expenditure, must be met by the richer classes. It was a very welcome suggestion. Everybody agreed. What is the method? It is that we issue bonds which will be bought up by the richer classes. Temporarily some money is raised from the richer classes. But the bonds are interest-bearing bonds. They have to be ultimately repaid. All that you have really done is you have temporarily borrowed money from the rich.

Every seven years or ten years, you put the burden on the working classes. Now this is exactly what we are doing. To meet our deficit, we are borrowing money, externally and internally, and internal borrowings will hit only the poor man. What do we do today? Today, we can raise funds. We see the public-sector bonds, the government bonds, the IDBI bonds, etc. get subscribed immediately. But the interest and the repayment can only be at the cost of the common man.

HAVE WE EXHAUSTED ALL MEANS?

Another interesting point here is this: have we exhausted all the means?

Suppose this is the problem, this is the expenditure of the country. What has the finance minister done to curb expenditure? In the Western countries, in America, in England, etc., the government expenditure goes up every year because salaries and other expenses go up. But in these countries it is made up by increased revenue because the private sector is also making more profits and they are getting more by way of taxes from their people. In the socialist countries or the communist countries, there is no private sector.

In India, Pandit Nehru, during the formative years of our freedom, chose the path of mixed economy, though during the last three years the government has made a lot of policy changes. But I understand that the government is still committed to the Industrial Policy Resolution of 1956, the Industries (Development and Regulation) Act, 1951, and largely the policies of Nehru. Now, the policy of 1956 is largely and basically Nehru's policy, which was for a mixed economy, in which there will be a private sector and there will be a public sector. Later on, during Smt. Indira Gandhi's time, the policy was that the public sector should have the commanding heights. Nevertheless, it is an agreed thing that the private sector and the public sector must coexist, which means that the private sector, when it makes profits, must pay taxes to the exchequer, which the government must use for welfare. That money must be supplemented by profits from the public sector.

But what is actually happening is that we are collecting money from the private sector, which has a saturation limit, because we do not have laissez-faire economy and we do not give any blanket permission to make profits and there are certain regulations. That money is not adequate to meet our expenditure. Not only that, a part of that money and those resources we have to give to the public sector to meet its losses. Nowhere in the Constitution, nowhere in the Industrial Policy Resolution, has that been envisaged. Public sector is very important.

NOT THE WAY TO RUN A WELFARE STATE

I can understand that if you run schools or hospitals or medical centres, there can be a deficit. But nobody said that there should be deficits in a steel-making unit. This is not the way to run a welfare state and that could not have been the scheme envisaged by Nehru. So, the correct and the proper way to meet this deficit is to increase our accruals from the public sector undertakings. Here, I want to refer to the long-term fiscal policy announced by this government in December 1985.

The first question that arises is whether this policy is still followed. In the absence of the government saying that the policy is no more valid or announcing any other policy or a new policy, this policy is very much valid because this is a policy for three years and one of the postulates of the policy is that the taxation rates would not be changed for three years. When there is a demand for the reduction of rates or for any other change, the finance ministry says that the long-term fiscal policy prohibits it and that they stand committed to it. Let me illustrate what that policy sought to achieve.

It is said that the balances from the current revenue (BCR) will be negative during the Seventh Plan period. The previous figures of current revenue have been given and the policy itself says that the highest balance from current revenue was in 1978–79. These are government figures. And that was about 2 per cent of the gross domestic product.

At no time before has the public sector ever given more than nominal accrual to the exchequer. But since the balance from current revenue is negative, the long-term fiscal policy postulates that they expect 3.4 per cent during 1986–87, which is the year gone, 3.7 per cent during 1987–88 and 4 per cent during 1988–89 from the public sector.

FUTURE GENERATIONS WILL NOT EXCUSE US

I want to know from the finance minister what the alternative avenues of raising resources are, since the public sector is not going to give us this money. After a few months if the money does not come, you will again borrow money from the people and they will again pay more tax.

So the basic management of the economy hinges around returns from the public sector. Now, during this year, even the defence expenditure listed is only ₹13,000 crore as against ₹12,000 crore last year.

I do not understand with Sri Lanka operations how there is an increase of only ₹1,000 crore, which represents inflation. So the projected figure this year is less than last year's. It is a preposterous proposal. Even the common man who does not understand economics will not swallow this. Ultimately, what will happen is that the defence expenditure will go up which, in the national interest, we have to all agree, is all right.

Non-plan expenditure you will not reduce. The public sector

will not generate money. Ultimately we have to come back to the poor man. We put more burdens on his head. Directly it will not be put. So it will be indirectly put—some deficit financing, some market borrowings, etc. It is a slow poison for him. This is a major issue. In my opinion, the long-term policy needs to be reviewed. I would request the finance minister to please review it.

On borrowings, the interest burden this year is ₹14,000 crore. During 1980–87 our interest burden has gone up from ₹2,600 crore to ₹14,000 crore. This burden will just go up and a stage will come when like Mexico and Brazil, our currency will cease to have any meaning. Future generations will not excuse us.

EXPORT PROMOTION HAS FAILED MISERABLY

My next point is about external borrowings. Internal borrowing is already a problem. How can external borrowing be repaid? It can be repaid only by two methods. Either you borrow to repay, which we are doing, or you repay by increasing your own foreign exchange earnings. The present finance minister is also the commerce minister[1]. I must say a word of appreciation. Since he has come, he is trying to put all his efforts for export promotion. But our export base is very weak.

> We never tire of saying that we have the third largest body of intelligent manpower. It may be a fact. But what is the use of that manpower if we cannot become an export trade surplus country?

Over the last twenty–thirty years, our policies with regard to export promotion have failed miserably. Now we are trying to give all sorts of incentives for export promotion. Those are petty things. When you give some concession to trade or commerce, the Chamber of

---

[1] Narayan Dutt Tiwari

Commerce and Industry says that this should be 10 per cent less or more. Now these are very minor things. The major thing is that a country of the size of India, with this size of the budget and with all the resources, should have more exports.

We never tire of saying that we have the third largest body of intelligent manpower. It may be a fact. But what is the use of that manpower if we cannot become an export trade surplus country? Small countries like Korea and Singapore, not to speak of Taiwan, have increased their exports. They have thrown us out of our established markets. Therefore, the export policy deserves to be examined on a war footing. What we need is not a 10 per cent or 20 per cent increase in exports. What we need is a 500 per cent increase in exports.

Let us put all our industrialists together. Let us call a meeting. Let us tell them that this is the country's income. It is not a question of A, B or C making profit. But the country must get the foreign exchange. What have we seen during the last ten or fifteen years? None of the large houses who get industrial licences from the government were able to generate foreign exchange. It is our masons, our carpenters and our craftsmen who have gone to the Middle East and to Southeast Asia who have earned the money and sent it to India. The ultimate strength of the country still lies in the small man. We have to make policies by which more foreign exchange can be earned.

FOREIGN EXCHANGE REGULATION ACT HAS TOTALLY FAILED

We hear of it only when some industrialist is arrested for some violation of Foreign Exchange Regulation Act (FERA). This act needs a sea change. There was a time when, due to ideological consideration, it was decided that foreign companies should not have more than 40 per cent share-holding in the companies. Now the companies which had 60 per cent or 70 per cent or 100 per cent ownership floated their shares in the Indian market and a lot of public money went into these companies, which they sent abroad. The country is poorer of foreign exchange to that extent and the control of the company is still with them. So we have achieved nothing. FERA has totally failed.

Every fifteen days you come out with the news 'hawala racket busted' and so many crores of illegal foreign exchange seized. Obviously we are operating on an artificial exchange rate. Till the artificial exchange rates exist, the hawala racket will exist. No doubt the enforcement machinery is there. We should give all encouragement to the enforcement machinery. The ultimate solution to foreign exchange, the ultimate solution to exports, lies elsewhere. It lies in the fiscal policies of the government. The government must have a relook at the entire gamut of policies by which money supply, inflation, taxation, public sector and exports are interlinked.

The private sector in India began by one family starting a company or an enterprise, the motive being return on their money and occupation of the family. This is vastly different from large corporations, as in America, or now in India. We have the Associated Cement Company or the Tata Iron and Steel Company with lakhs of shareholders. Those shareholders are also owners. These owners are not interested in an occupation. They are happy with a reasonable return on investment. They tell the board of directors to take whatever decision, but they should give a good dividend and bonus shares to them.

What is public sector? If the public sector is unable to generate a dividend, if it were a large stock-holding company, in the annual general body meeting, the managing director would find it hard to conduct the meeting. The shareholders would boot him away. But here, they are protected because the public does not deal with them. One of the suggestions as to where the immediate test of public sector can come in is that the government should offload 50 per cent or 60 per cent of its shares to the public. Let the shares be quoted on the stock exchange. We will know how the company is functioning. The management of the company will face the shareholders in the annual general meeting. This is the quick test in a democracy. As far as the government is concerned, it loses nothing. The control remains with the government while 60 per cent of the shares will go to lakhs of people. In the joint sector, there is one entrepreneur. I am against it. The Birlas and the Tatas are allowed to run their company with 5 per cent or 6 per cent.

BUREAUCRATS WILL RUIN PUBLIC-SECTOR COMPANIES

It is far from my mind that the public sector should be closed. If the public sector is closed today, then we are sunk. We are now in a situation where even that option is no longer open to us. We have to run it, and run it successfully. We cannot run it to allow a few to make money and then justify to the public that it is required for a social welfare programme.

The managing director (of a public-sector union) should be told that for three years or four years he will not be removed. Otherwise, what security has he got in the job? Before he learns his job, he is more interested in seeing that his confidential report is all right, that no remark comes against him. If the company runs in a loss, why should he care? Unless we have people of commitment—commitment to the public sector, commitment to make profit—public sector cannot survive. Again there is a fallacious argument. People say [that] in private sector there is motivation for profit. In public sector there is none. It is wrong.

> Now, of course, you can say that ONGC is also public sector and is making money. But to make money in oil does not need any brains or effort.

How is Tata Iron running? There is an employee who is running it. He is running it for his salary. He can run the Steel Authority also. We need a cadre of people who can run companies. Giving public-sector companies to bureaucrats to run will ruin them. Because bureaucrats know that the nature of their job is to control and to regulate, not to push production. By the nature of their job their duty is in a way to act as a constraint while the manager's duty is to push through. It needs a different type of training.

Unfortunately, over thirty–forty years, the public-sector investment today, minus the railways, which I am not even counting: ₹28,317 crore is the capital and ₹33,286 crore is the government loan. I am not even talking of borrowing from the commercial banks and bonds. That is beyond that ₹61,600 crore of the public money which the finance minister and his predecessors have collected with much patience and agony, and after hearing so many abuses, this money is blocked up here. What is the return? The entire public sector has made a profit of ₹1,450 crore this year.

Now, ₹1,450 crore of profit looks all right. But out of ₹1,450 crore, the oil sector, ONGC profit is ₹1,484 crore. Actually, there is a loss. Now, of course, you can say that ONGC is also public sector and is making money. But to make money in oil does not need any brains or effort. Unless public sector generates money, the entire economic structure on which the finance minister is trying to build his edifice will crash. Year after year we will discuss the same thing. We will pass on the burden to the common man in the name of the rich man. That is all we can do.

TAX STRUCTURE IS IRRELEVANT TO THE MODERN TIMES

The Finance Bill proposals, in the light of the constraints I just now mentioned, are a very difficult task. The finance minister cannot do much. But the inadequacy is there. Now, for instance, take income tax. I do not think I am letting out a secret if I say that a majority of the tax assessees in this country are fudging their tax returns. There was a time, fifteen years ago, when you could blame some business houses, some people, of not paying taxes properly.

Your whole tax structure from the assessment to the recovery stage is totally irrelevant to the requirements of the modern times. If tax rates are to be rationalized, lower income tax categories need to be abolished. You will not lose any revenue. If a sensitivity study is made, you will find that if 60 per cent of the taxpayers are removed from the tax net and from the remaining 40 per cent we can collect correctly, there will be no loss of revenue; there will be a lot of saving on overheads.

Every year we see the number of income tax officers increasing. This is an exercise in futility. Secondly, on the higher income group, there has to be a rationalization. In the long-term fiscal policy it was mentioned that you are soon coming out with a simple direct taxes bill. And true to the promise, [the] government came out with a bill, Direct Taxes (Amendment) Bill; but it was not simple. Anyway, it was there. But the beauty is, before that bill comes into force, it has to be amended. We want to know, what are we trying to do? Are we trying to become the laughing stock of the people? What is our intention? I request the finance minister not only to keep that bill in abeyance but refer it to the Select Committee. Let Parliament properly study that bill and let proposals be floated to really simplify the tax structure.

I have got here with me Prof. Nicholas Kaldor's study on Indian taxation done in 1956 at the instance of Pandit Nehru. The figures mentioned in his study relate to the period 1956, and I quote:

> Everyone is agreed that apart from manipulations of various kinds which are broadly classed under the term 'tax avoidance' there is considerable amount of evasion in India due to fraudulent concealment of income secured through false entries in the account books and the accounts. It is generally also agreed that such practices have become more widespread since the last war. The important question is how much income is concealed in this manner in relation to the income which is assessed to tax. Conversations with individual business men, accountants and revenue officials

reveal guesses which range from 10-20 per cent of assessed income at the minimum to 200-300 per cent maximum...

In 1956, Prof. Kaldor found that concealment is double of the total income collected. I need not tell this House that everybody today is aware that concealment is many times more today; the morality level is much lower than what it was in 1956, in all spheres of our life. So, unless we produce a tax bill which is simple and which can be administered efficiently and effectively, I am afraid we are only creating more complications and opening avenues for corruption.

DISCRETIONARY POWER USED ONLY FOR THE RICH

I am sorry to say, our legislations are always drafted in a manner which will give some discretionary power to some people. I can submit a general argument that every discretionary power vested with any government official is always used in favour of the influential and the rich; the poor man will not be able to reach that official. So, there should be a law which gives minimum discretion to officials.

Prof. Kaldor himself says: 'The three prime considerations that should be taken into account in framing an effective tax system are equity, economic effects, and administrative efficiency.' But our present taxation system is neither equitable nor administratively efficient, and the economic effects are disastrous for all to see. My humble submission is that even at this stage, the Direct Taxes (Amendment) Bill should be formed by a motion from the finance minister himself. Nothing would be lost, I can assure you. The Direct Taxes (Amendment) Bill needs to be redrafted.

Sir, on the corporation tax, we had great hopes. But what do we find now? There are ad hoc, arbitrary deletions, disallowances and additions by the income-tax authorities. In the long-term fiscal policy, you promised a simple tax bill. Then we had a bill which was not simple. Again, we are told now that this bill may be amended. We find that arbitrary disallowances in corporation tax will only lead to more tax evasion. Business has gone on as usual in this country for the last forty years. If the aim of the government is to bring about more morality, better tax returns and simpler collection of tax, this is not the way to do it.

Here is what Prof. Kaldor has said in relation to company taxation. In company taxation, the general rule for allowances should be what is spent wholly for making profit during the year. Even when the income tax officer agrees that the money has been genuinely spent, he says, 'I will not allow it.' This kind of a provision will only lead to cheating. What I am trying to point out is that it will not work. Why do we make such laws which we all know cannot be implemented? Prof. Kaldor says:

> I am strongly of the view that the developments of the last fifteen-twenty years which imposed (nominally) fantastically high marginal rates of tax, while permitting the continuance of wide loopholes for tax avoidance. As Henry Simons said before the War the whole procedure smacks of a 'subtle kind of moral and intellectual dishonesty'. One senses here a grand scheme of deception whereby enormous surtaxes are voted in exchange for promises that they will not be made effective. Thus the politicians may point out with pride to the rates, while quietly reminding their wealthy constituents of the loopholes.

This was in 1956, when the general standard of morality was much higher than today. Today, we are making laws which we all understand cannot be implemented. Today, we are giving powers to an income tax officer to straightaway make a difference of crores of rupees. There is no correlation between the status of the person who enjoys the power and the power that he wields. An excise official has got the power to make a difference of profitability of crores of rupees. Is it workable? Common sense tells us that it will not work.

WHY PAY IF CHEAPER NOT TO PAY TAXES?

Rationalization of tax structure should be done in such a manner that it takes into account all these things. Prof. Kaldor's report is with the government. Some of the things which we have—code number, GIR number, etc.—are according to this report. We have taken [into account] all the points and additional regulations suggested by Prof. Kaldor. But the pitfalls we have not seen. For instance, Prof. Kaldor says: 'At a marginal rate of 90 per cent the return from tax evasion is 900 per cent on any particular amount concealed. At a marginal rate of 45 per cent, the return from successful concealment is only 82 per cent.'

By marginally changing the rate of tax, the benefit to the dishonest taxpayers can be substantially reduced. Ultimately, no citizen is dishonest. But the law should be made such where the honest get priority over the dishonest. If the law is made in such a manner where it is cheaper not to pay taxes, why would anyone pay taxes? Not paying tax should become a costly thing.

I come to the search and seizure by the enforcement machinery, popularly called 'raids'. In the early '60s, a proposal was introduced in this Income Tax Act that due to rampant evasion in income tax, authority should have the power to search the premises of a tax assessee and to seize any documents which show revenue concealment. I would like to know from the finance minister the total amount spent on conducting searches and seizures in the last twenty-seven years and the total revenue, if any, the government was able to get as a result of these searches and seizures.

BAD AND GOOD

Ten years ago, there was an atmosphere in the country that monopoly houses were not good and when a monopoly house was raided, it was big news. But what do we see today? One day we read in the paper that Mr So-and-So has been raided and so much concealment of income has been found. We have successfully destroyed his reputation, whatever he had, in the social circles.

What do we read next? The same industrialist is putting up a thousand-crore plant in the sector jointly with the government within a week. The minister of state of [for] finance gives a statement that the raids will have no bearing on this project; the project will go on. You cannot say the man is bad and good. He is bad because he is concealing income but he is very competent to put up another thousand-crore plant.

This kind of system which gives arbitrary powers to tax authorities is of no use. If we need those people to put up further industries then they deserve different ways of treatment. Blacklist them and do not give them any licence.

I will be the first man to support you if you catch a person who has cheated on taxes and recover the money. You have never recovered the money. The only thing is, you increase a few files in the department, you field some proceedings, those proceedings will go on for years and in the meantime that man has become ten times in size of what he was. This proposal, when it was introduced, was with the intention that there may be a few black sheep in the tax-paying community and the enforcement machinery should have the powers to deal with them.

Today, these powers are not being used against the influential and the rich; it is the small and medium men who are being harassed. You read that a raid was conducted and jewellery worth ₹1 lakh was found. Mr Narayanasamy, what is jewellery worth ₹1 lakh when gold is selling at ₹4,000 a tola? That would be twenty-five tolas of gold. Now, which house in Tamil Nadu or in India does not have fifty or hundred tolas of gold? That is part of the Indian tradition. Today you say 'jewellery worth ₹1 lakh was found' as if the man has committed murder. The people who had gone for the raid, I am sure, have got more unaccounted income than the person whom they are raiding.

GO AFTER THE BIG FISH

The tax authorities have no courage to catch the real tax evaders. Instructions go from Delhi. Mr V.P. Singh was the finance minister. He said: 'Go after the big fish.' What does big fish mean? It means the big tax evaders. But what does the chief commissioner of income tax do? The orders from the boss are, 'Go and catch the big tax evaders', but he makes a list of big taxpayers and goes and catches them. Let us catch the people who are not paying tax.

Your system is built in such a way that you are assuming that the man who is paying more tax is cheating you of more tax. The entire system needs to be changed. If I speak against the system, it is construed as if I am trying to support the people who are dishonest. The entire taxation department is [a] cesspool of corruption. Who can deny it? In the system, as it is today, the advantage goes to only the petty government officials who are armed with powers disproportionate to their size. It is the small and medium men who suffer because the rich who are raided can always meet the prime minister, the finance minister or any authority. Nothing will happen. In the interest of the nation, it is necessary [to] settle with them because only they can do the large projects.

DON'T PART WITH PRIME GOVERNMENT PROPERTIES

During the Special Mentions on 12 December 1991, Morarka spoke on the reported move of the government to give out the Centaur Group of Hotels to private bodies. He pleaded with the government not to sell off such prime property but to arrive at an arrangement with private parties so that even as the value of the land appreciated, it would be the public that would benefit. Incidentally, the report of the comptroller and auditor general, tabled in Parliament on 6 May 2005, passed strictures on the valuation method used in selling the two hotels then owned by the Hotel Corporation of India (HCI), a subsidiary of Air India. These were the five-star hotels in Mumbai, Airport Centaur and Juhu Centaur, which were sold to private companies in March–April 2002 by the National Democratic Alliance government.

I want to draw the attention of the government to the reported move to privatize the Hotel Corporation of India. The Hotel Corporation of India, as we all know, owns four hotels—two Centaur Hotels in Bombay, one Centaur Hotel in Delhi and one in Srinagar. The HCI and the India Tourism Development Corporation which owns the Ashoka Hotel and, I think, twenty or thirty other hotels, are the two public-sector units in the hotel industry. The Committee on Public Undertakings (COPU) has at least twice recommended merger of these two corporations into a single one. The HCI is a subsidiary of Air India (AI). The idea was that like the airlines abroad, AI should have its own hotel subsidiary which would get business from Air India. But it did not work out here because AI itself was not doing well enough.

A MONUMENTAL ERROR

The AI itself has had a chequered career. Therefore, the HCI did not come up to expectations and the Committee on Public Undertakings (COPU), after considering all aspects, decided that it should be merged with the ITDC. The ITDC has got the infrastructure to run thirty or forty hotels. The Ashoka Hotel in Delhi and the Centaur Hotels near the Bombay Airport and at Juhu are prime properties, and the value of the land goes up every day. To sell these to the private sector would be a monumental error.

The government should not part with properties which can appreciate, which can never lose. There are operational losses. But the operational losses of the hotels are minimal compared to what I mentioned earlier, the losses of the Delhi Transport Corporation (DTC), the Fertilizer Corporation and the Heavy Engineering Corporation (HEC), Ranchi, etc.

I asked a question in this session of Parliament: whether bids have been invited to give over the Hotel Corporation to the private sector, and if so, what are the details. I have got an answer from the minister, 'No, sir. Does not arise.'

Here is a news item in *The Economic Times* (11 December). It says 'HCI employees counter Manu Chabria's bid for Centaur Hotel'. The newspaper, on its front page, says that Manu Chabria, who is a non-resident Indian, has given a bid for the HCI. The hotel employees have given a counter bid. There is no denial from the government. The government has told me that they have not invited bids. I suspect that the reply is a technical one. Maybe the government did not invite bids but people sent them anyway.

KEEP THE PROPERTY WITH THE GOVERNMENT

We want to know from the government very clearly: (a) Whether there is any proposal to hand over these prime properties to the private sector, or worse, to NRIs or foreigners; (b) If the government contemplates such a move, what are the norms they are going to lay down, how are they going to decide this; and (c) My suggestion to the government is, please don't do this. The Taj Hotel in Delhi is actually the property of the New Delhi Municipal Corporation (NDMC). It is not the Taj Hotel's property. The management is by the Taj Hotel and there is a profit-sharing arrangement.

The government should go in for such an arrangement for all hotel properties. Keep the property with the government, enter into a management arrangement with the private sector and share the profit so that you don't have to suffer losses. And the value of the property, when it appreciates, accrues to the public sector and to the government and to the public at large.

BORROWING MONEY AMOUNTS TO POSTPONING THE PROBLEM

'The common man ultimately has to pay more for his daily requirements as a result of the fiscal and financial policies that we have been following,' Morarka says as he speaks on the Appropriation Bill (No 4), 1988, in August 1988. He says that it is very disturbing that the finance minister is presenting an additional demand within five months of the budget. '[...] we will have to increase the dearness allowance and wages of workers as a result of inflation. For that we need money. We will get that money again by printing more currency. This will be a vicious cycle from which we can never come out. I feel the time has come when the government should clamp down heavily on all government expenditure,' he observes.

At the outset, I wish to express my grave concern about the tendency to come in repeatedly with supplementary Appropriation Bills. As the Honourable Minister has just said, the total amount sought to be spent additionally is of the order of ₹1,593.18 crore. The minister has been kind enough to tell us that out of this, ₹925.47 crore will be met by savings or augmentation of resources and the gap will be ₹667.71 crore. He has further said what this ₹667.71 crore would consist of—the items which he has selected, probably; one would not be able to quarrel with because they relate to Punjab [and] Haryana for the Sutlej–Yamuna Link Canal.

However, the fallacy of the argument is that out of the total ₹1,593.18 crore, if the gap is only ₹600 crore, there is no way that we can allocate ₹667 crore to this particular item. We must see ₹1,593 crore in its totality and with a little more tightening of our belts, it is possible to entirely do away with the additional requirement of ₹600 crore, because this amount of ₹1,593 crore consists of various items, like payment of financial institutions totalling ₹6 crore, the subsidy of ₹100 crore of the industrial development department. There are items which certainly can be looked into and I do not see any justification why there should be a deviation from the budget figures, which has been passed only five months ago.

A DISTURBING TREND

It is a very, very disturbing trend that first of all, there is a large deficit at the time of the presentation of the budget and then within five months, we have to come with an additional demand, 40 per cent of which still remains uncovered. How are we going to make this ₹667 crore is not known. We can safely assume that it will be done by deficit financing, which essentially means additional money supply. I wish to place certain figures before the House. In the first sixteen weeks of this year (1988–89), from 1 April, figures are available for the first four months. The net Reserve Bank credit to the central government has increased by ₹8,171 crore against ₹3,909 crore in the corresponding period last year.

This is widely believed to be an indicator of the real magnitude of the budgetary deficit. In other words, [in] the first four months of the year itself, the budgetary deficit of the order of ₹8,000 crore is already looming large on the horizon. With our economy being what it is, and without any dramatic change in the situation expected in the remaining eight months of the year, it is not possible to see how we can take these deficits to a reasonable level. The net bank credit to the central government and the state governments, including the incremental credit from all banks, including the Reserve Bank, the increase is of the order of ₹10,841 crore against ₹6,943 crore last year.

This again is a very disturbing figure and there is no let up on commercial borrowing. Commercial borrowing from banks has increased by ₹3,103 crore as against ₹1,851 crore. Even on the front of the money supply or the total money in circulation, there is no let up. The net result is, seeding the broad basis of money supply in the first four months of this year, it appears that the money supply increase is in the range of ₹10,000 crore, as against ₹7,320 crore last year.

CAUSE OF INFLATION: INCREASE IN MONEY SUPPLY

We had mentioned while participating in the debate on the Finance Bill that increase in money supply is one of the major causes of inflation. At that time, friends from the other side did not like our sounding very pessimistic about the outlay during the year but if we have the first four months of the performance to go by and the official figures, this situation is very, very disturbing, to say the least.

I would like to mention two more features which have helped in our curbing the money supply or the liquidity, in spite of this situation. But though this helped to curb the money supply, there were negative repercussions in other ways. The first is the foreign exchange reserve. The foreign exchange reserve has declined in this period of four months by ₹1,264 crores, a decline of 23.1 per cent, as against a decline of ₹381 crore last year during the same period. This is a very steep decline. But for this decline, the liquidity or the money supply would have spurted much further. But though this has helped in not allowing the money supply to spurt, this has got other serious negative repercussions.

The net liabilities of the banking sector in this period have also gone up by ₹2,860 crore as compared to ₹1,160 crore last year. All these economic indicators point only to one thing and that is that we are having an overdose of currency in circulation, in comparison to the state of our economy. Ultimately, inflation has a direct relation with money supply.

I will also give some figures on the inflation situation. On 30 June this year, the general index for working class was 433.8. That is, the wholesale price index was 433.8, compared to 401.5 last year. This is an increase of 8.5 per cent, which is 32 points, compared to only a 5.8 per cent increase last year, which was 22 points. The wholesale price index is the basic indicator and it has an effect on all other indices as we have seen. Even on a conservative basis, 1 per cent increase in the wholesale price index means 1.5 per cent increase in the retail index. Therefore, the inflation rate is of the order of 13 per cent. The common man does not go by these figures. Cereals have increased by 13.8 per cent as against 3.7 per cent last year; pulses by 36.7 per cent compared to 6.5 per cent. The common man ultimately has to pay more for his daily requirements as a result of the fiscal and financial policies that we have been following.

A GOOD MONSOON NEED NOT MAKE US COMPLACENT

I want to bring the attention of the House to two or three more aspects. The first is the agricultural sector, which is a very important sector. The consumer price index for the agricultural sector has risen to 661 compared to 572, which is an increase of 15.5 per cent. The only ray of hope in the whole thing is a good monsoon. We read various newspaper articles, various statements, that there is a good monsoon and we are going to have no problems this year. I wish to caution the finance minister against undue complacency because of a good monsoon.

We should be very vigilant, especially with regard to the money supply position. The exact figure of money supply is available only up to 15 July. The increase in money supply is ₹8,335 crore compared to ₹4,150 crore last year. Mr Nani Palkhivala, who is an eminent jurist and economic thinker, has been very harsh on this. He has made a statement in Bombay that counterfeit currency is in circulation. What he meant was that the currency in circulation is far beyond what a prudent economic index would justify. I do not want to use such harsh words.

But the fact is that if our currency and money supply go on at this rate, soon a day will come when we will be caught up in a quagmire and a vicious circle from which we cannot come out. What will happen is, we will have to increase the dearness allowance and wages of workers as a result of inflation. For that we need money. We will get that money again by printing more currency. This will be a vicious circle from which we can never come out. I feel the time has come when the government should clamp down heavily on all government expenditure.

If government expenditure is curbed, if we show some austerity, I am sure this ₹600 crore can be met. There was talk of a 5 per cent cut in expenditure in all departments. But we do not hear anything more of it. I request the finance minister to immediately ask all the ministries to cut down their expenditure by at least 5 per cent. That will really help the economy. The other thing is, for augmenting the resources the working of public sector undertakings needs to be improved—again the only resource left with the government, which is basically the profitability of the public sector undertakings. We do not find a mention in the Appropriation Bill; I would request the finance minister to give us a picture of how the public undertakings are faring. Under the long-term fiscal policy they were supposed to be generating a large surplus in the plan period.

THE REAL SUFFERER IS THE COMMON MAN

I would request the finance minister to tell us whether the public sector undertakings are generating profit or we have still to pay money to them because here you have made an allocation for financial institutions. Of these ₹600 crore, how much of it is going to the National Textile Corporation and other such white elephants, we must know. If partly the money being raised is to finance the losses of the public sector, then we are going to face a very serious situation. Therefore, I request that there should be a proper debate in Parliament; a White Paper from the government on public sector should be published. Unless we augment our resources we cannot meet the situation. And we have to augment interest-free money.

No; borrowing money is not augmenting resources. That is only postponing the problem. Therefore, I would request the finance minister, even at this stage, there are still seven months to go; going by the indicators of the last four or five months I shudder to think what will happen to the economy in the next seven–eight months. As I said before, when the economy suffers, it is really the common man who has to pay more, and by the time we wake up to the real situation, it may be too late.

SEBI HAS UTTERLY FAILED

The SEBI is a 'half-baked' decision of the government which failed to sound the alarm about the scams taking place then, Morarka says, whilst speaking on the debate on Disapproval of the Capital Issue (Control) Repeal Ordinance, 1992, and the Capital Issue Repeal Bill, 1992, on 10 August 1992. Poorly staffed, an inept chairman, brought into existence through an ordinance without waiting for Parliament—this body is just a poorer version of its predecessor, the Controller of Capital Issues, he points out.

At the outset, let me say that this whole debate is a rather confused one. The opening speaker, Dr Jain, if I could understand him correctly, has complained that the Securities and Exchange Board of India (SEBI) has only replaced the Controller of Capital Issues (CCI); there is not much of a difference and hardly any deregulation has taken place; the government's main idea was to deregulate, but just now, SEBI is another form of CCI.

Of course, he has dealt with other subjects which I will come to later. The complaint of Shri Dipen Ghosh, on the other hand, is against this form of deregulation because the economy will not be in the control of the government and a lot of undesirable things will happen. But I do not understand Shri Vishvjit Singh. He is trying to tell us that the SEBI, in fact, will be more regulatory than the CCI. This is not the intention of the government. Let me tell him so. The idea is to deregulate. A man like me is not against deregulation by itself. But it has to be done cautiously; it has to be done in a controlled manner. And we have to see the feedback from the market.

ONLY THE NAME HAS CHANGED TO SEBI

I am totally against the way this government is deregulating because the economy has gone out of its control; the inflation rate has gone out of its control; everything has gone out of its control. That is a different matter. I do not want to enlarge the scope of this debate. But, on this matter, my friend Shri Vishvjit is totally wrong. He has quoted at length the duties and obligation of the SEBI. He has referred to the brokers as well. Let us understand and let us try to help this government come back on the rails. What they wanted to do was to create a body which could control the capital issues as well as regulate the stock markets because the CCI, as Shri Vishvjit rightly put it, gives clearances for capital issues, and has no control on the functioning of the various markets.

The SEBI was supposed to be a specialized body. Last time, when the SEBI ordinance came up for discussion—the minister, Shri Rameshwar Thakur, was here—I made the same point, namely, 'You are, as usual, doing a half-baked, half-cooked thing.' You have set up a SEBI in Bombay without proper people (staff). You have appointed as chairman someone who does not know the ABCD of the capital market. What is the use of doing it? As of today, nothing more has happened except that the name has changed from CCI to SEBI. The point of control has shifted from Delhi to Bombay.

Bombay has 62 per cent of the total share-market activity. If the government decides to shift it to Bombay, I have no objection. But let us know what we are doing. The SEBI today has got 103,000 complaints from investors. If they try to take up those complaints, they will have no other work to do. Let us understand what we are doing.

The moment you try to say that the current scam, of which

the country is seized, could be prevented by this machinery, you are just weakening your own case for this mechanism. The attitude of the ruling party is highly objectionable. Never since Independence have I heard that the prime minister of the country writes to his cabinet colleagues, to each one of them individually, to report to him if they are involved in the scam. On the basis of that statement, the prime minister has made a statement in the Lok Sabha that he has checked up individually on the basis of the information so furnished. He has not taken responsibility for his colleagues.

I don't understand in what kind of a system, in what kind of an age we are living where the cabinet ministers, the members of the council of ministers in the Government of India, are under a shadow. I certainly object to members of the ruling party pushing the problem under the carpet.

If this government wants the SEBI to be effective, they must take urgent action. First, make such a person as the chairman of the SEBI who knows the capital market. I am sorry to say that the present chairman does not know anything about the capital market. The Unit Trust of India (UTI) is one of the powerful institutions with the government. What is the interaction of the SEBI with the Unit Trust of India? After all, when you have created a body, you are trying to claim that you have given the body teeth. It must be able to perform the job. As SEBI is constituted today, it will be a poorer version of CCI. The minister referred to an exemption order issued in 1969. All that was required today for adjusting for inflation is that you could have issued another exemption order up to ten crores of rupees, saying it has been freed. Half the problems could have been solved. But no; this government wants to raise itself towards some economic reforms, etc.

If you believe in free market economy, if you believe this country can sustain a free market economy—I don't, but if you believe—then you must understand that if there is no regulation, there will be scams, there will be cheats, investors will be cheated. In America, every year these companies go bankrupt. Are you ready for that? And if we are not, then we must not try to wear a mask.

We talk of free market. The minister wants us to believe that SEBI means deregulation. And his party colleagues want us to believe that it is a tighter regulation. Now we want to know for what. I object strongly to the fact that this whole measure has been brought through two ordinances. Parliament has met several times. In the days of Jawaharlal Nehru, he had made it very clear that unless the measure was urgent and could not wait for Parliament to meet or if the measure was of such a sensitive nature that it has to be done suddenly, ordinances should not be issued. This government, unfortunately, has a record of issuing ordinances. When the SEBI was constituted by an ordinance in January and the bill came before the House, I said the same thing.

What was the necessity of an ordinance? The finance minister in his reply said, 'No, no, no. The economy is suffering. In these days, the share market is going up.' And they thought it was because of their budget. They thought, 'The economy is now going ahead at a fast pace, we can't wait and, therefore, we have issued the ordinance and now the SEBI has taken over. We have to give teeth to SEBI.' The 'teeth' were given to SEBI in January and all the scams had taken place after those teeth were given. So let us not try to run away from the problem. SEBI has utterly failed. If it was meant to regulate the securities market, then only on that one account alone, SEBI should be wound up because SEBI knew that the market was substantially going up. SEBI knew that large securities were being transferred from one bank to the other, it knew that large amounts of money are coming from sources which cannot be identified so easily.

It was SEBI's business to find out from where the money is coming and they could have found out long back. If SEBI was doing its work properly, in March, in April, they would have known and told the finance ministry about this bungling that was taking place. SEBI has already failed on that account. The chairman of SEBI has failed. Everybody in the government knows who the honest people are who are knowledgeable about financial banking.

Finally, again, the CCI was abolished by an ordinance. Why? I don't know. The CCI could have been wound up by the Parliament. But this practice of issuing ordinances where they are not strictly required ought to be condemned. I want to tell the minister that the stock market now is just in a total state of limbo. Since they are so serious about the SEBI, etc., they must sit down with the stock exchanges' chairmen and the people who know the subject and find a way that the normal stock exchange operations are continued, where there is no artificial boom or artificial disaster. There should be a proper regulatory mechanism. If you give tax concession naturally the market will go up. But the market cannot go up twenty times.

LIBERATION FROM ACCOUNTABILITY AND RESPONSIBILITY

The securities scam of 1992, or what was popularly known as the Harshad Mehta scam, created an uproar that involved not just the banking and political world but became a public talking point for years. In this short duration discussion on 9 July 1992, Morarka is at his acerbic best, wanting to know whether a scam had taken place at all, considering that no one in authority seemed to be responsible for it. He also noted that while the stockbrokers were pilloried, the bank officials and worthies seemed to be innocent of all wrongdoing.

What I have understood is that the finance minister[1] need not resign because he was not even aware of it; he came to know it only from the newspapers, just like all of us. The governor of the Reserve Bank of India need not resign because he was the person who found out the theft. The chairmen of the banks need not resign because some chaps lower down did it. I would like to know whether a theft has at all taken place. I do not know whether it is a fact that ₹3,000-odd crore of public money has been embezzled. I do not see why they are afraid to take the responsibility.

Sir, those of us who are not prepared to bear responsibility for failures should not enter public life. Nobody has forced anyone to come to Parliament. It is entirely a voluntary activity. I would like

---

[1] Dr Manmohan Singh

to quote from paragraph three of the finance minister's statement which says:

'The findings of the Committee confirm that unscrupulous brokers, in collusion with certain bank officials, have manipulated securities transactions of banks...'

The adjective 'unscrupulous' is only for the stockbrokers. Bank officials are clean. If this is not pushing things under the carpet, what is it? As I understand, brokers are free citizens of this country. The law will take its own course. If anyone has done something wrong, he is answerable to the law. But bank officials are the custodians and trustees of public funds, accountable to Parliament. We have accepted that the banks do not come under the purview of the Public Accounts Committee because we were told that the watchdog for the banks was the Reserve Bank. The Banking Regulation Act, 1949, has given vast powers to the Reserve Bank. The powers are so vast that the Reserve Bank of India can virtually do anything with the banks—it can merge banks, can take over banks, it can supersede banks and it can liquidate banks. And today we are told, 'What could the Reserve Bank do?' Reserve Bank has been referred to by the Supreme Court as a watchdog expert body.

Then I quote: '...in clear violation of the established rules, guidelines and prudent business practices.' What has happened is a criminal activity and very mildly he tries to save bank officials. I understand, in Parliament sometimes it becomes necessary to protect the officials under you, but this is not one such case. Though there are the Janakiraman Committee[2] and CBI inquiry reports and the matter is serious enough for Parliament to appoint a Joint Parliamentary Committee at the same time, we have an array of members trying to whitewash this matter.

My objection is not what the JPC will do or will not do or what the government is doing or not doing. My objection is to

---

[2]Under R. Janakiraman, then deputy governor of RBI, who inquired into the matter.

the attitude of this government, the ministers and the members of the Congress party. In the last one year they have led this country's degeneration into a state of licentiousness. Liberalized economic policy may be a matter of debate. No economic policy has been liberalized. What you have done is that you have liberated the mind from responsibility and accountability. The governor of the Reserve Bank is not here. He has given an interview to *The Week*. I will read from it. The statement is long but the main point is along these lines, 'I found out the fraud, I nailed it, so why are you asking me to resign?' He says, 'It is unfair for politicians to criticize. They have allowed the system to flourish; they are responsible for all this.'

> The adjective 'unscrupulous' is only for the stockbrokers. Bank officials are clean. If this is not pushing things under the carpet, what is it?

Who is responsible for it? Who should resign? Not the finance minister, not the governor of the Reserve Bank, nor the chairmen of the banks. I have studied this matter. No politician is involved in this scam. Ask me why? For the last one year after this government has come to power, if you asked the man in the street who is running this government, they will say, 'Shri Narasimha Rao' or 'Shri Manmohan Singh' or 'Shri Chidambaram'. They have not heard of a fourth minister. Except the finance minister, even if the ministers of state ring up a bank chairman even to transfer an official, they (the chairmen) don't listen. I might be mistaken. The man in the street has heard of two more ministers: Shri Arjun Singh and Shri Sharad Pawar. Not because of their performance in the human resources development and defence ministries. The public thinks these are the people who may create trouble for the PM. I have no complaint against the prime minister. He has acted with proper form, but whatever he is doing is being undone by these kinds of statements, which betray total lack of any guilt or any remorse. On the contrary, the signal is: all is well with the banking system; carry on.

SACK THEM ALL!

The finance minister has mentioned the number of places raided and officials arrested. Now he says, 'Chairman, National Housing Bank, has resigned. Chairman, UCO Bank, and Chairman, SBI, were asked to go on leave.' No. Only Chairman, UCO Bank, was asked to go on leave. Chairman, SBI, had to be asked to go on leave after Shri Janakiraman gave his first report. And what happened in the State Bank? The managing director becomes the acting chairman. So it is Tweedledum and Tweedledee. How Parliament is going to get back the funds, I don't know. Has the government sent an officer of unimpeachable integrity to take charge of the State Bank? No.

> No economic policy has been liberalized. What you have done is that you have liberated the mind from responsibility and accountability.

What I understand from the corridors of power is that one of the managing directors, who is [the] acting chairman, is trying to become chairman. If that happens, then, I think, the JPC is a sham. There is no use of having JPC if the mind of the government is not clear to punish those who are involved in this scam or in the embezzlement. When we know officers have taken money, have enriched themselves and their relatives at the cost of public funds, it is not a system failure. It is dishonesty. Please sack them all. At least twenty-five to thirty top officials of these five banks should be sent on leave or their services should be terminated. Do it without any further loss of time.

IS THE GOVERNMENT SERIOUS ABOUT TAKING ACTION?

I am afraid of one thing. They have announced the JPC. Now they will say that any further action will be taken after the report of the JPC. That is not good. The JPC can give you further data. Every time Janakiraman goes into the matter, he finds names of two more banks. In Report No. 1, he gave some figure. In Report No. 2, he added two banks, one Ratnakar's company and ₹500 crore. Let him proceed further. This figure will go on increasing. The names of the people involved will be getting added. That is not the issue. The issue is: is the government serious about taking action?

On the question of the finance minister's resignation, my colleagues have demanded it. I am not demanding it, why? Because he is not involved and resigning or not resigning on moral grounds is entirely a personal matter. Morality differs from person to person. Lal Bahadur Shastri resigned. I don't think it was anybody's case that he was driving that train at Ariyalur or he had ordered that accident. He thought that since it took place, he should resign his position. Today, if somebody wants to follow Lal Bahadur Shastri or wants to follow other more illustrious precedents on the other side, it is entirely up to the individual.

Another thing I want to bring to attention is the attitude of the government. The government through this statement has very cleverly mentioned the Narasimham Committee Report and its implementation, and said that if computers were in use this fraud could not have taken place. I have not understood how dishonesty could be prevented by a computer. Sir, if the fire alarm does not go on, you say that the alarm has to be more effective. But if somebody has deliberately lit the fire, how does it absolve him?

Here is a case where you go on talking about the system failure. There are people who have deliberately done this fraud. Have you put them in jail? No. Have you dismissed them? No.

> When we know officers have taken money, have enriched
> themselves and their relatives at the cost of public funds, it
> is not a system failure. It is dishonesty. Please sack them all.

Do they still have access to you? Yes. How do you answer all
this? The CBI cannot do anything about it. All genuine borrowers
and depositors have come to grief ever since this has come out.
So, my first request to the government is that they must restrain
themselves while making a speech. It is for the finance minister
and the governor of the Reserve Bank to see how they will catch
the officials. That is their business. But my point is, stop saying
things to the press which signal that nothing has happened.

SHOW THAT YOU ARE TOUGH

The RBI governor says he was the watchdog. A watchman says, 'A
thief broke in, stole something and ran out. Why are you dismissing
me? I saw the thief; I detected who has broken in.' When he broke
in and stole, the watchman was sleeping. That is the problem.
We are not saying you were involved in the theft, but what we
are saying is that you failed to do the duty for which you were
appointed. This governor's term is expiring. It is up to the finance
minister if he wants to change him or not, but I want to ask him
to appoint a Reserve Bank governor who is tough. There are tough
people in the country whose mere appointment will immediately
lead to resignations of twelve bank chairmen. I can give the names
if you want.

To know who is corrupt and who is honest we do not have to
go to the CBI or to the Intelligence Bureau. Go to Udyog Bhavan.
The peon there will tell you which officer is honest and who is not.
Everybody in Bombay knows which bank chairman takes money
and which bank chairman is honest. If the government means
business they can bring the guilty to book within no time. But if
the intention of the government is to gloss over the whole thing and

make an excellent statement in parliamentary form and decorum, you can claim that immediately on reading in the newspapers you appointed CBI and the Janakiraman Committee. Immediately after the report has come we have agreed to the formation of the JPC. What more can the government do?

They can do a lot more to show that they are a tough government and that such frauds would not take place. We were not a part of the National Front government. In fact, we came out of the National Front. But today, an unkind remark about Shri V.P. Singh's son being in Citibank is not called for. Yes. Let somebody give the details about [how] Shri V.P. Singh's son being in Citibank got favours from the then government.

The nexus is to be established. I am surprised that this gentleman Shri Harshad Mehta has visited the North Block. Shri Krishnamurthy himself has agreed that he had brought him there. If that has happened, it is objectionable. When he was under the adverse notice of the Enforcement and Revenue Intelligence authorities, then that person had no business to visit the North Block.

On 26 July 1991, Shri Amitav Ghosh, the then deputy governor of the Reserve Bank, has written a letter about it, which is reproduced by the Janakiraman Committee in its first report. He had warned that these types of transactions are taking place and we should see that they do not take place. So, within one month of coming to power, they knew that some banks were misbehaving. The Reserve Bank of India could not detect it. From 1,000 crore of rupees of exposure of the State Bank of India, in ten–eleven months, it went up to ₹9,000 crore.

Today, Shri Jagesh Desai wants us to believe that when they found out about it, it was more than ₹22,000 crore. You have allowed it to mount. You have patronized it. You have glossed over it. You have given a signal to the officers that nothing will happen as long as you make money and the more money you make, the greater Indian you are. That is what Shri Harshad Mehta has done. He made lots of money. I repeat, this entire socio-economic philosophy will have to change. In a country like ours, where 90 per cent people are poor, where the total number of taxpayers is 1 per cent, all this will not work.

Dr Manmohan Singh's clarion call is that ministers should not interfere with the office of the chairman of a bank. The finance minister in his budget speech promised the writing off of farmers' loans to the extent of ₹1,500 crore. We had written off ₹10,000 per farmer and that was frowned upon as profligacy. Here, five parties have taken away ₹3,500 crore and you want us to debate it in the Parliament. You can be staunch because you are in a majority, [a] contrived majority, but you will not be able to face the electorate.

I am not worried if the government goes. We are here to elect a new one. But if the banking system collapses, all of us put together will not be able to make it all right again.

FOUR FOREIGN BANKS CORNERED TWO-THIRDS

My final point is rather touchy. It relates to the question of foreign banks. With our newly developed relationship with the International Monetary Fund and the World Bank, I can understand the government's hesitation in taking action against them. But after the Janakiraman Committee's report, ANZ Grindlays Bank's licence should have been cancelled. The total securities transactions in fourteen months are worth ₹9 lakh crore. And two-thirds of the transactions were cornered by four foreign banks.

At no time in history have foreign banks got such a large chunk of the security business. And two-thirds of ₹9 lakh crore is about twice the GDP of the country. One of these foreign banks, which has run into trouble, refused to pay. If we have a Reserve Bank, if we have a finance ministry, please send them packing. Grindlays Bank should be asked to get out of the country. We lose nothing. I was in Europe fifteen days ago. A banker there educated me more than anything I had heard here. They know everything. None of them approves of what has happened in Standard Chartered Bank or Grindlays Bank. Such banking practices in America will land them in prison. Nobody is going to excuse them.

But as I told the House earlier, this is not liberalization, this is liberated mind. They have liberated themselves from accountability and responsibility. In the whole statement of twelve pages, the words 'foreign banks' appear once. I take this opportunity to request the finance minister: please give a burial to the Narsimham Committee. Do not talk about it again. The talk of implementing the Narsimham Committee report is turning the chairmen of the banks into sovereign bodies. They think that soon there will be no department of banking; soon there will be no priority sector; soon there will be no lead bank scheme; soon there will be no service area approach.

IF THE BANKING SYSTEM COLLAPSES...

Everything that Smt. Gandhi did, everything that nationalization was meant for, has been quickly and rapidly undone in one year of this government. The earlier they reform their ways, rather, governance, the better for the country. I am not worried if the government goes. We are here to elect a new one. But if the banking system collapses, all of us put together will not be able to make it all right again. It is a thing much more difficult to put together than the government of the day. They must understand their limitations. My request to Shri Thakur is, please take a U-turn at least in your public pronouncements because they are giving totally wrong signals. They are giving the signal to the crook to go ahead and the honest and poor man is feeling frightened.

HOW TO WIN HEARTS IN PUNJAB

*Speaking in the discussion on the Punjab Appropriation (No-2) Bill, on 6
September 1991, Morarka makes it clear that political problems need political
solutions, not administrative ones. He repeats his stand that popularly elected
leaders of a region must be engaged in dialogue, even when they espouse separatist
causes, and won over.*

Punjab is under the central rule and this problem has been going
on for so many years. I do not want to waste the time of the
House by going into the background of the problem, how the
previous government tried to tackle it or aggravated it, how we
in the Opposition gave various suggestions on how the 'Punjab
problem' should be viewed and tackled.

I will straightaway come to what the present situation is and
what needs to be done.

POLITICAL SOLUTIONS FOR POLITICAL PROBLEMS

First and foremost, it needs reiteration—that our party stands for
a political solution to political problems. We do not stand for an
administrative solution to political problems. It is neither desirable
nor feasible. Anytime if you had tried in any part of the country
to solve the political turmoil by using administrative powers, you
could have succeeded for a short time, but the problem resurfaces

with a greater gravity.

Terrorism is a menace not only in India but all over the world. We must not make the mistake of thinking that every terrorist belongs to a political party, say, in Punjab the Akali Party, or that every Akali is supporting the terrorists. This kind of a formulation is very unfortunate. In the last ten years a general atmosphere, as if it is a Hindu–Sikh problem in Punjab, has been created in the country. Now this totally needs to be removed. We, who have the good fortune of representing our people in this august House and who move in an educated section of society, must understand that people of various religions are living in this country and that in Punjab there is no religious problem.

The problem is created by certain vested interests and, I am afraid, the problem gets aggravated because of wrong actions or inaction of political parties, whether they are in or outside the government.

PASSIONS OF THE MOMENT

The former Honourable Member, Shri Annadurai of the DMK, is on the record of this House demanding the secession of Tamil Nadu. In those days, the House used to listen to him and counter argue. After Shri Annadurai spoke, twelve speakers explained to him that in the interest of India and even in the interest of Tamil Nadu, what he was saying was wrong. And today, Tamil Nadu is a part of India just like any other part of India. Passions of the moment have to be dealt with in their own way.

Merely using an iron hand will not help. Temporarily, yes; but they will again come up. Shri Mann has made the unfortunate demand of UN supervision of the elections or something like that. There is no question of that and he must banish that thought. Take the case of Sheikh Abdullah. For twenty-two years he was put in prison and then again he was made the chief minister and he accepted the Constitution of India. Take the case of Laldenga. He burnt the

Indian Constitution, but then we made him the chief minister.

> We mention the Jallianwalla Bagh episode every now and then. The total number of people who died there was 150 and it shook the British Empire. What has happened now?

There are two or three things in Punjab which are pending and when we were in [the] Opposition, we had always been insisting that till action was taken on people who perpetrated the riots in Delhi, no solution was possible. According to government official records, 3,000 Sikhs were killed, and unofficially the estimates are much more. Nowhere in history have we a case where there is genocide of this order and not a single person is hanged. Now, what kind of a message are you sending through?

We mention the Jallianwalla Bagh episode every now and then. The total number of people who died there was 150 and it shook the British Empire. What has happened now?

PUNISH PERPETRATORS OF DELHI RIOTS

We have become insensitive when we see that thousands of our brethren are being killed. I say with all the emphasis at my command that till the perpetrators of Delhi riots are brought to book, we will never gain the understanding and sympathy of the Sikh community and we do not deserve it. I do not know what is holding up the further action when we have commissions, committees and affidavits—let us end this matter on a war footing, let us take action on the perpetrators of Delhi riots without fear or favour because that will be our first attempt to prove our bona fides.

There are a lot of arguments and counter-arguments. Somebody used the word 'Sikh Quam' and there is a big objection, somebody said 'sub-nationalism' and there is a big objection. I do not want to go into polemics, but the fact remains that India is a country of diverse religions, diverse ethnic groups, diverse linguistic groups and this fact cannot be ignored, and a government or a political party which ignores this reality will face these problems and will never be able to solve them. To paint India with one brush, to pretend that all Indians are the same, to pretend that equality is already there is to close our eyes to the real problem. We must understand that every region has its peculiar problems.

Punjab has its own peculiar problems and they have to be tackled in its own unique way. The perpetrators of [the] riots, Delhi riots, to be brought to book is the first priority. The second priority is rehabilitation of some of the Sikh brethren who left the army. This was part of the Rajiv Gandhi–Longowal Accord. Five years have passed but nothing has been done so far. If we are not able to do something for them, again the question comes whether the central government or the Punjab government of the day is at all serious about solving the problem and healing the past wounds.

I point out with a bit of anguish that even after this government has come into power the situation in Punjab, of course, continues to be serious. There has been a change of governor. But the state government unfortunately does not see certain hard ground realities, and one of the hard ground realities is that the director general of police, who was responsible for what one may most charitably call strict police action—objectively, much worse adjectives can be used against this gentleman—unless you change him, what sort of dialogue can you begin even with our misguided brethren?

The Punjab government, I am afraid, is making a great slip in not changing the police setup in the state. If a political dialogue with the extremists is called for, if we want a climate of confidence to be created, not only we should call the youth and discuss with them, we should also have discussions with even some [of] the Akali leadership. But then it will not happen till first a deterrent of this type is removed.

Coming to the Punjab politics, we in the Janata Dal and the National Front have very little at stake politically to be accused of having an axe to grind, because in Punjab we do not exist in a big way. But the Congress party is there. The Akalis are there, various factions of them. One thing I want to make very clear. This business of dividing and ruling, or trying to divide or derive a political advantage from divisions of a political party, may be a normally accepted political process. But in certain places it must end. And Punjab is one place where I think it is the duty of all of us to see that a viable leadership, a viable, acceptable leadership emerges.

TALK TO THE POPULARLY ELECTED LEADER

Unless you have a political leadership which has the support of the local people, it cannot deliver. I have to mention that great hopes were built around Shri Simranjit Singh Mann, Akali Dal (Mann Group), after the Lok Sabha elections. There was talk that the elections were not fair. This is hogwash, because if the elections were not fair, five Congressmen could not have won, the Janata Dal candidates could not have won. The elections in Punjab were as fair as in any other part of the country. Now, under that garb there is a movement that the Assembly elections should not be held because the elections will be held under the shadow of terrorism and there will not be fair elections. No, I don't subscribe to that. I want the government to take a decision. It is for the government to consider at an all-party meeting when elections should be held. In my opinion, the sooner the better.

> Whether we like it or not, political personalities emerge and they do not do so because of our charity or because of our benevolence, and they do not exist there because of our patronage.

Again we are trying to play the same politics and thinking that having a dialogue with Shri Simranjit Singh Mann is not called for in the national interest. Whether we like it or not, political personalities emerge, and they do not do so because of our charity or because of our benevolence, and they do not exist there because of our patronage. Take the case of Shri Sheikh Abdullah in Kashmir or Shri Laldenga in Mizoram or Shri Phizo in Nagaland. At various times, in all these places, there were a lot of tensions which were not acceptable and which were not within the Constitution of India. All these personalities did receive the unstinted support of their own people and that part we cannot ignore. If we ignore that, we would be ignoring the reality.

Now, whatever information we have from Punjab would only indicate that to feel that Shri Simranjit Singh Mann is marginalized or to start dialogues with the other Akali units which do not have the support of the people would only be a foolhardy process. Of course, it is not our duty to build up Mann's political party and it is entirely his job. But we, in our own subtle way, at the political level, even at the administrative level, must see that Punjab has a political party which is able to get the confidence of its people and rule the state, because the only system that we know in our democratic structure is a popularly elected government, a legislative assembly, and only that can deliver the goods. I do not see any other option.

AKALI UNITY IS ABSOLUTELY NECCESSARY

Therefore, Akali unit willy-nilly has become an absolute imperative as far as the political solution of Punjab is concerned. I know that technically, theoretically, one can argue, 'Well, who are you to talk about Akali unity? It is their problem.' But, as I told you, there are circumstances; there are places in history where individuals can play a very important role. But in the long term, history adjusts everybody. And once the Punjab problem is solved and Punjab is back on the democratic road, there can be again a change of government in the normal way. But today, unless we help in installing a popularly elected government in Punjab and unless we stop this mad killing, I am afraid we will not be able to get nearer to integrating the hearts and minds of the Punjabi population with the rest of the country and that is imperative now.

But we must talk to them. We must surely talk to them and we cannot say that because they have made preposterous demands, they have become irrelevant. Whether we like it or not, political personalities emerge and they do not emerge because of our charity or because of our benevolence and they do not exist there because of our patronage.

The time has come for us to understand that the problems of a particular place have to be resolved only by the elected leaders and the popular leaders of that place, and it is our duty to see that those individuals, instead of getting misguided or looking outside the frontiers of India, get woven into the Indian fabric. And this requires a lot of understanding on both sides, not tough talking—maybe tough action at a certain level, but understanding and compassion is what is required. Unless we do it, the problem cannot be resolved.

A LAW FOR PEOPLE WHO NEED NO PROTECTION

Speaking on the Delhi Rent Control (Amendment) Bill, 1988, on 29 August 1988, Morarka says that the proposed legislation did not touch 25-40 per cent of the poorest who need housing; neither did it cover the old and dilapidated buildings, nor the middle-income groups. It seems to be for people who need no protection. He also speaks about a concept that is gaining ground in congested cities like Mumbai now: constructing houses to be rented to the middle- and lower-middle-income groups.

Sir, the bill that has come before the House after a prolonged discussion and debate through the press among the people is a damp squib. It has not even scratched the surface of the problem.

Its objects are three: first, to rationalize the relation between the landlord and the tenant; second, to boost the housing activity; and third, to reduce litigation between the landlords and the tenants. None of these three objects can be fulfilled by this bill. At best, it can be called a starting point in the rationalization of relations between the landlord and the tenant, because the major debility in this bill is that only houses with a rental of ₹3,500 and above are sought to be removed from rent control.

Since this bill relates to Delhi, how many houses are there in Delhi where the rent is above ₹3,500? The percentage is very, very small. And who are the occupants of these houses? The income of the person who can pay a rent of ₹3,500 must be ₹20,000 per month. And a house which can fetch a rent of ₹3,500 must be belonging to a rich man. So it rationalizes the relations between the landlord and the tenant. But which landlord and which tenant? A very rich landlord and a very rich tenant! So the basic purpose, the avowed purpose, for which the bill has been brought, is not even touched by it.

PROVIDING HOUSES TO THE RICH

The L.K. Jha Committee, which went into this matter, had recommended that a rental of ₹1,500 and above should be outside the purview of rent control. Why it is increased to ₹3,500 is not known. Probably, there are good reasons. But the fact is that a very small number of houses will get outside the purview of the Rent Control Act and, therefore, reduction in litigation will not follow.

Nor will there be a boost to housing activity. I do not know which housing activity will get a boost. Yes, very rich people can construct houses and let them out to very rich people as a result of this act. I do not think it is the social purpose of this legislation or the policy of this government to provide houses to the rich. If we need a boost in the housing activity, it is for the poor. In India, I do not know whether we have companies or corporations which are willing to construct houses and rent them out to the poor. I don't think that kind of an institution exists and I don't think that by any legislation we will be able to induce the private-sector people to build houses and rent them out to the poor, unless we are thinking of removing ceiling from rent, in which case the poor man will have to pay more rent.

So no amount of legislation on rent control can give a boost to housing activity. This object is totally irrelevant to the purpose of housing activity.

TODAY, THE TENANTS ARE RICHER THAN THE LANDLORDS

I am surprised that one of the major objectives, which has escaped the attention of the government, is that there are dilapidated houses or old built-up houses. Even large parts of Delhi, which we call Old Delhi, have got this problem of collapsing houses or urban degradation. All the old cities of India have this problem. Delhi also has its share. This act does not touch that problem.

> In fact, it would have been much more appropriate if you had stated the objects of this bill as (a) to enable the government servants to resume possession of their properties after retirement. That one purpose is fully served by this bill.

In Chandni Chowk the rental of a shop is ₹36. Under this act, it will increase by 10 per cent every three years. Now this is nothing. The shop-owner is making a profit of crores of rupees. What should be done? All commercial premises should be taken out of the purview of the Rent Control Act. Anybody who is renting a shop does not need the protection of the Rent Control Act. The very concept was to protect the poor from the rich. There was a time when the landlords were rich and the tenants were poor. Today, it is not so. Today, the tenants are richer than the landlords in most cases or in a large number of cases. The government and the law should protect the weaker person, and not the tenant or the landlord [specifically]. Wherever the landlord is weak, he needs to be protected. Wherever the tenant is weak, he needs to be protected. The persons having business worth crores of rupees don't need the protection of the government.

The minimum that the government can do is to introduce indexation. After all, the same landlord has rented the same shop at ₹36. In 1924 or 1936, that was the prevailing rent. Now the rent should be raised. His rent should be raised according to the index. Now that will also not be solving the problem of upgrading all the houses. But by not touching the problem we have left a large area of people outside the ambit of whatever reform we are trying to bring.

GOVERNMENT SERVANTS CAN GET PROPERTY BACK

The other problem is that 25 per cent to 40 per cent of the population of Delhi, Bombay, Calcutta and Madras (Chennai) live in slums. Even today they are not under the protection of the Rent Control Act. They have their own system between the tenant, the slum lord, the policemen and the local politician. They are living in a world of their own. It is they who need some reform that we may want to make in the housing system and we must do something to see that ultimately the place where they are living belongs to them. How to do it?

It is a very complex problem. But I am trying to point out that this legislation which we are going to pass does not touch 25 per cent to 40 per cent of the poorest of our people. It does not touch the old and dilapidated buildings. Whom does it touch? It does not touch the Delhi Development Authority or the middle-income groups or the working classes. It touches a fringe of the people who, I may humbly submit, need no protection.

In fact, it would have been much more appropriate if you had stated the objects of this bill as (a) to enable the government servants to resume possession of their properties after retirement. That one purpose is fully served by this bill.

I am not saying that government servants should not get possession of their property. But as the bill stands today, the only major reform that is taking place is that the central government servants or the Delhi administration servants, one year before their retirement or one year after their retirement, will be able to get their property back without tedious litigation. Even if this is to be kept as it is, the minimum that we can add is that all persons above the age of sixty should be given this facility. How is a retired schoolteacher or a retired employee of a private sector different from the retired government servant? A government servant who owns three bungalows, I don't think, needs the protection of the act.

We have gone at a tangent from the direction in which we started this rent control discussion a few years ago and how we have ended it. I am not grudging government servants getting their property back, neither am I grudging the armed forces and their widows getting back their property. But we must extend it to other widows, for which, I am pleased to see, an amendment has been moved by the Honourable Minister. And a provision should be made that senior citizens, everybody above the age of sixty or sixty-five or seventy, whatever the government may think, should be able to get their property back without tedious litigation.

Sir, the other point is that the L.K. Jha Committee, in its wisdom, had decided on ₹1,500. Why? It is because they found that if you remove above ₹1,500 from the rent control, poor people will not be hit, but a large amount of litigation will be obviated, leaving the rent controller with enough matter which he can handle. Today, we call the rent control as a fast track. It is not. Even the rent controller is taking years to settle the matter. The whole idea of reducing litigation or reducing the volume of work was to keep the threshold at ₹1,500 because even at a rental of ₹1,500, the person will be getting a salary of ₹7,000 or ₹8,000.

The government, in its wisdom, should bring an amendment and reduce it to at least ₹2,000 because at ₹3,500 there will be hardly any difference in the number of cases or the number of people benefited by this legislation.

The other point which I want to make is about the agreement. Whatever is the old law, that is a different thing. Today, if the person who is giving [a property] on rent is a literate person and the tenant is a literate person, why should it be allowed that after signing the agreement, the rent control is applicable? The agreement must have the force of law. Any agreement entered into—we can have whatever safeguards you want—must have the force of law if it is a rent above ₹1,500. Instead of this limit at ₹1,500 or a monetary limit, we can have a limit of area, such as anybody staying in a flat of more than 1000 sq. ft. That will ensure that we are protecting the poor. Somebody who is living in a flat of 2,000 sq. ft or 3,000 sq. ft does not need our protection. He can settle with his landlord. So, the threshold should be either ₹1,500 or a suitable area, whatever can be worked out, to see that the poor are protected. The only protection should be the agreement between the tenant and the landlord, or rather, the lessor and the lessee, because the landlord is a misleading word, because today the tenants are the public-sector companies, multinationals, private-sector companies.

LESSOR AND LESSEE, NOT TENANT AND LANDLORD

I know of a lot of people in the Indian Airlines and other public-sector organizations who have rented [out] their flats but when they want it back they are in difficulty because the tenant is a multinational company, or a bank, or some rich person. So, the words landlord and tenant are misleading. It should be lessor and lessee. There should be sanctity of agreement. Agreement between two literate persons should have the force of law.

The final point is the income tax angle. One provision says that henceforward the return will be 10 per cent on the actual cost. Now this will lead to a lot of manipulation. The cost should be fixed. I do not think it should be 10 per cent of the actual cost. It should be 10 per cent of some notionally fixed cost on rational basis. For the old rental you have provided 10 per cent increase every three years. Again, 10 per cent increase of what? If the old rent is ₹130, 10 per cent means nothing. So again, this 10 per cent increase is on what basis, is not clear. We must first bring all old rents to a particular base and then apply the 10 per cent increase formula. Otherwise, the 10 per cent increase, even if granted, will not serve any purpose, although the purpose for which the government puts it is very clear to me. But this act will not serve that purpose.

THE WEST'S KISS IS THE KISS OF DEATH

'India is being pushed around in the corridors of world power,' Morarka observes while participating in the discussion to formulate a stand on the GATT Treaty on 9 March 1994. India has succeeded in all those sectors where she has been self-reliant, he reminds the government.

Much discussion has taken place on the new General Agreement on Tariffs and Trade (GATT) and the Dunkel proposals. I want to deal with two or three fundamental questions. The first one is that speaker after speaker has said that this new arrangement of the GATT is better for India than the previous one—the exports will rise, India's share in the world trade will go up, etc., etc.

I have to just remind them that in September 1986, when the Uruguay Round started, India's stand was diametrically opposite to everything that the government now claims to stand for. At that time, Shri Rajiv Gandhi was the prime minister of India. The Congress party had 400 members in the Lok Sabha. It was a strong government, representing the will of the Indian people. Without fear of contradiction, I may say that the stand taken in Punta-del-Este in September 1986 represented the ethos of the Indian people. At that time, the third-world countries were with India. Brazil was with India; Argentina was with India; Egypt was with India; ten countries, including Tanzania and Nigeria, stood solidly with India.

We were able to make America and some other countries agree that the original format of GATT would not be contaminated, I would like to say, by the addition of matters not connected with trade, namely, agriculture, intellectual property rights, investments and services. After 1986, a worldwide debate has been taking place on Trade-related Aspects of Intellectual Property Rights (TRIPS), Trade-related Investment Measures (TRIMS) and agriculture. Till 1988, it was widely believed that this round would fail; fail in the sense that America and other countries would not be able to substantially modify the original GATT.

> The basic problem is not that we are in a minority in the world comity of nations; not that India is weak. Now, India is seen to be a country governed by a weak government. India is being pushed around in the corridors of world power.

Between December 1988 and April 1989, the whole scenario changed and in 1989, the Government of India also had to agree to the introduction of all these elements. This is part of the record. What happened between September 1986 and April 1989? One is that America, by using bilateral methods like the Super 301 and Special 301, arm-twisted the various countries, the third-world countries that had stood by India. Second, India, which had a very strong government in September 1986, had a very weak government by April 1989. It was the same Lok Sabha. But the strength of a government does not depend on the numbers alone. It depends on the willpower of the people running the government.

THE INDIAN GOVERNMENT IS SEEN AS WEAK

I have to say, with anguish, that the basic problem is not that we are in a minority in the world comity of nations; not that India is weak. When we achieved Independence, America was the richest country; the Western countries were quite prosperous; India was a poor country; and China was a poor country. The basic difference that has happened is, apart from the third-world countries leaving us, now India is seen to be a country governed by a weak government. India is being pushed around in the corridors of world power. Why are we shying away from this fact?

This morning, there was a small discussion on Kashmir in the Question Hour. The same thing applies to Kashmir. Are we trying to deny that in the last six months Pakistan had been raising the Kashmir issue at all the international forums? The Kashmir issue is the same. What are you discussing? Accession, Article 370, the events of 1948—nothing has changed. The world perception about India has changed. Suddenly, they feel that India can be pushed around; suddenly, they feel that India is vulnerable. Why? Again, they will say that we are politicizing the issue. The issue is that the way we have gone around with the begging bowl to the IMF and the World Bank, we have opened ourselves to being vulnerable.

The fact is that only in sectors where India has had its own swadeshi form of policy, we have succeeded. We have something to boast of. Where we have aped the West we are an abysmal failure.

Unless India goes back to the path of Jawaharlal Nehru and Indira Gandhi, we will be in trouble, because the world is a cruel place and nobody gives you your due unless they know that you have the spine to ask for it. It is not right to say that we are in a minority. How can one-sixth of the world population be in a minority? We are one-sixth. It is five-sixths versus one-sixth. That is a wrong way of looking at it. And, if you can make China come with you, it is one-fourth versus three-fourths. You can never be ignored. It is a question of psychology. I am surprised that the speakers on the other side have given all the arguments that we would give. But at the end of the argument, they say, we support the GATT.

I submit that we have made progress only in the fields where we have not submitted ourselves to the West. We have made progress only when we are 'isolated'. Which are the areas in which India can claim to have achieved success? Agriculture, atomic energy, missile technology, these are the very areas where we have not followed the West. We have had our own agricultural system, maybe, full of subsidies, and the subsidy may be unsustainable from the financial point of view. We have made our own basket; we have had our own method of fertilizer subsidy, some procurement price, some newer subsidy. We have made our own swadeshi form of agriculture and it has succeeded. Why are we ashamed of it?

It is because some white man can come and tell us that we have not followed the international norms. We are feeding one-sixth of the world population. Nobody is going hungry. Why are we ashamed of it? We have not become Somalia. We have refused to sign the Nuclear Non-Proliferation Treaty till today. According to the world powers, we would be deprived of heavy water, we would be deprived of plutonium and so on. We have done everything on our own. We do not need to take assistance. We have not adhered to the Missile Technology Control Regime and with our Agni success, they are scared. Why are we closing our eyes to the reality?

SUCCESS IN SELF-RELIANCE

The word 'isolation' may be very frightening to some people. It is a psychological frame of mind when someone feels isolated. But the fact is that only in sectors where India has had its own swadeshi form of policy, we have succeeded. We have something to boast of. Where we have aped the West we are an abysmal failure. Take the Indian industry. All the top twenty [business] houses of the country are net foreign-exchange losers year after year. They import equipment, they import technology and they are not able to compete in the world. It is on record.

Today, I ask the question which they are asking. We are isolated. We need foreign exchange. Why do we need foreign exchange? For oil? We have our own oil. If we develop our oilfields, we do not have to go to them for oil. Why do we need foreign exchange? For import of capital goods and raw materials? For whom? For [an] industry which cannot export, and for [an] industry which cannot look after itself. For agriculture, we do not need all these things. We have got our own fertilizer factories now. We have our own method of seed reproduction. We are fairly self-sufficient. I am not suggesting that we should cut ourselves off from the world. We are one-sixth of the humanity. They need us as much as we need them.

But we must draw a line of national self-respect. In the inter-country negotiations, each country likes to bargain for what is good for her, specially at a stage like this when the basic rules of the game are being changed. In the whole negotiations of the World Trade Organization (WTO), every country likes to put a rule which favours them or avoids a rule which is likely to go against them. That is fair enough. It is our own negotiating ability, our own conviction that will ultimately lead us from where we are. My complaint to the House, to the country, is that this government has been in power for the last three years. Why have they not taken the people into confidence? I was a little surprised at the very angry response of the commerce minister when our Jaipal Reddyji suggested that the GATT 1947 should be circulated. He said, 'There is a library and you can go to it.'

We agree with him. But when a bill comes before the House, the Statement of Objects and Reasons is printed for our ready reference. The minister can say that since the act is available in the library, the members can go to the library. The act is lying there. But that is not the issue. The issue is that when a matter of such importance, which is likely to have [an] effect on the country for the next two or three decades, is being discussed, the more information you disseminate, the better it is for everybody. I am sure this is not the contention of this government that the effect of this new trade organization is going to be felt only for one or two years but not in the next twenty years, thirty years or fifty years.

Why shouldn't the Parliament, the members, be taken into confidence? How many people today really know about the Dunkel Draft? I have met informed sections of the population—industrialists, economists, bankers—they do not have a clue as to what the Dunkel Draft is. They are all talking in a vacuum. I request the government to bring up, even now, a question-answer format for the things that are really agitating the minds of the people. For example, seeds for the farmers. Whenever we raise an issue, the minister will reply, 'No, no, it is not going to be like this. The farmers will not be affected.' Is this issue covered under the GATT provisions? We do not know. The government should come out with some comprehensive document in simple language. The common man must understand the plus and minus points of what they are about to sign.

> I have suggested in my earlier speech, and I repeat, that any treaty which has an importance over decades must be passed by the Parliament before it becomes a binding law for the country. You are binding it on all our future generations and you are doing it by yourselves.

Pharmaceutical prices will go up. Everybody knows they will go up. If it is the government's case that it will go up only on certain items, what are those items? Why don't you come up with a list? My request to the government is, at this stage it should see whether we can retrieve the situation by following the suggestions of Dr Ashok Mitra[1] because he has dealt with it in a very technical and detailed way. I am not aware whether India can take that stand even now, whether you can say that your legislature has to pass it. In my opinion, that was one of the lacunae in our Constitution. America and the Western countries have to go to their Parliaments. You can sign it without coming to us! So I do not know the constitutional amendments.

---

[1]Marxist economist, politician and writer.

LISTEN, BUT DON'T FOLLOW THE ADVICE

I have suggested in my earlier speech, and I repeat, that any treaty which has an importance over decades must be passed by the Parliament before it becomes a binding law for the country. You are binding it on all our future generations and you are doing it by yourselves. I do not think that it is fair. There is nothing good about this GATT as far as their interference in agriculture is concerned; their interference in internal affairs is concerned. Even Prof. [John Kenneth] Galbraith[1], who had been an American ambassador here, an eighty-five-year-old man, has publicly said, 'Indian agriculture has done well. You listen to the IMF, hear them patiently, but don't follow their advice.'

He has said that while every country has its own method, everybody gives loose examples of China and the Soviet Union. China is like India. China has progressed only where it has nothing to borrow from the West. It has come up on its own. Russia was dismembered and it has disappeared the moment it took advice from the West.

My advice to the government is, please take only such advice which will be good for us. Don't listen to the West. Their kiss is a kiss of death. I am very clear on that. I am not blaming America. America is a great country. They have been so great that for the last forty years they have been batting under GATT and we have been fielding. Because other countries have come up, now it is our turn to bat. Now, they have switched over from cricket to football. They say that everybody should be able to kick the ball equally. They are changing the game. Why? They are doing so because they don't want to do the fielding. They always want to bat. Now they say, 'Let us play football.' Whoever scores a goal will be the winner. They are changing the whole game.

I blame us. Even now our strong point is, at low consumption

---

[1] Influential economist and writer.

level we are reasonably happy. Let us not try to disturb it by suddenly increasing our consumption level.

I challenge the basic premise of export of wheat and sugar. Why should this country export wheat and sugar? We need wheat and sugar. Our people are suffering from malnutrition. This is the bankruptcy of mind. If you are exporting manufactured goods, that is one thing. If you say that our whole progress depends on export of wheat and sugar and our people should go hungry, then the basic premise has to be arrested. I am not challenging the fine print of that. You know better about the fine print.

I am challenging your whole philosophy. In a country of 85 crore people, where 40 per cent [of the] people are below the poverty line, how can you export foodgrains? Are our people here well-fed? Are they getting two meals a day? Do we have surplus wheat and sugar? You are exporting wheat and sugar because we need foreign exchange to import goods to be used by a handful of industries which are running inefficiently. I think this is a totally lopsided economic philosophy. The government must look at it.

FOOD CORPORATION—PASSING THE LOSS TO THE CONSUMER

The Right to Food and legislations and schemes regarding it has become something of a vexed and controversial issue of late. In this debate on the Food Corporations (Amendment) Bill, 1988, on 16 August 1988, Morarka points out that 'the whole purpose is to see that the farmer gets a fair price for his produce and that it is channelled to the consumer at a fair price. This purpose would be lost if the operations of the corporation itself become heavy as far as expenses are concerned.'

The Food Corporations (Amendment) Bill, 1988, is before us on a limited issue of providing more resources to the Food Corporation for its functioning. The manner of raising resources raises a crucial issue as to the cost of capital. If we see the Food Corporation's working for the last six or seven years, we observe that the sales turnover as a total turnover of operation has gone up from ₹2,800 crore in 1981–82 to ₹5,200 crore in 1986–87. It is a stupendous increase—it has almost doubled in six years. The alarming feature is the expenses of operation.

The operational expenses as a percentage of sale is understood to go up when sales go up. Normally, in a commercial enterprise, the percentage of expenses would come down because there is an element of fixed costs, which does not go up in direct proportion to the turnover. The unfortunate feature of the Food Corporation is that the expenses ratio has gone up from 27.86 to 35 per cent in this period, i.e., from 1981–82 to 1986–87. In fact, in the year 1984–85, the percentage was 38.9 per cent and probably, the alarm bells must have rung and thus the department of Food and Civil Supplies took a serious view. In the 1986–87 annual report, it was mentioned that a programme for reduction of expenses with a target was undertaken. The target was of ₹195 crore during 1986–87 and they have been able to reduce much more i.e. ₹238 crore. For 1987–88, the target is ₹232 crore. For 1987–88, the target is ₹232 crore but the figures are not yet before us.

PREMISE ON WHICH FCI STARTED

I want to point out that in an organization like the Food Corporation of India, which does not have a manufacturing unit of its own and which is largely a trading organization, the whole purpose is to see that the farmer gets a fair price for his produce. At the same time, the produce is channelled to the consumer at a fair price. This purpose would be lost if the operations of the corporation itself become heavy as far as expenses are concerned, because the FCI is supposed to replace the private trading infrastructure. The premise on which the FCI was formed or state trading in foodgrains started was based on the fact that the wholesale and retail dealers in foodgrains were making a fat profit and the consumer was made to pay much more.

> The annual report mentions that this corporation is supposed to function on a no-profit no-loss basis. What does this mean? From where will the expenses come? You will charge more from the consumers or you will try to pay less to the producers. Ultimately, the burden is being borne by the consumer.

Now we are procuring wheat and rice, which are the two main items dealt with by the FCI, at a certain price fixed by the government, and we are selling through the public distribution system (PDS) where again the price is fixed by the government. What will happen? Two things will follow. If the expenses are more, then the FCI will make a loss. The annual report mentions that this corporation is supposed to function on a no-profit no-loss basis. What does this mean? From where will the expenses come? You will charge more from the consumers or you will try to pay less to the producers. Ultimately, the burden is being borne by the consumer.

DANGEROUS IF EXPENSES UNBRIDLED

Before the House allows the FCI to issue debentures or bonds for which this bill is being introduced and has been passed by the Lok Sabha, we should very carefully examine whether the utilization of funds is proper because in a situation of monopoly—not strictly monopoly, but oligopoly, because they are controlling more than 25 per cent of the total procurement of foodgrains—it will be very dangerous if the expenses of the FCI are unbridled. What happens is, when we create a corporation like this, on ideological grounds, we do not feel like criticizing it. After all, we feel we are doing a good turn to the farmer. The corporation is required to do a good turn to the consumer without realizing the inherent, inbuilt inefficiency in our own machinery that we have set up.

The figures are really alarming. From 1981–82 to 1985–86 the percentage expenditure has gone up from 28 to 35 per cent and this is a very serious matter. I would like the minister himself to look into it personally, because cutting expenditure is a very difficult task, especially in a public-sector organization. There would be employees, there would be overhead expenditure and the cycle of increase would be going on. But in spite of all these, it must be our attempt that with the increasing scale of operations, the percentage of expenses must come down. Only then will we be able to give real service to the consumer.

Especially on the interest, we find, in 1981–82, on the operational scale of ₹2,800 crore, the total interest paid by the corporation was ₹262 crore. In 1986–87, on double the scale of operations, the interest paid was about three times the earlier figure, i.e, ₹650 crore. Last year, it was ₹709 crore. This could be due to the increased lending rates of banks. But when we discuss commercial banks, we always come up with the theory that their operations are not economical because they are lending to the FCI and the agricultural sector at subsidized rates of interest.

> We have examples like the Amul Dairy, which is a cooperative and has been able to maintain a balance between what it pays to the farmer and what it charges from the consumer. I am not suggesting that the FCI should be abolished and handed over to the cooperatives. But we feel that, in any case, its functioning should not be at an efficiency level which is lower than that of the cooperatives.

If our banking system is lending to the FCI at subsidized rates and its interest payment is going up disproportionate to the increase in its sales turnover and its total operations, it is a red signal. Either the inventory levels are not correct, or they are having too much of stock, or the stocks are not rotated correctly, or they are operating at rates higher than what are prescribed. I do not know how they will be empowered by this bill. Will they go in for public funds? Will they go in for Unit Trust funds? Or will they go in for bonds at cheaper rates of interest? Whatever it may be, as for the interest on the total borrowing, the average interest rate should be fixed by the government, by the Department of Food.

I see from the latest report that the debt-equity ratio is 1:6. I do not know whether the government thought it prudent to do so. Only two years ago, their capital was increased. Till 1984–85, the debt-equity ratio was adverse. The government has increased the capital. Now the debt-equity ratio is 1:6. The question is whether for trading companies with such a heavy burden, the ratio of 1:6 is justified, because interest is a major component of their expenditure.

This aspect should be examined before we give the FCI the power to borrow funds.

LOSS PASSED ON TO CONSUMER

It is in the nature of a monopoly organization. Once the government gives permission, it will go ahead borrowing more money and thus paying more interest. The more dangerous part of it is, since it is supposed to operate on a no-profit no-loss basis, the loss will be passed on to the consumer. So, who is going to pay for this inefficiency? It will be the consumer. Therefore, on the expenditure, especially the interest, the department of food must come out with standard costs, which should be strictly adhered to.

> But the country has been put to a loss and, I am sure, loss running into several crores of rupees. Because of this deal and the way it has been handled, I would request the Honourable Minister to order a full-scale inquiry into this particular deal in the light of these facts which the newspaper has published, along with the photocopies of the various transactions which have not been refuted.

It should not be that in 1985 we wake up and say, 'In the next two years, please reduce the expenditure. Our target of reduction is ₹232 crore.' This is not proper because that means, over the years, a lot of extra expenditure is built in and a stage has come when we have to make efforts to reduce the expenditure. An organization like the FCI, which has no production facility, which is only trading and which has got the added advantage of trading with a monopolistic position of strength, can definitely assure us of this. We have examples like the Amul Dairy, which is a cooperative and has been able to maintain a balance between what it pays to the farmer and what it charges from the consumer. I am not suggesting that the FCI should be abolished and handed over to the cooperatives. But we feel that, in any case, its functioning should not be at an efficiency level which is lower than that of the cooperatives.

I do not want to talk of the private sector efficiency because it is not possible to ascertain at what margin levels they work, since it is an unorganized sort of trade. But the FCI being in a commanding position, this is the elementary thing that should be done before we give them the carte blanche. I want to now to come to a specific issue which has become a major issue in the newspapers, and that is the Korean rice deal. The *Business Standard* (13 June)—I am sure the minister must have read it—carried this huge headline, 'MMTC forces acceptance of North Korean rice deal.'

NOT A STRAIGHT DEAL

I am sorry to say that, from the reply given by the MMTC's senior general manager to the press, things do not appear to be straight, because it appears that the whole thing was handed over to the MMTC. I find that there is a countertrade involved in it. On the price, very easily, by a simple telex or telegram, the FOB (free on board) and the CIF (cost, insurance and freight) prices have been interchanged. Anybody familiar with international trade knows that there can be a difference running into crores of rupees if the price is changed from CIF to FOB and FOB to CIF. This is not known to the people who are not familiar with this or to the average newspaper reader, unless of course the newspaper points it out.

But the country has been put to a loss and, I am sure, [a] loss running into several crores of rupees. Because of this deal and the way it has been handled, I would request the Honourable Minister to order a full-scale inquiry into this particular deal in the light of these facts which the newspaper has published, along with the photocopies of the various transactions which have not been refuted. So, in the interests of the functioning of the Food Corporation, in the interest of removing all the doubts, this should be done.

We are losing money even on what we are purchasing or

importing in foodgrains. Therefore, I demand a full-scale inquiry, which is the minimum which is required to get at the bottom of the rice deal with North Korea, which is handled by the MMTC. Normally, the MMTC should not handle this and, basically, this should be handled by the Food Corporation. This is my first objection. But I see from the newspapers that countertrade is involved in this and so, the MMTC is handing it.

Then, in Rajasthan, the Food Corporation asked a number of people to construct open godowns for them. For increasing their storage capacity, the FCI has this policy that instead of investing its own funds, it asks private parties to construct the godowns. They (the private parties) will take some time.

NOT KEEPING A PROMISE

In Rajasthan, the Vyapari Sangh has complained to the state government that after they invested in constructing the godowns, the FCI says that it does not want them any longer; I do not know these people and I am not acting as their advocate. But I must say that since a public-sector corporation is a part of the government—there are several court judgments saying so—the promises that they make should be strictly followed or fulfilled. A trader or a person who has built godowns for you should not be suddenly told that you do not need them. He cannot use it for anything else because basically, these are meant for foodgrains. However, this is what has happened.

Finally, I want to say that the total management and operations of the FCI leave much to be desired. Organizations like the FCI, the State Trading Corporation of India, the MMTC, etc., all came into existence in the '60s and '70s as a result of a definite and deliberate policy and the political decision to take over the wholesale trade by the government. But at no point of time was it the policy either of the Congress party or of Jawaharlal Nehru or of Smt. Indira Gandhi that having taken over everything, the consumer should be put to a loss or the producer should be put to a loss and only the top-heavy management should eat away whatever little margin is there or, ultimately, they should run into losses for which the government was never prepared and is not prepared.

STRONG OBJECTION TO 'ORDINANCE RAJ'

'I will have to say with anguish that the general tendency is to bypass Parliament or take Parliament for granted,' says Morarka, while disapproving the National Highways (Amendment) Ordinance, 1992, on 25 and 26 November 1992.

I beg to move the following resolution: 'That this House disapproves of the National Highways (Amendment) Ordinance, 1992 (No. 19 of 1992), promulgated by the President on 23 October 1992.'

I want to put on record my strong objection to this Ordinance Raj, which appears to have become a routine affair with this government. I wish to bring to the notice of the government that never has there been a year in which nineteen ordinances have been issued. This particular ordinance was issued on 23 October 1992. Parliament met on 24 November, only one month after that. What was the urgency?

There is a statement explaining the circumstances which had necessitated immediate legislation by the National Highways (Amendment) Ordinance, promulgated on 23 October 1992. To my utter disappointment, this five-paragraph statement does not give us the circumstances which necessitated it. It gives the reasons why this bill has come: the highways are in a bad shape, money is required, there is a resource crunch. We may all support the need to raise resources to maintain the highways better. The issue is, you must tell us why the ordinance had to be issued.

Let me remind this government: Smt. Indira Gandhi was a very powerful prime minister. In her regime, one ordinance was issued for the nationalization of banks—and there was a furore in Parliament as to why that ordinance had to be issued when Parliament was going to meet in the next few days. She had a valid reason—that nationalization by itself was a thing which had to be done without notice. It was not advisable to bring a bill before Parliament. Now, these reasons do not apply to the kind of ordinances that this government has been issuing.

> I will have to say with anguish that the general tendency is to bypass Parliament or take Parliament for granted.

WHAT IS THE URGENCY; WHAT IS THE REASON?

They have issued an ordinance to create SEBI. Between the last session and this session, seven ordinances have been issued, each one of them wholly unnecessary, wholly irrelevant. The urgency aspect is not there. There is one ordinance on the Industrial Finance Corporation of India to convert it from a corporation to a public company; I don't understand what the reason is for an ordinance in this case.

I thought the statement would tell us that government had to impose a fee or octroi on a particular bridge urgently. Nothing of the sort is there. The statement doesn't say anything. I would like to know from the minister whether, after the promulgation of the ordinance, till today, if they have used these powers. If they have not used these powers between 23 October and now, it proves my case that the ordinance was wholly unnecessary.

I will have to say with anguish that the general tendency is to bypass Parliament or take Parliament for granted. There are so many instances I can give, which are not relevant to this case. I request the prime minister to look into these things himself. Every ministry sends matters and says that those are most urgent. But an ordinance can be issued only after the cabinet approves it. The prime minister should not allow ordinances to be issued in this cavalier fashion. This is my first objection.

I will conclude after making one or two requests to the minister. On the substantive part of this bill, the whole House will agree with the minister that the highways are really in a bad shape. There was a proposal for the National Highways, which are in bad condition. The main National Highway No. 1, which used to be the pride of this country, is really in a bad shape. We agree with the contention of the minister that the highways need repairs. They need resources. On that, there is no doubt.

NO INFORMATION, ONLY DEMAND FOR BLANKET POWERS

How will you raise the resources? There are no details, except taking blanket powers. We do not know exactly the total quantum of resources [is] that you think [you] will be able to raise by levying octroi or other levies for bridges or ferries. We would like to know from the minister whether the ministry has worked out how much annual resources can be raised by levying some sort of a fee on the traffic.

Will the money raised for a particular highway be used only on that highway, or will there be a pool? Who will administer that pool? If the National Highways Authority [of India] has not come into being, who is going to repair those highways? Will the money be given to the state governments? We would like to know these details. We definitely support your intention behind the bill, but we want to know more details. We do not approve of this fashion of issuing an ordinance and not even acting on it for one month after you have issued it. If you have acted on it, we would like to be enlightened on it. It should have been mentioned in the statement. Why was the ordinance required to be promulgated? These are my main objections.

Therefore I recommend to the House that this ordinance should be disapproved, while I have no objection to the objects and reasons behind this bill.

HOW WILL THE NEW STEEL POLICY HELP?

Letting public-sector units in the core steel industry run below capacity while encouraging the private sector is a dangerous practice, says Morarka, in this debate on 29 May 1990 on the government's new Steel Policy. Asking for a White Paper, he points out that while the public sector blast furnace-producing units were being kept idle, the private steel industry was being permitted to import them.

The new Steel Policy is before us. After reading it, I find it is a major announcement. Blast furnaces will now be permitted in the secondary sector. The blast furnace technology was under the primary sector and the electric arc furnace in the secondary sector. If the government in its wisdom is taking a decision to allow smaller companies to go in for the blast furnace route, well, I am afraid it will not be in the secondary sector anymore. That is number one. Number two, I do not know which is the indigenous blast furnace technology available in the country for up to 250,000 tonnes. I think, once you allow this, it will go to a million tonnes, whether we like it or not.

Over the years we have seen how the Monopoly and Restrictive Trade Practices (MRTP) Act has been totally diluted. It has gone beyond recognition today. In fact, in this policy also, the first clarification I want to get from the steel minister is: is it only the steel ministry's policy or has he coordinated with the industry minister and the finance minister? Because once you allow this, they will merge projects and that means [that] the MRTP Act, the industrial licensing policy and other policies have to be coordinated. The government may come to the conclusion that steel is in short supply, that instead of importing steel we are now going to allow the private sector to go in for steel-making in a big way.

COUNTRY NEEDS MORE INFORMATION

But then, we should know that allowing the private sector to go the blast furnace route is a departure from the Industrial Policy Resolution of 1956, whether we like it or not. I have been complaining when I was sitting on the other side that the previous government in the last ten years had made major departures in the resolution, cloaked in the kind of language which I have never appreciated. For instance, by a simple notification we have removed all major industries from the MRTP Act—cement, paper—under the guise that the country needs it. When the MRTP Act was introduced by Smt. Gandhi, she never said that she was introducing this for industries. Steel is still under the MRTP Act. Would the government remove steel from the MRTP Act? Will it remain under the MRTP Act? This is one of the major changes in the steel policy for which the country is entitled to have more information.

Together with this, my second request to the steel minister is that having made this policy announcement, a White Paper on the steel industry should be placed on the table of the House because all the major steel plants have undergone modernization. Two years ago, Shri Ram Awadhesh Singh had very rightly drawn the attention of the House to major modernization schemes in the public sector, whose cost calculations were disproportionate to all available information. The Heavy Engineering Corporation in Ranchi is grossly underutilized. Yet, we are importing blast furnaces.

> The public-sector units should be worked to their optimum capacity. Only when you do that can the cost of steel-making come down.

The TISCO has been allowed to import equipment, which is made by the HEC in Ranchi. Durgapur and Burnpur are being allowed to import equipment which can be made in India. Not only that, we are also having consultancy from abroad when Indian consultancy organizations in the public sector and the private sector very much exist. Steel is a major core sector industry of the Indian economy. I think it is not enough to make this policy statement. A White Paper on this, the status of the steel industry, its present status, the future plans for the next ten years as the government perceives them, is required because there are pending projects: the Visakhapatnam Steel Plant, the Vijayanagar Steel Plant in Karnataka, the Salem Steel Plant, which was later converted into an alloy steel plant. For these the foundation stones were laid in 1971 by Smt. Gandhi.

Because of lack of resources, these projects were not implemented. Later, we were told that the demand for steel was not enough. Today, a stage has come when there is a spurt in the demand for steel, to the extent that we are saying that the private sector should come in. The public-sector units should be worked to their optimum capacity. Only when you do that can the cost of steel-making come down.

AN UNWISE STEP

You are maintaining the public-sector plants at 1-million-tonne capacity, not expanding them, and are allowing a number of smaller blast furnaces to come in. I am not a student of economics. I will seek your help in that respect. But from whatever knowledge I have as to business and industry, I don't think that this is a prudent thing to do. The whole world is going in for economics of scale.

In Korea, the Polang Iron and Steel Company, a single steel

unit, is making some 12 million tonnes of steel. Our Bokaro Steel Plant, which is our largest steel plant, is yet to reach 5 million tonnes of steel. It is still at 3 million tonnes or some such figure. So, the time has come when the whole perspective should be on economies of scale. Maybe electric arc furnaces on the western coast, based on imported scrap or on gas-based sponge iron, can produce steel at a lower cost. But, if we allow this route, I am afraid that the public-sector steel plants will be put to a permanent disadvantage and the country will have to bear losses for a long time to come. So, I would like to know from the minister by way of a clarification if all these aspects have been kept in mind.

> Most of the private-sector units in India are based on government money. It is from the IDBI, IFCI and ICICI. Ninety per cent of the money invested in the private sector is from the public sector.

Maybe it is my conjecture because I have some knowledge of how the Government of India functions. The Government of India functions in the same way, whichever government comes into power. The sponge-iron plants are there. The sponge-iron manufacturers are clamouring that their goods should be sold. So, my third clarification is whether it is a fact that ₹150 crore was sanctioned a few months ago for import of scrap and whether that money is not being released because the sponge-iron people do not want scrap to be imported.

I understand [that] if sponge iron is produced in India, we should use it, but if its production in India is not enough to meet the demand of electric arc furnace, for some time you will have to import melting scrap. So, import of melting scrap, production of sponge iron, new units of gas-based sponge iron and even import of sponge iron—all these will have to be taken into consideration as an integrated policy for steel-making, keeping in mind that we already have a huge investment in the steel sector e.g. the Steel Authority of India Ltd.

PRIVATE SECTOR IS BASED ON GOVERNMENT MONEY

The Indian Iron and Steel Company Ltd, the two public-sector plants and all those three plants at Visakhapatnam, Vijayanagar and Salem—I again repeat those three because I remember very clearly [that] over the last twenty years, Visakhapatnam and Vijayanagar at least were staggered only on this basis. First, because the demand was not enough. Second, we do not have enough resources. By way of clarification, I would like to know whether it is because of our resource crunch that we are slowly moving away from the public sector to the private sector, because in India the private sector has no resources. Most of the private-sector units in India are based on government money. It is from the IDBI, IFCI (Industrial Finance Corporation of India) and ICICI (Industrial Credit and Investment Corporation of India). Ninety per cent of money invested in the private sector is from the public sector. The track record may show better profits in the private sector, because private entrepreneurship is probably helping them function better.

That is a matter of detail, but the fact remains that the resource base being the same, how will this policy really help? The overall national picture is not clear to me. Because such a large issue cannot be settled by way of clarifications, I would again request that a White Paper on the status of the steel industry with the overall policy perspective for the next ten years should be placed in the House and we should have a full discussion on the subject, probably in the next session.

STOP FERTILIZER SUBSIDY, SAYS IMF; DOES THE GOVERNMENT LISTEN?

The government seems to be convinced about the IMF's argument to stop fertilizer subsidy, Morarka observes, during the special mention of 17 September 1991 on the Need for a White Paper on Fertilizer Subsidy. However, if this means that foodgrain production falls, that can never be good news for the people, he adds.

I wish to draw the attention of the government to the very vexed issue of fertilizer subsidies, which is current at the moment. In 1980–81, when we were negotiating the last IMF loan, under those very stringent conditions we had hiked the fertilizer prices, first by 40 per cent and then by another 25 per cent. For the next three years after that, the foodgrain production in India was stagnant because fertilizer consumption went down and food production also went down.

I understand the balance of payments difficulties, I understand the government negotiating an IMF loan, which may be inevitable, but I want to remind the government that this country had earlier passed through very difficult days on the food front. For years and years we were under obligation to the US PL 480[1]—the vocabulary has been forgotten by the people today, the new generation probably

---

[1]One of the US food aid programmes that gave foodgrains to poor countries at a very low cost, under the Food for Peace, or Public Law 480 (PL 480).

does not even know what the country suffered twenty years ago.

> The fact of the matter is that fertilizer prices in India are high
> according to international standards. Actually, the subsidy that
> we are paying today is not to the farmer but we are really
> subsidizing the inefficiency, the corruption and the initial high
> capital cost of the fertilizer plants.

It was only after the introduction of fertilizer subsidy in 1977 that we have had a stable and regular increase in food production. I will just give two figures. In 1976–77, when the subsidy was introduced, the production was 111.2 million tonnes. It increased to 126.4 million tonnes in 1977–78 and 131.9 million tonnes in 1978–79. After that there was an increase in fertilizer prices, and the production got stagnant. Only in 1983–84, when the fertilizer subsidy was reintroduced, there was again an increase of production to 132.4 million tonnes and, after 1983–84, though the fertilizer subsidy has been rising at a pace which may not be comfortable for the finance ministry, the fact is that foodgrain production has been rising steadily, and today we have 170 million tonnes.

> No import would be required, provided we can use the
> indigenously produced fertilizer efficiently.

SUBSIDIZING INEFFICIENCY

In this context, the obvious question to any analyst would be, though the subsidy may be required, the country cannot go on paying endless subsidies. The fact of the matter is that fertilizer prices in India are high, according to international standards. Actually, the subsidy that we are paying today is not to the farmer but we are really subsidizing the inefficiency, the corruption and the initial high capital cost of the fertilizer plants. It is surprising to know that each fertilizer plant in India has been put up at a cost of, at least, ₹400 crore higher than similar plants in other parts of the world. If the capital cost of a plant is ₹400 crore higher, obviously the cost of production is higher, over the years.

It is a national problem and I want the government to bring out a White Paper giving all the figures and statistics, and have a national debate as to how we can tackle this problem. Dr M.S. Swaminathan, the foremost agricultural expert in India, of international renown and repute, has observed that though the IMF loan may be essential, though correcting the BoP may be essential, but if that results in our foodgrain production going down, it will be an unacceptable trade-off by any standards in a developing economy. He has further observed that foodgrain production may not be directly connected with fertilizer consumption because fertilizer efficiency is very essential.

> If the capital cost of a plant is ₹400 crore higher, obviously the cost of production is higher, over the years.

The small farmers in India are unable to do water management. The nutrients of the Indian soil, which has been cultivated for thousands of years, have got destroyed. According to Dr Swaminathan, in terms of NPK (nitrogen, phosphorous, potassium) the 9 million tonnes of indigenously available fertilizer should be enough to sustain the existing foodgrain production. No import would be required, provided we can use the indigenously produced fertilizer efficiently. My submission to the government is that because this problem will come up year after year—this year they reduced the subsidy, then again they restored a part of the subsidy—and the next year's budget will face the same problem, much before that there should be a proper debate on this.

A SERIOUS MATTER

According to Dr Swaminathan, between 1985–86 and 1989–90

with the NPK availability, the foodgrain production should have increased by 30 million tonnes, but it has increased only by 20 million tonnes. Considering all these facts, I feel that the government should come out with a comprehensive document. The Government of India is going by the IMF argument in April 1981, favouring stopping the fertilizer subsidy. Probably that argument has been very convincing to the government. But if the price that we pay for it in the long term would be a decline in the foodgrain production, it will be a very serious matter.

Across party lines there is the Agriculture Consultative Committee. There are other committees too. This matter should be discussed fully, and we should arrive at an acceptable solution in the interest of the country.

SELF-SUFFICIENCY IN OIL

In the long run, the only thing that can bring stability to the country's economy is self-sufficiency in the energy sector, apart from the food sector, says Morarka in this speech during Special Mentions on 3 March 1992.

I wish to draw the attention of the government to the declining oil production in the country. In the last seven–eight months, we have heard about the macro-economic adjustments the government wants to make.

In the recent budget, there has been a lot of focus on the balance of payments position and the foreign exchange reserves. The figures for the last four years show that on one item alone, namely, oil, crude oil, as well as other petroleum products, we have been spending a lot of foreign exchange. The oil bills have gone up from ₹4,000 crore in 1988–89 to ₹6,000 crore in 1989–90 to ₹11,000 crore in 1990–91 and now ₹12,000 crore in 1991–92. From 1988–89 to 1991–92, it has gone up three times.

MAKE OR MAR

Oil is one item which can make or mar the future of the country. But when the budget comes, the immediate discussion is on some tax. Somebody gets some tax relief. Some excise duties are increased. Some customs duties are increased. On the basis, that the newspapers write that it is a good budget or a bad budget. In the long run, the only thing that can bring stability to the country's economy is self-sufficiency in the energy sector, apart from the food sector.

In case of food, in the 1970s, because of the Green Revolution, fortunately because of the policies of the late Smt. Gandhi, we are in a position today where we do not have to import foodgrains. I do not want to digress on the subject. I hope this policy will continue even if it means continuation of fertilizer subsidy, etc. But on the energy sector, I am very clear that the government must take it up on a war footing.

> **Oil is one item which can make or mar the future of the country. But when the budget comes, the immediate discussion is on some tax.**

Already three rounds of bids have been completed to involve international companies in oil drilling and exploration. Of course, I am firmly opposed to so many policies being followed by the government to involve foreign companies; opening the door to multinationals. We have foreign cold drinks companies like Pepsi cola and Coca Cola here.

But when it comes to oil, we say that the foreign companies cannot come. We must make our programme for the next five years, as to what will be our quantum jump in oil production. Just now, the production has declined, from 33 million tonnes to 30 million tonnes. We cannot afford this at a time when the consumption is going up. As you know, because of the Gulf crisis, the oil prices shot up. A stage has come when we must understand that our entire trade balances is dependent on oil. Of course, there is the new trade policy. The details are yet to be known. But the government would be setting aside 40 per cent for oil import. I am afraid, if the oil bill alone is ₹12,000 crore, even this 40 per cent will not be sufficient. Moreover, they also want to use it for fertilizers and essential imports.

DRAFT A NATIONAL ENERGY POLICY

My submission to the government is that a National Energy Policy should be announced immediately. We must have a time-bound oil programme. We must also have a power generation programme. Even 1 per cent increase in the plant load factor of power plants would mean an extra generation of 500 MW. We all know that the major consumption of petroleum products is by way of diesel by the farmers. This is because we cannot give them electricity. Diesel is costlier than electricity. If we can give them electricity, diesel can be saved. Therefore, this is one action we should take.

The ONGC should draw up a corporate plan to increase oil production. The present production is 33 million tonnes. You should plan for a 40-million-tonne production over the next few years. I agree that it requires a lot of resources, you may require foreign exchange, but that is the one sector where you may have a high-level group which can talk to the American companies, ask them to get into the sector and get the results. Instead of that you are issuing notifications, you are liberalizing. There should be a Cabinet Committee on oil and energy and they should take up this matter seriously. I request the prime minister to personally look into it.

THEN THE ENTIRE BOFORS MYSTERY WILL BE RESOLVED

Speaking on the Bofors Investigations debate on 13 May 1992, Morarka clarifies that he neither suffers from Bofors-mania nor from Bofors-phobia. However, for the first time there is clear-cut evidence of a cover-up and an attempt to erase evidence, and it is this angle that must be pursued as the most promising lead, he argues.

In the five years since the [Bofors] issue has been engaging the attention of the country, this is the first time that an attempted cover-up has been found out. That distinguishes the matter from all the previous discussions that we have had earlier on Bofors. I am one of those members who do not suffer from Bofors-mania, as if it is the most important subject to be discussed.

> In this case we have got a lead for the first time. There is a person who has tried to extinguish the investigation. The police must do nothing else except to relatively pursue this character and find out who is the person.

I think this is an issue where alleged enrichment by some middlemen in the largest defence deal that this country had has been in the news from various quarters. The CBI has been entrusted with the task. The issue has come up in the House again and again and unfortunately, it is the newspaper which has leaked some documents from time to time, whatever may be the veracity of the documents.

Since Shri Narasimha Rao has become the prime minister, he has had nothing to do with this deal. It was done at a time when he was neither defence minister nor prime minister. Shri Solanki[1] has been found out in a very crudely and blatantly attempted cover-up to which he became a party, wittingly or unwittingly. He is a colleague of ours. I have no reason to disbelieve him. A document was planted on him, which he unwittingly gave to the Swiss foreign minister. The government has already tried to mitigate the damage by writing to the Swiss authorities, 'Please ignore all that and carry on the investigations.'

THE MURDERER ALWAYS RETURNS TO THE CRIME SCENE

I am on a different point. The CBI is investigating this matter. They are searching for a lead. The single biggest lead they have got is the person who has planted this document. Who will be interested in the cover-up? Obviously the people who have received the money. It is a common police parlance that the murderer always returns to the scene of the crime. The police always is on the lookout for this biggest clue, for the person who has done the murder is the chap who has tried to come and erase the evidence.

In this case we have got a lead for the first time. There is a person who has tried to extinguish the investigation. The police must do nothing else except to relatively pursue this character and find out who is the person. Then the entire Bofors mystery will be resolved. Let us not spend government money. Let us not go on fighting in the Swiss courts. Why don't you nab this lawyer? Shri Solanki is one of us. He owes a duty to this country to give all the information that he has. If he does not know the name of

---

[1] Union Foreign Affairs Minister Madhavsinh Solanki, accused of allegedly attempting to influence the investigations.

the lawyer, he must tell us how he met him. Who introduced him [Solanki] to him [the lawyer]? He must give a clue. The police must interrogate him and also prosecute him.

Shri Solanki should be able to give from his memory, from his recollection, every single piece of information he has about that person, because in identifying that person lies the solution to the Bofors scandal. I just want to end by saying that the prime minister must know that unless this episode is resolved, the clouds will hang on this government. They must remember that in President Nixon's case it was not the Watergate scandal that resulted in his ouster, but the cover-up. Please do not cover-up for anybody. Please find out the identity of this person. Therein lies the solution.

DO NOT REPRESS OR SUPPRESS
THESE MOVEMENTS

Speaking on the resolution regarding the situation created by the Bodo Movement and ULFA in Assam on 23 May 1990, Morarka says that the various separatist movements in the country occur due to our inability to cope with the conflicts, to tolerate a different viewpoint and the failure of political leadership. We should 'not seek peace in the absence of conflicts. We should seek peace in our ability to cope with conflicts,' he argues.

The resolution before the House is a very important one in the present context in the country. I would request the Honourable Members from both sides to reflect more seriously into the causes of such conflicts. It is not only Assam. We have Punjab. We have Kashmir. Let us not run away from the fact: we can have such movements in other parts of the country.

I do not share the perception that such movements can be stopped by giving an oil refinery here or a steel project there. Thereby, we are insulting the intelligence of our people. These conflicts were expected by the founding fathers of our country. If you see the speeches of Mahatma Gandhi, Jawaharlal Nehru, Jayaprakash Narayan, you will see that in those years they had foreseen the conflicts in a multi-ethnic society. I do not think the central government or the state government or any of us should seek peace in the absence of conflicts. We should seek peace in our ability to cope with conflicts.

INABILITY TO COPE WITH CONFLICTS

The reason why the country looks as if it is on fire today is not because anything is wrong with the people, it is our ability to cope with the conflicts that has gone down, our ability to tolerate a different viewpoint has gone down and that is the main problem in the whole country. The number of youth who come out of universities and colleges exceeds the number of youth that came out of colleges at the time of Independence. To give one statistics, I can say, today the number of the Scheduled Caste youths passing [out of] university every year is equal to the total number of graduates passing [out] at the time of Independence. You must understand that the sections of society which were neglected, whether they are the Scheduled Castes and Scheduled Tribes, hill areas, backward areas…today, their level of consciousness, their level of education, their level of restlessness has grown and, therefore, we should not be surprised if they want a share today in the national prosperity.

The whole problem is that the consecutive governments either at the Centre or in most of the states have not been enlightened enough. A friend from the other side said that the Asom Gana Parishad (AGP) government is our government. For the last four years they have been in power.

They forgot to ask a question. How come they came to power when they were not even a political party? They came to power because the Congress (I) government in Assam failed to respond to the people's aspirations. If the AGP government fails to do so, well, the democratic process will throw up another government. Therefore, nobody should think that staying in power is their monopoly. Whoever wants to be in power in this country must understand that power is not the power of 1947 or 1952.

FAILURE OF POLITICAL LEADERSHIP

From 1990 onwards, if you want to stay in power, you must have the ability to cope with the contradictions of the society. And I must say a word in praise of the West Bengal government which, I feel, has been able to solve—resolve—the Darjeeling Hill issue by resolving the contradiction inherent in the problem, i.e. the unity and integrity of the country on the one hand and aspirations of the local people on the other.

These contradictions will come everywhere. The central government will always have a role to play but we must understand that it is only enlightened leadership, and I was happy when Shri Pachouri mentioned that the Assam Accord[1] should be implemented, though it is late. How come it has not been implemented so far? It is the central government's responsibility. I do not think it is a problem where we should go according to party lines. It is a question of the unity of the nation. It is only—in one sentence—the failure of political leadership that brings about all these movements. Unless we have better and more enlightened political leadership, I am afraid, Balkanization of the country will stare us in the face. I do not have a ready solution, but I do have one solution. I can say what not to do and that is, do not try to repress or suppress these movements. They cannot be suppressed. Anything that we suppress will come out with greater fury after a number of years.

---

[1]Signed in 1985, the accord dealt with the issues of illegal immigrants and sealing Assam's borders with Bangladesh.

SHIFTING THE INTERNAL SECURITY ACADEMY FROM MOUNT ABU

Speaking during Special Mentions on 29 August 1991, Morarka pleads that the Internal Security Academy should not be shifted from Mount Abu to Bangalore. The academy continues to be in Mount Abu.

I wish to draw the attention of the government to the proposal, rather to the threat, of shifting the Internal Security Academy from Mount Abu to Bangalore. This matter was raised first by Shri Mufti Mohammad Sayeed when he was the home minister.

Apparently, for the expansion of this academy, some additional land is required. Now, Mt Abu being a hill station, land was not available immediately. But the Rajasthan government had offered alternative land sites in the nearby areas, in Sirohi district itself. In July 1991, suddenly, the state government was sent a telex by the home ministry saying that unless by the end of the month land was allotted in Mt Abu itself, the government would proceed with the shifting of the academy to Bangalore. The chief minister of Rajasthan immediately contacted the director general of the CRPF and the matter was discussed, and it was agreed that the director of the academy would go and inspect the alternative sites available.

On the fixed dates in August, unfortunately—16 August was the date which was fixed—the director [of] the academy did not turn up to inspect the sites. So, the collector of Sirohi went to Mt

Abu, but the director and the deputy director were absent. Then again, a telex has been received by the Rajasthan government to the effect that if by 31 August, 150 acres of land is not made available at Mt Abu, the academy will be shifted. Some unilateral decision will be taken.

A MATTER OF PRIDE FOR RAJASTHAN

I would request the Government of India—the home minister is also here just now—to see that something is done in the matter. The academy has been there for decades and for the people of Rajasthan, it is a matter of pride that the Internal Security Academy is there. There is a lot of local resentment and the entire state of Rajasthan will feel deprived if any effort is made to shift the academy. And if the only reason is availability of land, I am sure some method can be found and if land is not available and the Rajasthan government can settle it with the Government of India, it should be seen that the academy is not shifted.

I would request the home minister to direct the officials to sit with the chief minister of Rajasthan and find a way out so that the proposal to shift the academy is dropped.

INVITING THE SUPREME COURT INTO THE POLITICAL DOMAIN

Speaking in the debate on the Approval of President's Rule in Meghalaya on 27 November 1991, Morarka points out, 'We have brought this ignominy on ourselves that the Supreme Court has interfered with the legislature affairs.'

Many times we have discussed many states where Article 356 had been invoked, but in the political history of this country after Independence, this is the strangest and the queerest case that the House is discussing. In most cases, there is a doubt about the loyalty of the MLAs on one side or the other. Therefore, the speaker is confused, the governor is confused. [This is] The constitutionally funniest case, in which not one MLA has defected, not for one day has the chief minister lost his majority, not even for five minutes was Shri Lyngdoh[1] in a minority in the House and yet they say the constitutional machinery has broken down. What has happened is this: one gentleman who occupied the chair of the speaker has been consumed with the overwhelming ambition to become chief minister. In politics, that is all right. I have no quarrel with anybody trying to become chief minister, but he has to quit as speaker. What has happened? What are the facts of this case? Everybody is arguing eloquently about morality. I don't want to discuss the

---

[1]B.B. Lyngdoh

political morality of the Congress party just now, but what are the facts of the case?

The Governor's Report, on the basis of which the Centre has promulgated the President's Rule, I presume, is acceptable. That report says [that] the governor has come to the conclusion that there are thirty MLAs on one side and twenty-six on the other side. But the speaker has given out his intention to disqualify four MLAs. Despite knowing these facts, the governor is asking the chief minister to summon the assembly. In most cases, I submit there is a lot of confusion about the MLAs' loyalty outside the legislature. Therefore, we all agree that the strength should be tested on the floor of the House to clear the confusion.

Here is a case where the governor knew that confusion will be created on the floor of the House. There was no confusion outside. Even the governor knows thirty people are with the chief minister and twenty-six are with the other party. He knows the speaker's intention. The governor has said in his report that the speaker is conspiring to become the chief minister. I have never heard such a report from any governor. Look at the conduct of the speaker. The House meets. He declares four people disqualified under the Tenth Schedule. No show-cause notice was issued; no reason was given. Four MLAs have not resigned from any party. They have not applied to the speaker. The speaker suo moto says, 'You are disqualified.' Okay, as a Parliamentarian agreeing with this great Congress party, I will give the benefit of doubt to the speaker. He genuinely thought that these four people are disqualified. So he disqualified them.

After he took a vote, it was twenty-six versus twenty-six. To remove all doubts about him, he cast his vote with the Opposition. He wants to make it clear: please do not accuse me of impartiality. My intention is clear. I disqualified four members and I will disqualify any number required so that I can declare that this government is in a minority.

ARTIFICIAL MACHINATIONS

The constitutional machinery in Meghalaya never broke down. It is an artificial machination to prove that the constitutional machinery has broken down. I humbly submit that the governor should have refused to call the assembly. He should have disciplined the speaker in his own way. He should have told the chief minister, 'You continue in office.'

However, theoretically, the floor of the assembly is the best place to test the majority. Okay, you call this twenty-six versus twenty-six. Even at that time [when] those four MLAs had moved the Supreme Court, the court had given an interim order saying that their votes should be counted for determining the majority of the government. The speaker has blatantly, openly declared: 'I will not allow the Supreme Court to have jurisdiction in the legislature affairs.' I, in my individual capacity, do not approve of judiciary versus legislature. But if we want our autonomy to be maintained, we must have self-discipline. You cannot run amuck. You cannot have a speaker like that. While remaining as the speaker, he declares himself the leader of the Opposition and stakes his claim to form the government. That means the system has broken down. We have brought this ignominy to ourselves that the Supreme Court has interfered with the legislature affairs. What is the government's stand? You say, what can the central government do, it is twenty-six versus twenty-six, the speaker has cast his vote—we have no choice. They had a choice because there was an interim order of the Supreme Court. They could have told the governor to direct the speaker to count those votes. You did not do it. Your invocation of Article 356 is on the thin thread of disregarding the Supreme Court's interim order. The speaker of Meghalaya's intention is known. Somebody talked of political morality. I do not want to go into that discussion. The Congress party is within its right to send its emissaries and try to engineer defections. That is the game of politics. The Anti-Defection Act was brought by Shri Rajiv Gandhi and not by us.

Through his speeches, he wanted to cleanse the politics. Sir, see the action of the Congress party. Have they suspended the speaker from the membership of their party? Have they told the speaker that he should not stake his claim for the chief minister-ship? What is the signal they have sent? The signal even today they are giving is: 'We will not allow a popular government to come back, unless the majority is with the Congress party.' The next thing is, you will have the Supreme Court interfering whenever you invoke Article 356. One day the Supreme Court will say: 'We will judge whether Article 356 has been correctly invoked or not.' What we are inviting is the Supreme Court's entry purely into a political domain. We are inviting them because of our behaviour, because of our misdemeanour. What has happened in Goa? What has happened in other places? Speakers have gone amuck in this country. This Tenth Schedule has been reduced to the judiciousness of the speaker. Speakers are openly acting in a partisan way. I am most baffled to see that in this case, which is a transparent and open case, Shri Jacob is not doing anything. I expected Shri Jacob to get up and say that we are restoring Shri Lyngdoh as the chief minister. I am not against change. If Shri Lyngdoh tomorrow does not have majority, your man will come. I heard Shri Jacob saying, to my surprise, that the detailed judgement of the Supreme Court is awaited. It has no relevance. The operating order has no relevance. The operating order is binding on you and Section 7 has been struck down. The five MLAs have right to vote and Shri Lyngdoh's majority is beyond doubt. The earlier they restore Shri Lyngdoh, the less damage they will be doing to the democratic structure of the country. Thank you.

THE PRICE OF FAILURE IS PAID BY ALL

'Your stabilization programme, structural adjustment programme—all will go haywire if you cannot arrest inflation to a single digit. Postpone the Exit Policy and the Narasimham Committee report. Let us not go too much into the tunnel of the World Bank and IMF,' pleads Morarka with Finance Minister Dr Manmohan Singh during this discussion on the Appropration (No-2) Bill, 1992, on 7 May 1992.

Two and a half months have passed since the budget has been passed by the Parliament. I just want the minister of state for finance[1] to take note of a few points by way of evaluation as to what has happened in this period. We had said at that time that inflation can undo all that you are trying to do. Your stabilization programme, structural adjustment programme—all will go haywire if you cannot arrest inflation to a single digit. Despite the government's best efforts, the inflation even now is 13.3 per cent. It is a serious matter. I do not know what the finance ministry's game plan is. Whatever plan they have made and whatever plan they want to carry through, whether we like it or not, even to make that successful, unless you bring the inflation down to 9 per cent, to a single digit, your programme will fail and the country will be in bigger trouble. We will not be happy to see that the government

---

[1]Shri Shantaram Potdukhe

has failed. After all, the price of failure has to be paid by all.

On the budget deficit, after the budget was presented, certain figures have come to light. The budget deficit figure on 20 December 1991 was ₹15,547 crore and within a week, on 31 December, at the end of the calendar year, it came down to ₹11,503 crore. It came down by ₹4,000 crore in one week. Probably somebody can explain that to me. But within a week after that, it went back to ₹16,000 crore. I do not say that these figures are fudged. But definitely, these figures deserve an explanation. 31 December is an important date. 29 February is a more important date for the finance minister and, therefore, the 29 February 1992 figure shows an even steeper decline. I have got the quarterly figures of budget deficits for the last four or five years. You will be surprised to know that in the two years, 1989–90 and 1990–91, which are much maligned by this government, the year-end budgetary deficit figures are slightly higher than the quarterly figures, which is how they should be. The quarterly figures are tentative and at the year-end, you try to consolidate and you find the deficit slightly higher. This year, the quarterly figures are much higher and the year-end figure suddenly and dramatically drops.

> [...] unless you bring the inflation down to 9 per cent, to a single digit, your programme will fail and the country will be in bigger trouble. We will not be happy to see that the government has failed. After all, the price of failure has to be paid by all.

MONETIZATION OF DEFICIT

It is my apprehension that after 29 February the figure must have again gone up. I am not saying this to run down the method of presenting statistics. I am on a much more serious problem and that is the monetization of this deficit. In 1990–91, the monetization was 23 per cent and in 1991–92 it is 28 per cent. The target given by the finance minister[1] was 20 per cent.

This explains inflation. We do not have to go around trying to find out why inflation has occurred. The reason for inflation is in the figures themselves. Unless the budget deficit is controlled, unless the monetization of that deficit by the Reserve Bank of India is controlled, I am afraid you will not be able to control inflation. So, I want to draw the attention of the finance minister to this and to ask him to take serious steps to stop this profligation. If this kind of money supply goes on, it is difficult to control inflation.

Postpone the Exit Policy and the Narasimham Committee report. Postpone the second tranche. Let us not go too much into the tunnel of the World Bank and IMF. Not as a matter of confrontation or saving the economic sovereignty, etc.

That leads me to the next question. Your promise to the IMF was to contain the money supply at 11 to 13 per cent. It is even now reigning at 19 per cent. I understand that the IMF now does not want to part with the second tranche of their loan because these conditions have not been met. They also want the Exit Policy and the Narasimham Committee Report[2] to be implemented. My request to the government, at this stage, is this: we have taken the first tranche of the loan. Our BoP position is much better, thanks to whatever steps you might have taken. At this time, let us all sit together and see whether we can do without the second tranche because I do not think that this country can afford the Exit Policy; I do not think the Narasimham Committee report is a very wise decision to implement in full because that will be negating what Smt. Indira Gandhi did in 1969. After years and

[1]Dr Manmohan Singh
[2]Shri M. Narasimham was the thirteenth governor of RBI and headed the first committee appointed in August 1991 against the backdrop of the balance of payments crisis.

years of understanding and study, she nationalized banks. All right, banks as such may have a lot of things to be corrected. I am not on that. Please take corrective measures. But implementing the Narasimham Committee report would undo what Smt. Gandhi did to a large extent. And not only that, we will add problems which will be difficult to cure or rectify for the next five or ten years.

DO REST ON YOUR LAURELS

I think the time has come when you can rest on your laurels, if I can call it that. The BoP has improved. You have breathing time. Postpone the Exit Policy and the Narasimham Committee report. Postpone the second tranche. Let us not go too much into the tunnel of the World Bank and IMF. Not as a matter of confrontation or saving the economic sovereignty, etc. I am not on that subject. I am on a very, very pragmatic and practical note. Let us not take a loan if we can do without it. It increases our debt burden.

In Maharashtra, I went to a place called Panvel, which is 50 kilometres away from Bombay. You can hardly call it an interior. I found [that] the price of 'jowar' there, which was one rupee a kilo, is two rupees a kilo now. It is the staple food of the poorest of the poor. And if this is the condition near Bombay, I shudder to think of what is happening in the rest of the country. We will have starvation problems. We will have massive problems. That reminds me that the wheat procurement this year has been the lowest in the last twenty years. The procurement price is ₹280 while the market price is ₹5 a kilo. Who will give you wheat? God forbid, if our monsoon fails, you will not have wheat for your consumption. Four years ago, in spite of two consecutive failures of monsoon under Shri Rajiv Gandhi, you could manage this system because you had a buffer stock of foodgrains because of an excellent procurement. What will you do now? Please don't take these things lightly. Take it on an emergency footing and do something about it.

WE ARE AGAINST DEFECTIONS

Speaking on 16 May 1990 on the alleged Constitutional Crisis in Nagaland, Morarka points out that the National Front government led by V.P. Singh at the Centre is forced to grapple with a crisis which was not only created by the Congress–I, but that the latter 'fiddled' instead of trying to resolve the issues that trouble the northeast part of the country specifically.

I wish I could respond the way Shiv Shankerji[1] wants me to respond. On the principles that he has enunciated, I think the House should be unanimous. Number one, defections are bad. The principles of politics that we have enunciated are the very principles on which the National Front[2] was founded, on which we have fought elections and, I dare say, the very principles on which the people have elected us to power. There is no question of our going back from the well-stated principles that we are against defections in public life. On principle, the correct method to determine the majority in the legislature is the floor of the legislature. We stand for it.

In Nagaland, according to the information that we have got, after it was reported that twelve people from the ruling party decided to split their party, the chief minister[3] made a public statement that there was no crisis in the government. The chief minister should

---

[1]Shri P. Shiv Shanker was the leader of the Opposition.
[2]Led by V.P. Singh
[3]S.C. Jamir

WE ARE AGAINST DEFECTIONS • 255

have gone to the governor following the well-laid-down principles and said, 'Please call the legislature. I want to prove majority on the floor of the House.'

CONGRESS-I IN NAGALAND

Shri Shiv Shanker raised an interesting point—that of the Tenth Schedule, Clause 3 and a split in the original political party. What is the original political party? According to the act, the party is the legislature party. This is very unfortunate. When the Anti-Defection Act was enacted, there were people like Shri Madhu Limaye who wrote articles in the newspapers warning, 'You are setting a dangerous precedent because you are making the legislature parties independent of their parent organizations.' Now the test that you have to put is whether the Congress-I legislature party in Nagaland has split or not.

Many people have left various political parties since 1985, to whom the speakers have given recognition too. If that interpretation holds good, then those decisions are illegal. I just want to raise two points (Article 167) which Shri Shankerji has raised. I do not want to go into the legality because it has already taken much time. The sum and substance is this: one-third of the ruling party there has split and formed a party of its own and staked its claim to form the government. The (ruling) chief minister did not call the assembly. The governor had recourse to his own decision. Therefore, the Sarkaria Commission's recommendation, in our opinion, has not been infringed in any manner. This has been our stand also and this has been the substance of what we were demanding when we were in the Opposition.

NF HAS NO AXE TO GRIND

Shri Shiv Shanker was talking about healthy political practices. Surely we can have a debate outside the House and an all-party meeting can be held on this matter. He referred to the Northeast and said that it is a sensitive area. We agree with him. But it is his party that was playing quacks and drakes with the Northeast and which has brought the Northeast to its present condition. They have been fiddling with it. The Northeast is in trouble and the Bodoland and the Darjeeling and other movements have been there even while their government was in power there.

The Northeast has been suffering. From the time of Jayaprakash Narayan and Rev. Michael Scott[1], these people who are sitting here have been trying their best in Nagaland. We will do nothing to disturb the condition there. Let me add, for the information of the members, that the present government there is not the National Front government and we have no axe to grind. They are local parties, they have split and they have formed the government there, and these people have lost the majority. There is nothing unconstitutional in this.

---

[1]An Anglican pastor who, along with JP, was part of a Peace Mission formed in April 1964 to resolve insurgency issues in Nagaland.

FAMILY PLANNING PROGRAMME HAS MADE NO DENT

Speaking during the debate on the Constitution 1st Amendment Bill, 1990, on Delimitation of Constituencies, on 29 April 1992, Morarka says that freezing of reserved representation on the basis of the 1971 Census to encourage the Scheduled Castes/Scheduled Tribes to adopt family planning had failed. He also says that the health and family welfare ministry must pursue some other vigorous programmes to control population growth and only this electoral reform will not help.

At the outset, let me congratulate the government for deciding to pass this long-pending measure, which was introduced by my late friend, Shri Dinesh Goswami[1], to whom I pay my humble tribute. He made a lot of efforts to arrive at a consensus on electoral reforms and whatever little consensus emerged at the all-party meeting, he brought that [about] in the shape of this bill. I am also thankful to the law minister for bringing forward this amendment for delimitation of seats on the basis of the 1991 Census, since the 1991 Census results are now available.

First of all, the freezing was done by the 42nd Amendment Act, as we all know, with two purposes in mind. The first was that since the government was to step up the family planning

---

[1] Dinesh Goswami was law minister in the V.P. Singh government. He died in a road accident on 3 June 1991 at the age of fifty-six.

programme, it was felt that all those states which carried out that programme more efficiently should not be put at a disadvantage and their number of seats should not stand reduced, and there should be some sort of protection against not proceeding with the family planning programme.

In regard to the second purpose, it was felt at that time by the late Smt. Gandhi that if the family planning programme was vigorously pursued, it was likely that our Scheduled Caste and Scheduled Tribe brethren might be adversely affected because of the zeal and enthusiasm of the officials and, therefore, they should be protected and the reserved seats should be frozen at the present level. What happened in the last few years has, unfortunately, brought out the fact that the family planning programme has hardly made any dent. My friend, Shri Muralidhar Bhandare, has very rightly pointed out that family planning is one of the most important things to be done and I would like to quote Shri Madhu Limaye, who had raised this issue.

COMPREHENSIVE FAMILY PLANNING NEEDED

Shri Madhu Limaye had a running correspondence with the late prime minister, Shri Rajiv Gandhi, who seemed to agree with his analysis. Unfortunately, I have to say that there were people in the Congress (I) party at that time who talked very loudly about social justice, but who advised Shri Rajiv Gandhi against this and it got stuck.

I would like to quote Shri Limaye:

This proposal is to reverse representation of the states and the Scheduled Castes and the Scheduled Tribes in the Lok Sabha and the assemblies till the end of the century on the basis of the 1971 Census. It is said that freezing of this representation will act as an incentive and the states and the Scheduled Castes and the Scheduled Tribes will take to family planning more readily as a result of this stabilization of popular representation at the 1971 census level. But by itself, this will not have much impact on the population problem, unless there is a concrete and comprehensive programme of family planning, unless it is applied vigorously to all states and classes of people, etc. If all this is done, then, probably, freezing of representation will help.

Unfortunately, this has not happened. So, my first submission is that, basically, they (the government) should have a relook to find out whether freezing should continue. We should annul the 42nd Amendment and de-freeze and go back to the pre-42nd Amendment position. In fact, when the 45th Amendment was brought forward by the Janata government, only that part of the 42nd Amendment could be reserved which was agreed to by consensus. Unfortunately, on this there was no consensus at the time. Now, the government should seriously consider whether it should be de-frozen.

NO BENEFIT TO THE SCs/STs

Another aspect of this is that the freezing, which was supposed to protect the SCs and the STs, is today working against them. In the 1991 Census, if you keep the figures as they are and if the freezing continues on the total number of Parliament seats, at least the inter se representation between the general seats and the reserved seats—that freeze should be removed. On the basis of the 1991 Census, the SCs' and STs' representation will, in my calculation, go up by three to four seats in the Lok Sabha. And, therefore, they will get about three to four seats more if the total number of seats is kept as they are. Even if there is no total de-freezing, at least the Delimitation Commission should restore the balance according to the general population and the SC and ST population, so that the freeze which was done to protect them, and which is now working against them, should be corrected.

The other point that I want to mention is about the seats of Bombay and Delhi which, I think, your present amendment will take care of. The one-man-one-vote and one-woman-one-vote has already been negated in great measure, because in Delhi there is the New Delhi constituency and there is the Outer Delhi constituency. The voters' ratio is 1:5. The same problem is in Bombay. I may humbly submit that due to the influx of population from the rural areas to the urban areas, the concentration of the poor in the urban areas is increasing. The result is that that population is not getting adequate representation because they are concentrated and delimitation is frozen.

CREATING MORE DISTORTIONS

So if you want a fair representation on the basis of one-man-one-vote and one-woman-one-vote—especially in growing cities [like] Bombay, Delhi, Bangalore, Calcutta and Hyderabad, this problem has assumed menacing proportions—I would like the law minister to react and I hope the Delimitation Commission will correct that also. This is not only a question of rotation. I hope the constituencies would be re-demarcated in a manner that there is more even balance of the voters throughout the country.

Finally, I can only say that though we happily support this measure, we request the government to look into the total de-freezing. Within the present, if you do not de-freeze the total, then allow the SCs and STs to get more number of seats, as per the 1991 Census. And, of course, the largest issue, and that is, if you want this to act as an incentive for family planning, I feel that the health and family welfare ministry should take up a more vigorous programme because forcible family planning has already failed, and I think we have all accepted it. How to get it done is a totally different matter. I don't think that such a welfare measure can be attached to this small thing, which is only creating more distortions.

KEEP PRESIDING OFFICERS OUT OF THE PURVIEW OF THE COURTS

Speaking on 24 March 1993 on what he termed a 'piquant situation' involving the House and the judiciary, when the speaker of the Manipur Assembly had to appear before the Supreme Court, Morarka says that the dignity of the legislature must be preserved.

I want to draw the attention of the House to a very serious constitutional matter. I am glad Mr Bhardwaj[1] is here and I would like him to take note of it. Yesterday, the Manipur speaker[2] had to personally appear in the Supreme Court as a result of a long-winded controversy between the Manipur legislature and the Supreme Court. Madam, it has been hailed by judicial officials as a great day for the Supreme Court.

But we are parliamentarians. I feel that any confrontation between the legislature and the judiciary is anathema to our constitutional system. It will be a sad day if the presiding officers of the Houses of Parliament or the legislatures are hauled up before the courts. The Supreme Court made a very fine distinction yesterday and said, 'We have called the Manipur speaker here adjudicating in

---

[1]Hansraj Bhardwaj, minister of state in the ministry of law, justice and company affairs.
[2]Borobabu Singh

his capacity not as the speaker but the authority under the Tenth Schedule,' which means the reference is to the Anti-Defection Act. Now, Bhardwaj-ji knows very well that the Anti-Defection Act was passed. The speaker will have to give the judgement and if the judgement is justiciable, the speaker will be put in an awkward situation.

At that time, a clause was inserted that the proceedings under the Tenth Schedule will be considered as proceedings of Parliament and will be outside the purview of the courts. Now, the Punjab and Haryana High Court in a particular case struck down Clause 7, and that is why it became justiciable. Because of this, a piquant situation arose yesterday and the Manipur speaker has been literally forced [to appear before the court]. He himself feels humiliated. His lawyer went on pleading with the Supreme Court even yesterday morning: 'Please exempt him from personal appearance. He has come to Delhi. He is lodged in the Manipur House. But please exempt him.'

The judges did not agree. He came in the afternoon. The judges said 'We are happy he has come. Now the contempt proceedings are dropped.' That was done in a very dignified way.

But it raises certain basic issues regarding the functioning of our Constitution. I shudder to think that if the speaker of the Lok Sabha is similarly called by the Supreme Court tomorrow for any judgement he gives in the anti-defection matter, where do we go? Dr Balram Jakhar, a former speaker, is here. Shri Bhardwaj is here. He knows the Tenth Schedule. I think if there is some lacuna in the legislation, we should correct it. We should definitely keep our presiding officers outside the purview of the courts either directly or by a fine distinction. Otherwise, I am afraid, in the long run, the very dignity and independence of the legislature will be at stake.

RICH STATES OF POOR PEOPLE

'There is something wrong with our entire structure that the spin-off of the entire economic activity does not reach the poor,' Morarka points out in the discussion on The Cess and Other Taxes on Minerals (Validation) Bill, 1992, on 2 April 1992. 'Banks are lending money only in the urban areas and only for big industries and other things. So the areas which have a large population, which are based on agriculture or agro-based activity, need special attention. A stable mechanism has to be devised by which proper transfer of resources to the states takes place, not by the mercy of the Centre through the budget but as a matter of right. You are transferring a small portion to them and show it as if you are making a larger devolution of funds.'

This bill, though a very small one, gives a very good opportunity to the House to focus attention on this very long-standing and important problem in the country. Bihar, Orissa and Rajasthan—all these states which have got minerals are not poor states. They are rich states in a country consisting of poor people. And if the people are poor, the people are not responsible for their poverty. There is something wrong with our entire structure that the spin-off of the entire economic activity does not reach them.

BANKS LEND ONLY IN URBAN AREAS

Before I come to minerals, the other case which is very apparent is the credit-deposit ratio of banks. It is clear that though the deposits are going up because of the agriculture sector and small people from the states, the credit-deposit ratio is very poor. Banks are lending money only in the urban areas and for big industries. So the areas which have a large population, which are based on agriculture or agro-based activity, need special attention. Coming to the specific point on minerals, the Ninth Finance Commission in its report has touched on this point, not only for minerals but also for oil.

There is a long-standing problem of Maharashtra and Gujarat for oil and gas. These are similar problems. At the time when the Constitution was drafted there was no offshore oil, so obviously, that problem could not be dealt with. But the fact remains that a stable mechanism has to be devised by which proper transfer of resources to the states takes place, not by the mercy of the Centre through the budget, but as a matter of right.

Today, we see in the budget the transfer that is made to the states—it is shown as if it is going up. But this is a fallacy. Actually, the transfer is going down because they are not even getting their money for the real wealth created. So what we are transferring to them is out of appropriation that we have made at their cost. You are transferring a small portion to them and showing it as if you are making a larger devolution of funds. What is required is—I would request the government; the Tenth Finance Commission, I understand, is under formation—there should be special terms of reference. The Ninth Finance Commission was not on specific terms of reference. The Tenth Finance Commission should specially deal with this problem.

THE STATES ARE ALWAYS IN A JAM

With regard to cess on minerals, what should be the fair distribution for the states and the Centre, should statutorily be laid down. It should be statutorily laid down by the Tenth Finance Commission. I have mentioned in the budget speech about how the Centre has got recourse to deficit financing to meet its gap in the budget. But the states do not have such a facility—they take overdraft from the Reserve Bank and the central finance ministry has frowned upon them.

The states are always in a jam. Some of the states are backward and, I repeat, it is because of the peculiar structure. If 75 to 80 per cent of the total money goes for establishment expenses, what development can they do with 20 per cent? We would be having a serious social and economic upheaval if this matter is not put on a proper footing. I agree with Mr Ram Awadesh Singh—Jharkhand and other movements are ultimately an offshoot of long-standing aspirations of people not getting due recognition. I request the government to take this matter seriously before it is too late and ask the Tenth Finance Commission to go through it and lay down logical rational criteria to devolve the funds to the states, not from the budgetary allocations, but as a part of the wealth being created there.

SCAM-TAINTED BROKER AND THE PM'S SON

Speaking in the debate on a loan of ₹2 crore allegedly given to a company belonging to the prime minister's[1] son on 24 March 1993, Morarka pleads for a government statement on the allegation and not to ignore the newspaper reports.

The Janakiraman Committee's fourth report on the securities scam has been submitted. It has confirmed the charges that were published in the *Indian Express,* which Smt. Margaret Alva wanted us to ignore. Now, it is not a question of the *Indian Express.* The Janakiraman Committee has confirmed that a loan of ₹2 crore was given to the company of the prime minister's son.

THE CREDIBILITY OF THE PRIME MINISTER IS AT STAKE

They don't believe the press. Now they say they don't believe Janakiraman. We have to believe somebody in this country! The deputy governor of the Reserve Bank of India, Shri Janakiraman, has found that a loan was given by the scam-tainted broker to the company belonging to the prime minister's son. Now they are trying to say that the loan is given to a public limited company, it can never be for a director. It will be a gross violation of the

---

[1]P.V. Narasimha Rao

Companies Act. If a loan is given to a company, it has to be for the benefit of the company. It cannot be for the benefit of a director. Now they want to say that the loan was for the benefit of another director, and not for the prime minister's son.

It is a very serious matter. The credibility of the prime minister is at stake. The government should come out. I am not making any personal charge. The fact is, detailed reports with photostat copies have been published in the newspapers. The reaction of the minister of state in the ministry of personnel, public grievances and pensions was very sad. She is trying to tell us, ignore what the *Indian Express* says.

The newspapers are central to the functioning of any democracy. Members are entitled to a quote from the newspapers. It is not a question of the *Indian Express*. The government must come out with a statement.

The issue is not whether it is a loan or a grant. The issue is, was there a transaction between a scam-tainted broker and the prime minister's son's company? The prime minister's son is involved in corruption. Jayalalithaa has withdrawn support. One hundred of their own MPs have protested about Shri Sharad Pawar's removal from the cabinet. The government is collapsing.

www.ingramcontent.com/pod-product-compliance
Lightning Source LLC
Chambersburg PA
CBHW020658270326
41928CB00005B/171